# STATE AND FINANCE
# IN THE PHILIPPINES,
# 1898–1941

YOSHIKO NAGANO

# STATE AND FINANCE IN THE PHILIPPINES, 1898–1941

*The Mismanagement of an American Colony*

NUS PRESS
SINGAPORE

© 2015  Yoshiko Nagano

*Published by*:

NUS Press
National University of Singapore
AS3-01-02, 3 Arts Link
Singapore 117569

Fax: (65) 6774-0652
E-mail: nusbooks@nus.edu.sg
Website: http://www.nus.edu.sg/nuspress

ISBN  978-9971-69-841-6 (Paper)

All rights reserved. This book, or parts thereof, may not be reproduced in any form or by any means, electronic or mechanical, including photocopying, recording or any information storage and retrieval system now known or to be invented, without written permission from the Publisher.

**National Library Board, Singapore Cataloguing-in-Publication Data**

Nagano, Yoshiko, 1950-, author.
    State and finance in the Philippines, 1898–1941: the mismanagement of an American colony / Yoshiko Nagano. – Singapore: NUS Press, [2015]
    pages cm
    Includes bibliographic references and index.
    ISBN: 978-9971-69-841-6 (paperback)

    1. Money – Philippines – History. 2. Banks and banking – Philippines – History. I. Title.

HG1262
332.109599 -- dc23                              OCN896810594


First published in 2015 by Ateneo de Manila University Press.

Printed by:  Mainland Press Pte Ltd

# CONTENTS

Map and Illustrations     vi
Figures and Tables     viii
Preface and Acknowledgments     xi

INTRODUCTION: Understanding the Philippine Financial Crisis, 1919–1922     1

## PART I. OVERVIEW
CHAPTER 1: The Philippine Currency System under U.S. Rule     21
CHAPTER 2: The Emergence of Modern Banking in the Philippines     41

## PART II. START-UP
CHAPTER 3: The Agricultural Bank of the Philippine Government     69
CHAPTER 4: The Philippine National Bank and Lending in Agriculture     91

## PART III. DEBACLE
CHAPTER 5: The Wood-Forbes Mission and the Financial Crisis     119
CHAPTER 6: The Philippine National Bank and Credit Inflation     141
CHAPTER 7: Reconstructing the Philippine National Bank and the Currency System     165

Conclusion     187

Notes     195
Bibliography     224
Index     240

# MAP AND ILLUSTRATIONS

**MAP**

1. The Philippines, c. 1920. (Prepared by the author)        xiv

**ILLUSTRATIONS**        Follow page 66

1. Escolta, Manila, the then "Wall Street of the Philippines" in the bustling District of Sta. Cruz in Manila, 1916. (U.S. National Archives, RG350-P-E-11-2-3)
2. The Masonic Temple at Escolta on the Pasig River, the first Manila skyline in the late 1910s. The Manila office of the Philippine National Bank was located on the first floor. (U.S. Library of Congress, Prints and Photographs Division, Foreign Geographical File:46215)
3. The members of the Board of Directors of the Philippine National Bank at its establishment. From left to right: Leon Rosenthal, V. Singson Encarnacion, Venancio Concepcion, H. Parker Willis, Samuel Ferguson, William H. Anderson, and Charles C. Robinson. (*Bankers Magazine* 95, no. 2 [Aug. 1917])
4. Staff of the Manila office of the Philippine National Bank. (*Bankers Magazine* 95, no. 2 [Aug. 1917])
5. H. Parker Willis, first president of the Philippine National Bank. (*Bankers Magazine* 95, no. 2 [Aug. 1917])
6. Venancio Concepcion, third president of the Philippine National Bank. (*Far Eastern Review*, Sept. 1923)
7. Silver certificate, ten pesos, series of 1912, issued 1916–1918. (Author's collection)
8. Philippine National Bank note, five pesos, series of 1916, issued 1920–1921. (Author's collection)

9. Manuscript of the telegram drafted by Governor-General Francis Burton Harrison jointly with Senate President Manuel L. Quezon in Washington and sent to Vice Governor-General Charles E. Yeater in Manila on 7 April 1919. (U.S. National Archives, BIA 6769-207after)
10. New York agency of the Philippine National Bank in Manhattan's financial district. (*Bankers Magazine* 95, no. 2 [Aug. 1917])
11. The Bank of the Philippine Islands, 10 Plaza Cervantes, Manila in the late 1910s. (*Bankers Magazine* 96, no. 3 [Mar. 1918])
12. Sergio Osmeña, House Speaker (left), Francis Burton Harrison, Governor-General (center), and Manuel L. Quezon, Senate President (right). (*The Philippine Review* 2 no. 12 [Dec. 1917])

# FIGURES AND TABLES

**FIGURES**

| | | |
|---|---|---|
| 1. | Philippine Currencies in Circulation, 1910–1940 | 33 |
| 2. | Aggregate Amount of Assets, Loans/Discounts/Overdrafts and Deposits in Banks in the Philippines, 1909–1938 | 53 |
| 3. | Relations between Major Banks, Traders and Producers | 60 |
| 4. | Paid-up Capital, Loans/Discounts/Overdrafts, Deposits of the Bank of the Philippine Islands, 1853–1927 | 63 |

**TABLES**

| | | |
|---|---|---|
| 1. | Status of the Gold Standard Fund, 1909–1912 | 28 |
| 2. | Loans and Investments of the Gold Standard Fund, 1912–1918 | 29 |
| 3. | Annual Average Amount of the Gold Standard Fund and the Treasury Certificate Fund, 1923–1934 | 37 |
| 4. | Shares in Philippine Foreign Trade by Region and Country, 1903–1940 | 44 |
| 5. | Shares of Major Export Products in Total Export of the Philippines and Shares of the United States in Major Philippine Export Products, 1901–1940 | 46 |
| 6. | Investment in Major Export Industries, as of 31 July 1935 | 47 |
| 7. | Process of the Establishment of Banks in the Philippines, 1851–1940 | 55 |
| 8. | Number of Branches and Several Items of Balance Sheet of Banks in the Philippines, as of 30 June 1940 | 58 |
| 9. | Application and Approval of Loans in the Agricultural Bank of the Philippine Government, FY1909–FY1915 | 85 |

10. Number of Loans by the Range of Amount in the Agricultural Bank of the Philippine Government, FY1909–FY1913 — 86
11. Number and Amount of Loans in the Agricultural Bank of the Philippine Government by Province, FY1909–FY1915 — 87
12. Deposits of Provincial Funds in the Agricultural Bank of the Philippine Government, FY1909–FY1915 — 89
13. Balance Sheet of the Philippine National Bank, as of 25 May 1916 — 100
14. Balance Sheet of the Philippine National Bank, as of 31 December 1916 — 101
15. Outstanding Loans and Discounts of the Philippine National Bank by Sector, as of 31 December 1925 — 113
16. Outstanding Agricultural Loans of the Philippine National Bank by Crop and Branch, as of 31 December 1928 — 113
17. Export of Manila Hemp, Sugar, and Coconut Oil, 1911–1918 — 143
18. Financial Statements of the Philippine National Bank, 1916–1925 — 143
19. Estimated Losses of Loans and Discounts of Manila Hemp Trading Firms to the Philippine National Bank, as of 19 May 1921 — 147
20. Liabilities of Coconut Oil Companies to the Philippine National Bank, as of February 1922 — 149
21. Estimated Losses of Loans and Discounts of Coconut Oil Companies to the Philippine National Bank, as of 19 May 1921 — 149
22. Outstanding Loans and Credits to Sugar Centrals Provided by the Philippine National Bank Outstanding, as of 29 November 1919 — 153
23. Liabilities of Sugar Centrals and the Philippine Sugar Centrals Agency, as of February 1922 — 156

# PREFACE AND ACKNOWLEDGMENTS

THE THEME OF THIS BOOK was conceived during the late 1980s after the publication of my first book, *Firipin Keizaishi Kenkyu: Togyo-shihon to Jinushi-sei [A Study of Philippine Economic History: Capitalism and Hacienda in the Sugar Industry]* (Tokyo: Keiso Shobo, 1986). In my first book I analyzed the characteristics of the Philippine sugar industry, focusing on the American period. In the course of this research it became clear to me that the Philippine National Bank had played a crucial role in the formation of the colony's sugar manufacturing sector, and that the management of domestic capital under U.S. rule manifested the distinctive features of the Philippine colonial export economy. Thus a study of the history of the Philippine National Bank became the next topic of my research. However, shifting my research from the history of the sugar industry to banking and financial history required me to overcome various barriers: Not only was it necessary to study banking and financial systems, but it also proved essential to develop insights into the political system in a colony profoundly linked with the political economy of the United States.

The most difficult issue that I had to tackle was the overall clarification and analysis of the Philippine National Bank's collapse after World War I. The standard interpretation of this "scandal" in most of the works I consulted was that the Bank's crisis after World War I was due to mismanagement by Filipino bank officials who conducted lending without sufficient expertise in modern banking, relying rather on personal connections. However, as I pursued my study it became apparent that previous scholarship in economic history failed to draw a full picture of the crisis. I soon discerned, first, that it was important to analyze the role of the Philippine National Bank in maintaining the currency system in the colony at a time when no central bank was present; and second, that, in order to clarify the relationship between the crisis and the instability of the currency system, it was indispensable to understand the political and administrative system of the Philippines in relation to the political influence of the Bureau of Insular Affairs (BIA), an agency of the U.S. War Department. By now it had become clear to me that the discourse on the "corruption scandal of the Philippine National Bank after World War I" in previous studies should be recognized rather as the "Philippine financial crisis after World War I," involving not only local mismanagement of the Bank but also the major economic misjudgment of the BIA in "reforming" the Philippine currency system, an error that led inexorably to the grave debacle that shook the foundation of the American colonial state. However, I was also aware that I lacked the requisite knowledge of Philippine political history to clearly develop my hypothesis that the widely accepted view constructed during the American colonial period of the Philippine National Bank's "scandal" was incomplete and misleading.

In order to overcome my deficiency, intensive reading in the literatures of Philippine political history during the American colonial period was clearly required. My opportunity came in 1998–1999 when I took a year's sabbatical from Kanagawa University, Yokohama. Fortunately, I was able to take advantage of my affiliations with the Center of Southeast Asian Studies at the University of Wisconsin-Madison and the School of Economics at the University of the Philippines, Diliman, to concentrate on this research and in particular on the banking history of the Philippines.

The first results of my extensive research were published in Japanese as *Firipin Ginkoshi Kenkyu: Shokuminchi-taisei to Kinyu [A Study of Philippine Banking History: Colonial State and Finance]* (Tokyo: Ochanomizu Shobo, 2003). I presented papers at various international conferences: Euroseas in London (2001), AAS in New York (2003), ICAS in Singapore (2003), and conferences of ICOPHIL in Manila (2000), Leiden (2004), and (most recently) East Lansing, Michigan (2012). During a sabbatical year (2009–2010), I prepared the English manuscript based on my Japanese book, but adding some material that had been fully or partially published in the *Journal of Southeast Asian Studies*, *The Philippine Review of Economics & Business*, the *Philippine Political Science Journal*, and the *International Journal of Asian Studies*.

In the course of the decade during which this book was in progress, I used research materials from the following libraries and institutions, to the staffs and administration of which I express my gratitude: the U.S. National Archives and Records Administration; the U.S. Library of Congress; the Harry S. Truman Presidential Library; the New York Public Library; the libraries of Harvard University, Yale University, Princeton University, Columbia University, The George Washington University, the University of Wisconsin-Madison, the Wisconsin State Historical Society, and the University of Hawai'i at Manoa; the Philippine National Library; the Lopez Museum; the University of the Philippines, Diliman; Ateneo de Manila University; the National Library of Australia; The Australian National University; the National Diet Library of Japan; Hitotsubashi University; the Institute of Developing Economies (IDE-JETRO); the University of Tokyo; Tokyo University of Foreign Studies; Sophia University; and Kanagawa University.

To complete my final draft for submission to the press, I express my heartfelt gratitude to a number of scholars in the United States, the Philippines, Japan and some other countries. Benito J. Legarda, Jr., Daniel F. Doeppers, Germelino M. Bautista, and Bernardita Reyes Churchill read the first version of the introduction and gave me invaluable comments and useful suggestions. The entire manuscript was copyedited by Terence Hegarty in Boston, who worked to align my English with that of Anglophone academia. I should also add that many scholars and friends encouraged me by extending various kinds of support during the long process of research and writing. To mention a few: Cynthia Banzon Bautista, John D. Blanco, Oscar V. Campomanes, Michael Cullinane, Emmanuel S. de Dios, Kyoji Fukao, Paul D. Hutchcroft, Reynaldo C. Ileto, Akinobu Kuroda, Allan Lumba, Alfred W. McCoy, Konoshuke Odaka, Rene E. Ofreneo, Rosalinda Pineda Ofreneo, Vicente L. Rafael, Temario C. Rivera, Michael Salman, Shiro Saito, and Willem G. Wolters. My special thanks go to Maricor Baytion of the Ateneo de Manila University Press and to Paul Kratoska of NUS Press at the National University of Singapore for turning my draft into a book. Finally, and it goes without saying, I greatly appreciate my entire family for being understanding of my research life.

Yoshiko Nagano
Tokyo
May 2014

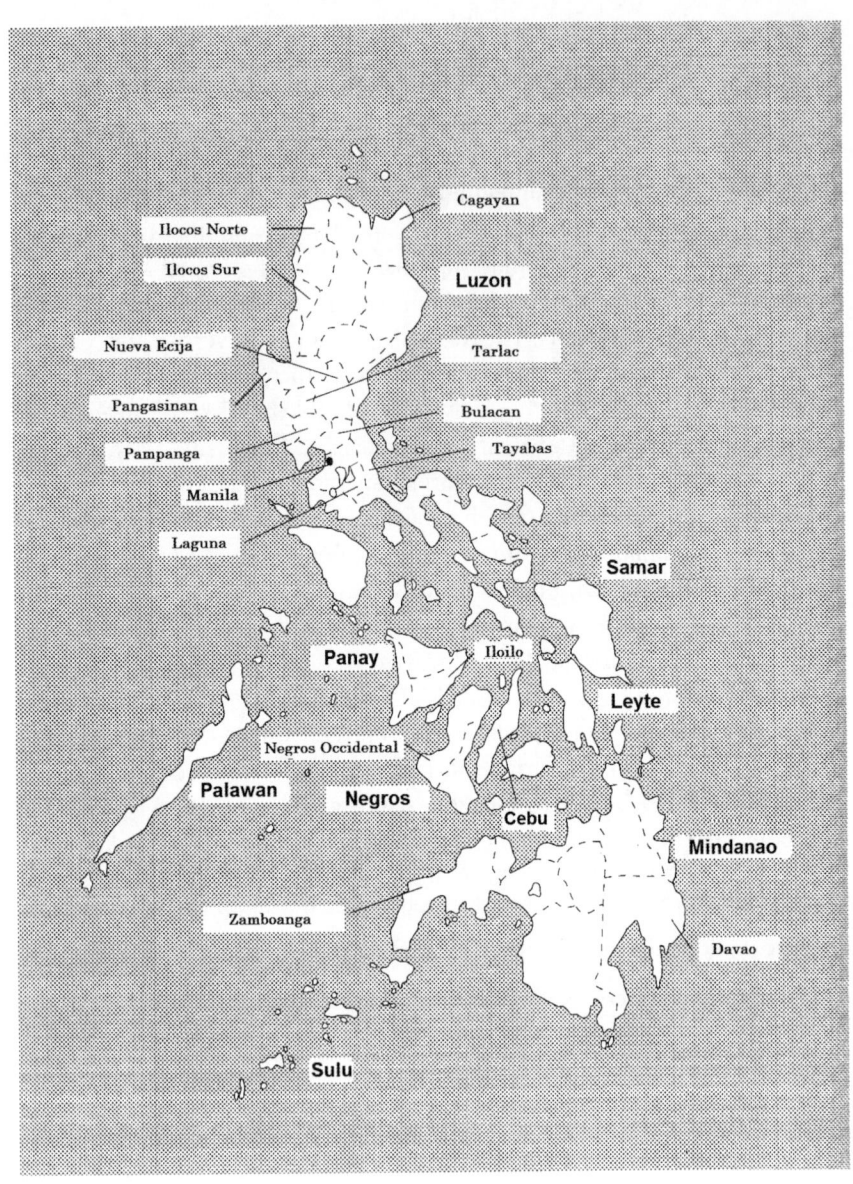

*Map*. The Philippines, c. 1920. (Prepared by the author)

INTRODUCTION
# UNDERSTANDING THE PHILIPPINE FINANCIAL CRISIS, 1919–1922

IN THE RECORDS of a long-defunct U.S. government agency, the Bureau of Insular Affairs (BIA) at the War Department in Washington, there is a handwritten unedited draft of an undated telegram jointly signed by Francis Burton Harrison, Governor-General of the Philippines, and Manuel L. Quezon, President of the Philippine Senate, probably written on 7 April 1919. This was to be sent to Charles E. Yeater, Vice Governor of the Philippines in Manila. It reads as follows:

> Yeater
> We have made examination of National Bank situation and believe that with the issues of emergency notes the crisis is averted and our currency will be stabilized however we are of the opinion that every effort must be made to support existing commitments in the New York Branch and to enable it to retain hold of hemp on hand until reasonable price offers. Also that no effort should be neglected to prevent Bank Philippine Islands from getting National Bank's business. Also that an active exchange market and telegraphic transfers must be maintained. Confidential Attorney General Paredes will be requested to look into [American vice-president of the Bank, J. Elmer] Delaney's activities.
> Harrison Quezon
> Please convey to Mr Osmeña my sincere sympathy with his accident and the hope that he has now entirely recovered.
> Harrison[1]

The message was written when Harrison was in Washington on leave from Manila for his third honeymoon, and Quezon was also in the U.S. capital heading the First Philippine Independence Mission to the United States.[2] Both of them had been warned by the BIA[3] at the U.S. War Department that the Currency Reserve Fund deposited in the New York agency[4] of the Philippine National Bank to support Philippine currency had dried up. With harried haste the message sought Vice Governor Yeater, in his capacity as acting governor-general in Harrison's absence, to act immediately to avert the imminent financial crisis. It may be noted that Harrison did not forget to send his regards to Sergio Osmeña, the Speaker of the House of Representatives in the Philippine legislature.

This message is of significance because it represents the earliest documentary recognition of the awareness of both American and Filipino high officials of the crisis. Why did this financial crisis happen at that time, and what were the consequences? Was the crisis caused by mismanagement and corruption associated with the Philippine National Bank, or by inherent structural inadequacies of the currency reserve system of the American colonial state? These are among the questions this book sets out to address.

Established in 1916 as a multi-purpose semi-governmental bank, the Philippine National Bank functioned as more than a mere commercial bank. In addition to providing loans for Philippine agricultural export industries, and doing business as a commercial bank, it also issued bank notes and served as a depository for the Philippine currency reserve funds. One year after the National Bank opened its New York agency in 1917, a large part of the Philippines' currency reserves was transferred to New York. During World War I the operations of the currency reserve were undertaken in two ways, both of them ill-advised.[5]

First, after the United States declared war on Germany in April 1917, the U.S. government began to issue Liberty Loan bonds to fund the costs of the war. The Philippine government marketed the bonds and encouraged Filipino citizens to buy them. The Philippine Treasury converted peso proceeds into U.S. dollars, using the funds deposited in New York as payment to the U.S. government. This bond sale was the first time the Philippine government had sent U.S. dollars to the U.S. government. Previously, however, the dollars had gone the other way. From the onset of occupation it was the U.S. government that had sent dollars to the Philippines to maintain its army and navy presence. These military expenditures were first transferred to U.S.

banks designated as government depositories and then, on transfer to the Philippine Treasury, issued in pesos. However, with the sale of Liberty Loan bonds in the Philippines, which necessarily contracted the money supply, the American administration of the Philippine Treasury continued to issue and increase peso currencies, thereby precipitating currency inflation.[6]

Second, the Philippine National Bank was not legally permitted to use currency reserves for commercial banking purposes. However, with the economic boom that accompanied World War I, a large portion of the currency reserves in New York was transferred during the war years to the Manila office of the National Bank. Then—whether out of ignorance or pecuniary interest—Filipino and American bank officials began to disburse the currency reserves as their own capital, providing numerous large loans to export businesses, often supported by dubious collaterals of landowning borrowers, like overvalued export products. These transactions were conducted under the direction of the Manila office of the National Bank, usually without any formal approval or authorization of the Philippine Treasury. Inevitably, this loan activity brought credit inflation to the Philippine economy. With the sudden collapse of the export market at the end of the war in 1918, these loans could not be repaid, and landowners and traders in export businesses incurred heavy indebtedness.

The results of this twofold mismanagement of money supply and currency reserves are evident from data assembled in George F. Luthringer's important 1934 book *The Gold-Exchange Standard in the Philippines*. Luthringer shows that, as of March 1919, the National Bank had disbursed at least 41 million dollars of its currency reserve fund deposited in New York for the following:[7]

| | |
|---|---|
| Liberty Loans | US$ 15,399,500 |
| Alien Property Custodian | US$ 2,808,000 |
| United States Shipping Board | US$ 729,146 |
| American Red Cross | US$ 360,721 |
| United War Campaign | US$ 20,600 |
| Sold (transferred) to local banks | US$ 9,293,500 |
| Sold (transferred) to others | US$ 12,573,836 |
| Total | US$ 41,185,303 |

In an attempt to understand the crisis, Luthringer studied investigative reports to trace in detail the disbursement of these funds and loan extensions. He observed that this disbursement "undoubtedly played an important part in the increase of nearly 51 million dollars in the loans, discounts, and acceptances of the Bank during 1918 and 1919."[8] The uncovered bulk of this estimated disbursement and loans is shown in the following schedule of non-liquid assets of the National Bank, worth about 44 million dollars:[9]

| | |
|---|---|
| Hemp business advances 1918–1919 | US$ 9,386,590 |
| Sugar and sugar mills | US$ 11,814,400 |
| Exchange purchased without cover (speculative and with estimated loss of US$ 400,000) together with capital loans and excessive frozen assets | US$ 8,103,490 |
| Coconut oil interests | US$ 11,270,600 |
| Frozen loans on corporation stock and agriculture | US$ 3,660,000 |
| Total | US$ 44,235,080 |

As a result of the mismanagement of the currency reserves by both the Philippine Treasury and the Philippine National Bank, hyperinflation ravaged the Philippine economy and depleted the currency reserves in 1919. As an indication of the severity of the crisis, the Philippine government lost or had to divert almost 80 percent of the country's annual revenue from taxes and tariffs to replenish the depleted reserve. In April 1921, two years after the outbreak of the crisis, the BIA sent a special mission, led by Leonard Wood and W. Cameron Forbes, to investigate Philippine political and financial conditions. With the near-bankruptcy of the Philippine National Bank and the collapse of the currency reserve system, the Wood-Forbes Mission's object was to determine the country's ability to govern its financial and economic affairs as well as its political and legislative affairs. Disregarding the mismanagement of the American administrators of the Philippine Treasury and the BIA in Washington, the Mission attributed the cause of the crisis solely to the incompetence of Filipino bank officials. This conclusion was widely circulated in the Philippines and elsewhere, functioning as a colonial discourse that may be characterized as the "corruption scandal of the Philippine National Bank."[10]

With the resignation in November 1920 of Philippine National Bank President Venancio Concepcion and the end of Governor-General Harrison's term in March 1921, the issue of Philippine political leadership came to the fore—which of the two most powerful leaders in Philippine politics, Nacionalista Party members Osmeña or Quezon, would become the nation's top leader. Quezon was the first to open fire. At the end of 1921, taking advantage of his "number two" position in Philippine politics, he began to criticize Osmeña's leadership, asserting the House Speaker's responsibility for the financial crisis. The Nacionalistas then split into two parties, the Nacionalista Colectivista led by Quezon, and the Nacionalista Unipersonalistas led by Osmeña. Quezon emerged victorious, becoming president of the merged Nacionalista Consolidado party while Osmeña was designated vice-president.[11] Thus the financial crisis of 1919–1922 was a crossroads not only for the American colonial administration in the Philippines but also for Philippine politics.

The true history and deeper meaning of the Philippine financial crisis of 1919–1922 is still an unexplored area of study. More painstaking archival research into its underlying causes as well as its consequences could lead to the development of a new framework for historical and political-economic analysis. As it is, available perspectives on the financial crisis and its political consequences seem inadequate. In a study of the Wood-Forbes Mission, Michael P. Onorato discusses the political significance of the change from a Democratic governor-general (Harrison) to a Republican chief executive (Leonard Wood), but he fails to analyze the impact of the mission's particular recommendations on Philippine politics with the shift to a Republican administration.[12] Peter W. Stanley's work, *A Nation in the Making: The Philippines and the United States, 1899–1921*, describes the corruption scandal in the Philippine National Bank and offers some insight into the problems of the currency system, though it does not discuss the loopholes in the Philippine currency system introduced on the advice of the BIA in Washington, and the fatal problems that arose from the misunderstanding of the currency system and its mismanagement by the U.S. administrators in the Philippines. Moreover, his work does not account for the gravity of the crisis that shook the foundations of the American colonial state.[13]

George F. Luthringer's *The Gold-Exchange Standard in the Philippines* remains the work that has most extensively and successfully dealt with the Philippine financial crisis of 1919–1922. However, even in Luthringer's study some questions are not clearly addressed. For instance, *why* did the erroneous exchange operations occur between New York and Manila? *Who* were actually involved in both the United States and the Philippines? *To what extent* was this crisis related to the Philippine colonial system (which was linked with the BIA in Washington)? And *what* were its political consequences in the Philippines?[14] These essential questions will be addressed in this book.

In contrast to the various limitations and missing links of previous studies, this book provides a comprehensive and substantive historical analysis of the Philippine financial crisis of 1919–1922.[15] It unmasks and reveals the true nature of the crisis, and goes beyond the colonial discourse of the "corruption scandal of the Philippine National Bank." The discussion is not confined to Philippine economic history, but probes the political and administrative history of the colony to show the linkages between banking and currency and the colonial administration. Three broader concurrent developments in Southeast Asia provide a revealing regional colonial context in which to examine the Philippine banking and currency reserve system. These are: (1) the general nature of banking and currency systems in colonial Southeast Asia; (2) the shift from the silver to the gold exchange standard that occurred about this time, and the price and trade development that accompanied it; and (3) the role of moneylenders and banks in the export economies of Southeast Asian countries.

**EMERGING BANKING SYSTEMS IN SOUTHEAST ASIA**

When we analyze the formation and development of the modern banking sector in Southeast Asian economies, it is important to understand how financial policies were formulated and implemented. This understanding begins with the nature of their currency systems. From the late nineteenth century to the middle of the twentieth century, all the countries in Southeast Asia except Thailand[16] were under direct colonial rule; no central banks controlled the currency. In most cases, it was the so-called "colonial banks"—that is, branches of major banks of the colonial masters—that conducted banking business in the colonies. These banks had the authority to issue bank notes, under the guidance of a treasury bureau or department of colonial government vested with the authority to regulate financial policies in cooperation with the colonial overlords.[17]

In order to grasp the nature of banking business and the currency systems in colonial Southeast Asia, it is indispensable to understand not only the political and administrative systems in these colonies but also the roles of the colonial masters that directly or indirectly managed these systems and activities. Most literature on Asian financial history, however, lacks detailed attention to the complicated relations between the currency and banking systems and the political and administrative systems for both colonies and their colonial overlords. The specialized division between political history and economic history that typifies Southeast Asian studies tends to hamper our grasp of the overarching design of the colonial system.

In the case of the Philippines under U.S. rule, the Philippine Treasury in Manila was legally charged with the regulation of the currency system, but it was the BIA in Washington that in fact made most of the decisions involving the system's maintenance and reform. From 1917 on, the New York agency of the Philippine National Bank functioned as the depository of the Philippines' currency reserve funds. Thus, in order to illustrate clearly the nature of the financial sectors that collapsed in 1919, it is important to discern the underlying pattern that reveals the behemoth with which the following three entities were deeply involved and inextricably interwoven: the BIA in Washington, the Philippine Treasury, and the Philippine National Bank.

It is also important to understand the peculiar nature of the Philippine National Bank within the broader framework of the development of modern banking systems in Southeast Asia. The Philippine National Bank was among a group of banks locally established by colonial governments or private sectors. An understanding of these distinctive institutions illuminates the peculiar nature of financial sectors in the colonial economies of Southeast Asia. Although the history of Southeast Asian banking and currency has not yet been intensively studied, G. C. Allen and Audrey G. Donnithorne's *Western Enterprise in Indonesia and Malaya: A Study in Economic Development* offers valuable insights into the banking history of these two countries.

In the Dutch East Indies (now Indonesia), the Java Bank was established to stabilize currency in 1828. It served as the note-issuing bank throughout the existence of the Dutch colony. Later, following the decline of *cultuurstelsel* (an early, small-scale crop cultivation system) after 1870, *cultuurbanken* (agricultural banks) began to engage in agricultural financing, especially of the larger sugar and coffee estate plantations. The Nederlandse Handel Mij. (NHM), the largest *cultuurbank*, had been established in 1825 as a state concern and had become a major investor in estate agriculture by the 1860s. British banks also entered the market of the Dutch East Indies—the Chartered Bank of India, Australia and China in 1853, and the Hongkong and Shanghai Banking Corporation in the 1880s. Later, in the early decades of the twentieth century, the Chinese came on the banking scene, and Japanese banks like the Yokohama Specie Bank and the Bank of Taiwan opened their offices in the 1910s.[18]

On the other hand, the history of British Malaya's banking system formed a part of British overseas banking as a whole; the chief banks in Malaya were branches of British banks. The Chartered Bank of India, Australia and China opened for business in Singapore in 1859 and opened a Penang branch in 1875. The Hongkong and Shanghai Banking Corporation opened its office in Singapore in 1877 and in Penang in 1884, quickly penetrating the internal economy of Malaya. In 1888 the Chartered Bank set up agencies in Kuala Lumpur and Taiping. With the expansion of the rubber industry in the early twentieth century, both British banks opened many agencies. The number increased after World War I, with new banks managed by Indians and Chinese. The British banks conducted their business mostly through Chinese agents.[19]

With the opening of unrestricted trade under the Bowring Treaty of 1855, Ian Brown points out, the Hongkong and Shanghai Banking Corporation and the Chartered Bank of India, Australia and China appointed agents in Bangkok. The Hongkong and Shanghai opened its branch in 1888, followed by the Chartered Bank in 1894 and the Banque de l'Indochine in 1897. The major task of these branches was foreign exchange operations, and their principal clients were Chinese merchants who exported rice to Hongkong and Singapore. Recognizing the profitability of the banking business as Thailand's export trade expanded, the Thai royal family established the Book Club as a local bank in 1904 with an initial investment of 110,000 baht under the jurisdiction of the Thai Privy Purse Department. In 1907 the Book Club was renamed the Siam Commercial Bank, with foreign ownership limited to one-third of the bank's shares. The Siam Commercial Bank has continued to play a pivotal role in Southeast Asia with the strong backing of the royal family, despite repeated incidents of mismanagement.[20] Thus, the Siam Commercial Bank may be understood as a domestic bank promoted by the government in rivalry with foreign banks, even as Thailand held on to its political independence under unequal treaties with Western powers.

What, then, distinguishes the banking history of the Philippines from that of other Southeast Asian countries? To answer this question, we should keep in mind the unique circumstances in the Philippines during the general realignment of colonial rule at the turn of the twentieth century. First, unlike other Southeast Asian countries, the Philippines changed colonial masters during this period. Through the Philippine Revolution (1896–1898) and the Philippine-American War (1899–1902) rule over the Philippines was transferred from Spain to the United States. This change in political identity complicated the continuity of Philippine banking history at the beginning of the twentieth century.

As Benito J. Legarda, Jr. incisively discusses in his *After the Galleons: Foreign Trade, Economic Change and Entrepreneurship in the Nineteenth-Century Philippines*, before 1898 the Philippines, although politically a Spanish colony, conducted its export business under strong Anglo-Chinese influence.[21] The major institutions financing agricultural production for export were British and American agency houses like Russell & Sturgis or Peele, Hubbell & Co., with Chinese traders as their intermediaries. The first modern bank established in the Philippines, authorized to issue notes, was the Banco Español Filipino de Isabel II in 1851, with mainly local capital of *obras pías* or religion-based foundations. However, the balance of banking business shifted when the two large British banks opened Manila branches—the Chartered Bank of India, Australia and China in 1873, and the Hongkong and Shanghai Banking Corporation in 1875. Thus, what the Americans inherited when they occupied the Philippines was a commodity export economy controlled by local landed elites and financed by the two large British colonial banks.

In response to this situation, American occupiers first reorganized the Banco Español Filipino in 1907 under the name Bank of the Philippine Islands. This institution functioned as a private commercial bank with authority to issue notes throughout the American colonial period. In 1908 the Agricultural Bank of the Philippine Government[22] was established specifically to finance the agricultural sector, and it was this bank that in 1916 became the Philippine National Bank, intended to be instrumental in expanding agricultural export under Filipino land ownership, rather than to protect U.S. economic interests per se. This banking setup differed fundamentally from the banking arrangements of colonies (or dependencies) under Great Britain, France, and Japan. Legarda points out that in Malaya and Indonesia, for example, Western enterprises were solidly backed by their home governments, while in China and Japan they had to deal with national governments. The Philippines fell between the two models. Western (British or non-American) businessmen had to deal with an American colonial government that was not their own—a third party to every transaction.[23]

This book's analysis of the distinctive features of banking activities in the Philippines under U.S. rule serves to illustrate not only some characteristics of U.S. colonial policy but also the nature of the politico-economic structure already in place in the Philippines that led the United States to choose the policy it did.

## THE SHIFT FROM THE SILVER TO THE GOLD EXCHANGE STANDARD IN SOUTHEAST ASIA

It is important to take into consideration the reform and transformation of the currency systems. The period from the late nineteenth century to the early twentieth century was a crucial time in that currency systems in Southeast Asian countries were shifted from the silver standard to the gold exchange standard. In the middle of the nineteenth century all the currencies in Southeast Asia were based on silver. As Southeast Asian countries expanded their export economies in the 1850s and 1860s, silver shortages caused fluctuation in the value of silver, affecting the Straits Settlements, the Dutch East Indies, French Indochina, and the Philippines. Then a steady decline in the value of silver set in after the 1870s, due to the impact of major new silver discoveries in the United States. Countries in Europe and North America responded by shifting their currency standard from silver to gold, while selling silver in the international market and releasing it to make up their trade deficits.[24] The gold exchange standard was introduced in the Dutch East Indies in 1877, in the Philippines in 1903, in British Malaya in 1904, and in Thailand in 1908.[25] Silver coins remained in use in the colonies, however, and the value of silver was linked to the value of gold used as the monetary standard by their colonial masters. Gold coins, on the other hand, were never circulated domestically in the colonies; it was a "gold standard system without circulation of gold coin,"[26] as Tadao Yanaihara calls it in his study of the currency system of British India. Thus the gold exchange standard of the colonies necessarily remained dependent on the gold standard system of the colonial overlords.[27]

Among the important comparative studies of the history of the currency systems in Asian countries, Edwin W. Kemmerer's *Modern Currency Reform* and William F. Spalding's *Eastern Exchange Currency and Finance* are especially notable.[28] From these studies we may grasp the nature of the transformational process from the silver standard to the gold exchange standard beginning in the 1870s, and the characteristics of the gold exchange standard that prevailed in Asia before World War I. For the period from World War I to the 1930s, studies covering banking and currency reform in Southeast Asia in general are lacking, but we do have excellent studies of currency reform in particular countries during this period, notably Luthringer's *The Gold-Exchange Standard in the Philippines*.[29] Along with Luthringer's book, studies on Thailand and French Indochina offer background and insight on how currency systems fluctuated dramatically in Southeast Asia after World War I.

As has been discussed above, these currency fluctuations in Thailand and French Indochina immediately after World War I arose from three main factors: the export boom in agricultural crops, the exorbitant price of silver, and a large trade surplus. Since these three factors were in constant interaction during and after the war years, Thailand and French Indochina faced difficulties, first in maintaining the gold exchange standard, second in managing the silver standard. In the case of these two countries the crisis occurred because the treasury or the governor-general's office could not cope with the financial aspects of the export boom or the skyrocketing price of silver. However, while these governments avoided fatal errors in their management of currency reserves, the Philippines went into a financial crisis on account of the irregularity of the deposit of currency reserves at the Philippine National Bank and the use of these reserves to finance the production and export of primary commodities. With its entire currency system thus undermined, the Philippine economy succumbed to the fluctuations of currencies and commodity prices after World War I.[30]

In his book on the economy of Thailand (1971), James C. Ingram discusses the stable functioning of the gold exchange standard in Thailand from 1902 until the end of World War I. However, like the Philippines, Thailand experienced a serious financial and economic crisis in 1919–1922, with two clearly discernible factors that bear mentioning. First, after World War I, the price of rice skyrocketed, precipitating a rice export boom. The Thai Treasury was swamped with demands for baht from exporters and banks. To compensate for a scarcity of baht, the Treasury took the emergency measure of issuing paper currency, drawing on the country's currency reserves and allowing investment in foreign securities in pounds sterling. As a result, the volume of paper money doubled between 1918 and 1919. By June 1919 it had become clear that the rice export boom was endangering the domestic food supply, and rice export was banned except under certain conditions.

The second factor in the Thai financial crisis was the enormous rise in the price of silver in early 1919, at the moment when it became clear that the rice export boom threatened the domestic economy. The Thai government reluctantly inflated the value of the baht against the pound sterling in order to cope with the situation. However, the price of silver continued to rise, with devastating consequences. Faced with the prospect of crop failure owing to bad weather, the government totally banned rice export at the end of 1919. This ban, combined with the appreciation of the baht, resulted in a heavy demand for pounds sterling that was further augmented by speculative purchases and large orders from foreign importers. Thailand experienced a trade deficit for the first time since 1850, and the Treasury sold 5 million pounds sterling in 1920–1921 alone. This combination of factors deepened the crisis. Fortunately, however, a better crop harvest in 1920 permitted a renewal of rice exports in 1921 and the Thai government entered into agreements with commercial banks for the stabilization of foreign exchange. In 1923–1924 the rate of baht against pound sterling was finally stabilized in Thailand.[31]

During the same period, monetary stabilization became an important agenda item for the colonial administration in French Indochina, as Yasuo Gonjo's study of the Banque de l'Indochine (established in 1875) explains. In French Indochina the silver standard had been initially well-maintained. However, as the price of silver declined at the end of the nineteenth century, export and import transactions of silver were prohibited under decrees of the governor-general during 1903–1905. The silver standard was actually abandoned in French Indochina at this time, and the piastre was placed at floating rates against the French franc and other Asian currencies, destabilizing the Indochinese economy for some time. At the end of World War I the value of the piastre against the French franc rose sharply, necessitating a deliberate stabilization of the colonial currency. Accordingly, the appreciation of the piastre accelerated in 1919 due to three factors—the rise in the price of silver during World War I, the decline in value of the franc (which had become separated from the gold standard), and a large export surplus in foreign trade. In order to meet the increased demand of piastres, the Indochinese governor-general's office authorized the Banque de l'Indochine to increase the volume of bank notes in circulation. In 1920 the demand for piastres continued to increase with the expansion of rice hectarage. Under these circumstances, the governor-general's office introduced a gold and silver double standard system, which was soon abandoned for a direct exchange rate with the franc and then a re-introduction of the silver standard in 1922. Finally, in 1931, French Indochina adopted the gold exchange standard.[32]

## MONEYLENDING, MODERN BANKING, AND THE EXPORT ECONOMY

In the financial history of colonial Southeast Asia, the relations among export economies, modern banking, and the moneylending business should be considered. Southeast Asian economies from the late nineteenth century to the mid-twentieth century may be characterized as "commodity export economies."[33] The nature of such economies may be summarized as follows:

(1) In an emerging world economy controlled mainly by Great Britain, only a few crops or raw materials were exported, while industrial products like cotton goods were imported from Western countries. (2) From insular Southeast Asia, including British Malaya, the Dutch East Indies, and the Philippines, primary commodities like rubber, tin, petroleum, sugar, tobacco, and Manila hemp *(abaca)* were exported to the industrial countries of the West, while mainland Southeast Asia (French Indochina, Thailand, and Myanmar) exported rice to the parts of insular Southeast Asia that faced rice shortages due to the expansion of export crop production. (3) Under the above division of trade patterns between insular and mainland Southeast Asia, economies were linked to each other through the rice-trading network that partly functioned as the "intra-Asian trade."[34] (4) As a result of a large migration of peasants and laborers from China, India, and Java to work in tin mines or sugar cane plantations in insular Southeast Asia or the new frontiers for rice production in the mainland countries, the ethnic composition of the population changed in most Southeast Asian countries. Finally, (5) In the export agriculture or mining industries, not only Western enterprises or overseas Chinese but also local landowners invested capital, while overseas Chinese or Indians played important roles as merchants or moneylenders.[35]

The penetration of Western powers into Southeast Asia and the subsequent colonization, starting from the mid-sixteenth century, maintained the commercial character of long-distance trade until the early nineteenth century. Around 1850, however, the influence of the industrial revolution in Europe and North America engendered a demand for primary commodities, and the prime economic value of Southeast Asia began its gradual shift from trade or commerce to agricultural production, making land and labor in the colonies a major source of wealth for Western countries by the end of the nineteenth century. Most studies of Southeast Asian economic history during the period from the mid-nineteenth century to the early twentieth century focus on this shift to primary commodity production. Excellent studies by Michael Adas and others describe the interrelations among agriculture, commerce, and finance during this period. Adas's discussion of the rice-producing area of Lower Myanmar at the time of the Great Depression of the 1930s, where many peasants were deprived of their land as a result of indebtedness to Indian moneylenders called *chettiars*, is notable among them.[36]

These studies, however, emphasize agriculture and land tenure—not trade, commerce, or finance. Beginning in the late 1980s with studies of the economic activities of overseas Chinese, scholars embarked on full-scale research into the history of the moneylending business in Southeast Asia. This business played a part across a wide range of economic activities, including revenue farming, commerce, mining, and banking. Overseas Chinese acted as the agents of revenue farming in Singapore, the Malay Peninsula, the Dutch East Indies, Thailand, and even India throughout the latter half of the nineteenth century, becoming ubiquitous moneylenders and even bank managers.[37] "Bookkeeping barter," a common method of transaction in Southeast Asian countries, is germane in this connection. This method was used by overseas Chinese revenue agents in the 1920s and 1930s, notably in Singapore, which functioned both as the transshipment station of rice from the mainland and as the consolidation center of rubber from British Malaya. The Chinese agents collected rubber and distributed rice in the same regions through a barter system,[38] an indigenous business practice that had characterized the trading network of Southeast Asia since the early colonial period. The awareness of such practices helps us to see the commercial and financial history of Southeast Asia in a new way, shifting the focus to a structural analysis that seeks to explore significant dimensions of commerce and finance in colonial Southeast Asia that had escaped us previously.

However, overseas Chinese or Indian merchants and moneylenders were not the only people who engaged in finance in Southeast Asia during the colonial period. G.C. Allen & Audrey Donnithorne and Takeshi Hamashita describe the export business transactions of the Chartered Bank and the Hongkong and Shanghai Banking Corporation in the Malay Peninsula, Thailand, Singapore, and the Philippines.[39] Indeed, the major clients of these banks were overseas Chinese and Indian merchants, whose networks became the basis of these banks' expansion. Yasuo Gonjo, in his study of the Banque de l'Indochine, describes how, in collusion with Indian moneylenders, the Banque de l'Indochine extended large loans to Vietnamese landowners (or usurers) and French plantation owners. Prospective crop yields served as the major collateral for these loans (called "crop loans") until the 1920s and 1930s, when the bank began to demand land properties as collateral.[40] A similar situation obtained in the Philippines: for example, when the Philippine National Bank extended agricultural loans to large-scale Filipino landlords, not only landed properties but also prospective agricultural crops were used as collateral through the end of the 1920s.

The institutionalization of crop loans probably dates from the mid-nineteenth century, when export agriculture began to develop and Western agency houses became involved in the purchase of crops from Southeast Asia. This lending method used prospective agricultural crops as collateral at a time when land titles had not been legally authorized. In circumstances where land titles were improperly prepared, some modern banks in Southeast Asia still used crop loans even in the early twentieth century. However, it is probable that Western agency houses found their model of crop loans in the traditional business transactions of overseas Chinese merchants, who had provided advances to local landlords or peasants for the purchase of crops especially in major rice-producing areas as far back as the end of the eighteenth century. In this connection we may discern a continuity from early local commerce to modern banking—two areas of study previously placed in distinct historical and economic categories.[41]

**THE AIM OF THIS BOOK**

In this brief review of some issues in the financial history of Southeast Asia three historical developments have been discussed: relations between financial systems and political and administrative systems; currency standards, fluctuating currency values, and the need for reform; and the interrelation among export economies, modern banking, and moneylending business. The way is now clear to consider the following five points concerning the parts played by the Philippine banking and currency systems in the overarching regime of the American colonial state.

First, the American colonial period in the first half of the twentieth century should be divided into two periods, relative to World War I, with regard to the overall political and economic structure of the Philippine colonial state. Second, the Philippine currency system should also be studied according to these two periods, that is, the period of the gold exchange standard and the process of its transformation into the dollar exchange standard. Third, the rise of modern banking considered in relation to the development of the export economy and the survival into modern banking of indigenous moneylending should be examined. Fourth, the establishment and nature of the business activities of two government banks—the Agricultural Bank of the Philippine Government and the Philippine National Bank—should be studied in order to illustrate the distinctive features of the Philippine banking system before World War I. This should also be discussed in tandem with the role of landed elites in export industries (mainly sugar, coconuts, and Manila hemp) as the most powerful economic interests in the Philippines. Fifth, the Philippine financial crisis in 1919–1922 should be seen in relation to the debacle of the Philippine National Bank. Analyzing the response of the Philippine government to the financial crisis may reveal the characteristic nature of the Philippine colonial system under U.S. rule.

Within the above research framework, this book is divided into three parts and seven chapters. In Part I, chapter 1 discusses the introduction of the gold exchange standard and the process by which it was transformed to the dollar exchange standard, and chapter 2 describes the development of the modern banking system in the Philippines, with special reference to the formation of domestic capital during the American colonial period, by illustrating some case studies of major foreign and domestic banks. In this way, the first two chapters provide an overview of the banking and currency systems in the Philippines under U.S. rule. Part II (chapters 3 and 4) deals with the role of successive government banks established during the formational period of the Philippine colonial system in the economic structure imposed by the United States. Chapter 3 discusses the background and establishment of the short-lived Agricultural Bank of the Philippine Government in 1908 and its failure to fulfill its initial purpose, and chapter 4 describes the establishment of the Philippine National Bank in 1916 and discusses the characteristic dual loan structure of agricultural loans based on land properties and short-term loans such as those based on prospective crop yields. Part III (chapters 5 to 7) addresses the major issue of the financial crisis of 1919–1922, exposing the underlying pattern of the American colonial state in the Philippines. This crisis is analyzed in relation to the debacle of the Philippine National Bank and the collapse of the currency reserves, in which the BIA in Washington and the Philippine Treasury were both deeply involved. Chapter 5 examines how the Wood-Forbes Mission characterized the crisis and goes on to trace the process of formulating the colonial discourse of the "corruption scandal of the Philippine National Bank." This chapter also discusses the involvement of the BIA in a disastrous currency reform policy in 1918, as well as the political consequences of the crisis for the Philippine legislature. Chapter 6 explores the debacle of the Philippine National Bank by detailing specific loans to the industrial and commercial sectors during World War I. Chapter 7 discusses the reconstruction of the Philippine National bank and the currency system in the Philippines during the 1920s.

Colonial economies in Southeast Asia (including Thailand, which succeeded in maintaining a fragile independence) have been defined as "commodity export economies." While the inner structures of all these economies could be understood as "dual economies" or "plural economies," each of them experienced the general post-World War II economic turbulence in different ways, depending on the nature of the country's pre-colonial structure or its relation with the colonial master. In fact, aside from the much later effect of extensive damage during World War II, whether Southeast Asian countries were successful in modernization and industrialization or not largely depended on the characteristics of their economies before independence—characteristics that remained as colonial legacies long after independence. Therefore, in the case of the Philippines, it is important to elucidate how the characteristics of its colonial economy as a whole reflected the nature of the banking sector during the American colonial period. At the same time it is also crucial to show how the banking sector influenced the formation of the producing sectors under colonial rule.

If the financial sector is understood as part of the material basis of the colonial economies of Southeast Asia, it is important to also understand its linkages with the political structure. How do the distinctive features of the political and administrative systems reflect the characteristics of the financial sector? How does the policy-making process tackle financial problems, and how is the relationship between colonies and their colonial masters reflected in this process? What measures were taken by the colonial masters to mitigate the effect of the post-World War I financial turbulence on the colonial systems themselves? Here is an opportunity to discover what kinds of colonial discourse were used by colonial overlords to conceal the actual problems from local politicians, government officials, and the populace for the sake of maintaining "business as usual" in the colonial systems. It is especially important to understand how these colonial discourses were assimilated into the knowledge base of the colonies.

This discussion of the construction of colonial discourses and their function in colonial societies in regard to the post-World War I financial crisis makes it possible to illustrate the enduring nature of colonial rule in the context of banking history and to deepen our understanding of the political role of colonial discourses in colonial states. By analyzing the background of how the Philippine financial crisis of 1919–1922 was characterized for popular consumption as the colonial discourse of the "corruption scandal of the Philippine National Bank" in Philippine society, this book reveals the mechanism that affected even the change of leadership in the Philippines from Sergio Osmeña to Manuel L. Quezon after World War I.

Under U.S. rule, when the first general election for the Philippine Assembly was held in 1907, it was the Nacionalista Party headed by Sergio Osmeña and Manuel Quezon that won the majority of the seats. With several stages of conflict and despite its division into various factions, the Nacionalista Party continued to dominate the Philippine political process throughout the American period. The party came to power by fostering close personal and official ties with American proconsuls or military officers during the crucial first decade of colonial rule. Thus, the new Filipino political elite became the prime mover in establishing the so-called "colonial democracy" in the Philippines, with American encouragement based on pragmatic considerations for the sustenance of the administrative regime.[42] However, the struggle between Quezon and Osmeña during the financial crisis may be understood as a political scene manipulated by American colonial discourse. And it was within the framework of colonial discourse that "colonial democracy" strengthened its foundation in Philippine politics. In this way the book also seeks to explore the possibility of deepening our knowledge of the U.S. colonial system. Although it is primarily a study of the history of the Philippine banking and currency system, this book opens a new approach to the politico-economic history of Southeast Asia in general.[43]

# PART I
# OVERVIEW

CHAPTER 1

# THE PHILIPPINE CURRENCY SYSTEM UNDER U.S. RULE

WHEN THE U.S. CONGRESS enacted the Gold Standard Act in 1900, it was understood that the monetary gold standard would be extended to the former Spanish colonies in Asia and Latin America that the United States had gained as an outcome of the Spanish-American War. The Bureau of Insular Affairs (BIA) was established at the U.S. War Department to administer these colonies or dependencies and to supervise the transition of the colonies' currencies from the silver to the gold standard, thus binding these overseas territories economically to the United States.[1] As Emily S. Rosenberg argues, "The goal behind spreading this Americanized gold-exchange standard was not only to simplify international transactions, thereby facilitating trade and investment, but to create a gold-backed dollar bloc, centered in New York, to rival the gold-backed pound sterling that dominated international trade. America's gold-standard diplomacy expressed the nation's growing economic power . . . . Within the emerging profession of international economics, three men became especially influential: Charles Conant, Jeremiah Jenks, and Edwin Kemmerer."[2] It is also important to note that "[N]early all of the U.S. foreign financial advisers before the Great Depression of the 1930s began their careers in the Philippines."[3]

The United States acquired the sovereignty of the Philippine Islands from Spain under the Paris Treaty in December 1898. At that time the territory was part of the silver standard area and remained so until the United States introduced the gold standard in 1903. The growing economic instability of the ensuing years eventually led to a quasi-dollar exchange standard after the Philippine financial crisis of 1919–1922, and this de facto dollar exchange standard was finally legitimized by Act No. 4199 of the Philippine Commonwealth in 1935. This complex and arbitrary-looking process comes into focus when a link is discerned between the currency system and the role played by the Philippine National Bank in the crisis of 1919–1922.

This chapter describes and analyzes the transformational process by which the Philippine currency system evolved from the imposition of the gold exchange standard in 1903 to the dollar exchange standard that ultimately became the Philippine currency standard in 1935. First, the chapter describes the distinctive features of the Philippine Coinage Act and the Philippine Gold Standard Act, both passed by the U.S. Congress in 1903. Next, it examines the nature and background of the 1918 revision of the Philippine Coinage Act. Third, the chapter outlines the fluctuations of the Philippine currency system with the debacle of the Philippine National Bank in the financial crisis of 1919–1922, highlighting the various responses of the Philippine government, the colonial administration, and the BIA in Washington during the 1920s. Fourth, it traces the process leading to the introduction of the dollar exchange standard during the Great Depression in the 1930s.

**ADOPTION OF THE GOLD EXCHANGE STANDARD**

At the outset of U.S. rule, a Philippine Commission appointed by President McKinley played a major role in setting policy in accordance with the interests of the United States. The First Philippine (Schurman) Commission arrived in March 1899 to investigate and report on Philippine conditions; it was not empowered to govern the islands. However, the Second Philippine (Taft) Commission, which arrived in the Philippines in June 1900, assumed legislative and administrative powers. In 1907, with the inauguration of an elected Philippine Assembly, the Philippine Commission became an upper house (or senate), sharing legislative powers with the Assembly, which served as the lower house. When a formal bicameral Philippine legislature was established in 1916 under the Jones Act, the Philippine Commission ceased its function and was abolished.[4] It was during this period that the gold standard was established (in 1903) and maintained.

Any analysis of the adoption of the gold exchange standard in the Philippines must rely on Edwin W. Kemmerer's *Modern Currency Reform: A History and Discussion of Recent Currency Reforms in India, Port Rico, Philippine Islands, Straits Settlements and Mexico* (1916). According to Kemmerer, five different currencies were in circulation in the Philippines at the outset of the U.S. occupation: (1) Mexican pesos, mostly smuggled into the Philippines, each coin containing 377 grains of pure silver; (2) Alfonsino pesos, commonly known as Alfonsinos, that were minted in Spain as Philippine currency under a Royal Decree of 1897; (3) silver coins of 50, 20, and 10 centavos with pure silver content 11.2 percent less than that of the Mexican pesos; (4) various coins including Spanish pesos, silver coins from Spanish America (in addition to the above-mentioned Mexican pesos), and copper coins from Spain and other countries; and (5) bank notes issued by Banco Español Filipino (later renamed the Bank of the Philippine Islands) in Manila, under authority granted by a Spanish decree of 1896. At the end of the nineteenth century the supply of currency was so limited that all of the above currencies circulated in the Philippines at a value substantially higher than that of the Mexican peso.[5] As Kemmerer observed: "Strictly speaking, the Philippines were not upon the silver standard from the time that gold disappeared from circulation in the early eighties to the time of the American occupation in 1898. They were upon a fiduciary coin standard."[6]

The U.S. War Department estimated that the United States spent 177 million dollars in total from 1 May 1898 to 30 June 1902 for the pacification of the Philippine Islands.[7] One primary policy of U.S. rule in the Philippines was the establishment of a colonial government with political and administrative autonomy; another was the maintenance of a self-reliant financial system. As will be described below, the U. S. government continuously disbursed military funding for stationing its army and navy in the Philippines; yet, U.S. Congress never approved any funding for the Philippine government throughout the period of colonial rule.[8]

To run the colonial government under such budgetary constraints, the United States first needed to stabilize the exchange rate between the U.S. dollar and various monies circulating in the Philippines.[9] The Philippine Commission first attempted to maintain a rate of two Mexican pesos to one dollar in American gold.[10] However, when the Boxer Rebellion broke out in China, the exchange rate of the Mexican pesos rose sharply in 1900 owing to the strong demand for silver currency, only to fall again after the rebellion ended in 1901. During the period 1902–1903 the Philippine government (the so-called Insular Government established by the Philippine Commission in 1901) was forced to change the official exchange rates several times.[11] The instability of the exchange rate of the Mexican pesos not only had a negative impact on foreign trade, but also brought financial losses and considerable complexity in budgetary accounting for the Philippine government.[12] Many heated debates on the long-lasting reform of the currency system were held in the Philippines during the first decade of the twentieth century. In 1901 three different plans were proposed for currency reform: (1) to retain the silver standard, by re-coining the Mexican and Spanish-Filipino coins into American coins[13]; (2) to establish the gold standard by adopting the U.S. dollar; (3) to adopt the gold standard with a new peso equivalent to half the U.S. dollar.[14]

The first plan had the support of overseas Chinese and European exporters in the Philippines as well as British bankers. They did business with the neighboring countries of China and the Straits Settlements, which ran currency systems based on a silver standard as part of the British economic sphere. These businessmen preferred to maintain a silver standard in the Philippines similar to that of other Asian countries. However, because American and European importers incurred enormous losses resulting from silver devaluations, the Philippine government was not inclined to maintain the silver standard, so the plan for retaining the silver standard was unanimously opposed not only by the members of the Philippine Commission who dominated the legislative and administrative power in the Philippines at that time but also by the majority in the U.S. House of Representatives (although it was once approved by the U.S. Senate).[15]

On the second plan, about simply making the U.S. dollar legal tender in the Philippines, there were various opinions in the United States. Supporters offered three reasons: (1) it was the simplest way to introduce a gold standard; (2) it would encourage closer relations with the United States; and (3) it would bolster U.S. prestige among the Filipino people. Opponents argued that: (1) the Filipino people were accustomed to silver coins, so that the introduction of American money would cause confusion; (2) the American dollar was too large in value to be the unit of Philippine currency; (3) there was a danger that American dollar might be counterfeited in the Philippines; and (4) maintaining the American currency system in the Philippines would necessitate a substantial gold reserve and gold coin in circulation, and this gold would drain away to other countries in Asia. This plan was in fact adopted by the U.S. House of Representatives in January 1903, but rejected by the Senate and later abandoned by the House.[16]

The Philippine Commission regarded the third plan, a new gold-based peso, as the most suitable for the Philippines. Upon the transition to civilian rule in July 1901, U.S. Secretary of War Elihu Root sent Charles A. Conant to the Philippines to prepare a reform plan for a new currency and banking system.[17] At that time Conant was already widely recognized as a leading financial and banking expert by American government officials and bankers.[18] Conant, after conducting his investigations during the summer of 1901, proposed a new coinage and banking system in the Philippines in accordance with that favored by the Philippine Commission.[19] In January 1902, a bill for Philippine currency reform was submitted to both the U.S. House of Representatives and the Senate, but was withdrawn when it failed to secure approval.[20] Hence the basic plan for the currency system had still not been decided when the Philippine Organic Act of July 1902 was enacted, by which the general guidelines for Philippine colonial rule under a civil government were formulated.[21] However, with the strong recommendation of the Philippine Commission, the same currency reform bill was introduced once again to the U.S. Congress in 1903 and this time approved by both House and Senate, being finally enacted in March as the Philippine Coinage Act of 1903.[22]

The Philippine Coinage Act had thirteen sections, and its main provisions were as follows:[23] (1) the legal currency of the Philippine Islands would be the peso, at the rate in gold coin of one U.S. dollar for two Philippine pesos (Sec. 1); (2) the Philippine government was authorized to mint silver currency not exceeding 75 million pesos (Sec. 2), and to mint silver coins of 50 centavos, 20 centavos, and 10 centavos (Sec. 4); (3) to maintain the value of the silver peso at the rate of one gold peso, the Philippine government was authorized to issue a temporary certificate of indebtedness not to exceed 10 million dollars (Sec. 6); (4) the Insular Treasurer was authorized to issue silver certificates and to retain the reserves to back them (Sec. 8).

Under these provisions, a new currency system was introduced in the Philippines, in the form of silver coins based on a gold coin whose denomination was a peso pegged to the U.S. dollar. Charles Conant, who had been instrumental in the introduction of the new system, was called the "Father of the Philippine currency system," and the silver coin first issued in the

Philippines in 1903 was named the "Conant." After his death in 1915, his half-length portrait was printed on the one-peso bill issued by the Philippine government.[24]

This was the gold exchange standard that was introduced by the United States in the Philippines. As will be explained in the next section, it was not unusual for a silver standard pegged to the gold coin of the colonial masters to be the currency system of choice for colonies or dependencies.[25] This form of the gold exchange standard, in which silver currency was backed by the price of gold, meant that the Philippines would be in a subordinate position to the United States, its colonial master.

While the Philippine Coinage Act of 1903 reflects the general outline of Philippine currency system as laid down by the U.S. Congress, the Philippine Gold Standard Act (Act No. 938), enacted by the Philippine Commission in 1903, established various detailed regulations for the government institutions to implement the Coinage Act and the establishment of the currency reserve. The Philippine Gold Standard Act had fourteen sections and its main regulations may be summarized as follows:[26] (1) The Gold Standard Fund was established as a trust fund at the Bureau of the Treasury in the Philippine government to be used for the purpose of maintaining the parity of the silver Philippine peso with the gold standard peso. This fund drew on various sources: the proceeds of the certificates of indebtedness; all profits of seigniorage made by the Philippine government in the purchase of bullion and coinage, and in the issue of Philippine pesos and subsidiary and minor coins; all profits made by the Philippine government from exchange between the Philippines and the United States; and all other receipts taken by the Insular Treasury (Sec. 1). (2) A Division of Currency under the Bureau of the Treasury was created for the purpose of facilitating the circulation of the currency and maintaining parity with the dollar (Sec. 2).[27] (3) To maintain the parity of Philippine currency with the dollar, the Insular Treasurer was authorized to deploy three convertible systems: (a) to sell on demand drafts on the Gold Standard Fund both in the Philippines and the United States; (b) to exchange U.S. bank notes or treasury notes for Philippine currency; and (c) to exchange U.S. gold coin or gold bars for Philippine currency (Sec. 7). (4) Detailed regulations were prepared for the printing and issuance of the silver certificates and the reserve vault of the certificates (Sec. 10).

Thus, a Division of Currency was created under the Bureau of the Treasury in the Philippine government and the Gold Standard Fund was deposited both in the Philippines (Manila) and in the United States (New York). For currency conversion the abovementioned three methods for maintaining parity with the dollar were stipulated, but it was in reality the sale of drafts on the Gold Standard Fund in the Philippines and the United States that put the Philippine currency system onto a gold exchange standard.[28] In short, the gold exchange standard functioned in the Philippines, while the Gold Standard Fund was deposited both in Manila and in New York and the drafts sold at a fixed rate on the fund, thereby maintaining the parity of the currency by government regulation of foreign exchange without circulation of gold coin. The Philippine government in Manila and the U.S. War Department faced various difficulties in maintaining the gold exchange standard from the time of its introduction—for example, the problems with the issuance of new currencies in 1903, or the sharp increase in the price of silver between 1905 and 1907—but these difficulties were not serious enough to lead to currency reform in the Philippines. A more severe problem, which the Philippine government and the U.S. War Department were to encounter later, was a shortfall in the Gold Standard Fund caused by a change in the function of silver certificates.

## THE TRANSFORMATIONAL PROCESS OF THE GOLD EXCHANGE STANDARD

As a general rule, to sustain the gold exchange standard in the colonies it was important that the currency system of the colonial masters be stabilized under a gold standard, at the same time as the colonies maintained an export surplus. However, as Luthringer correctly points out, the gold exchange standard was stabilized in the Philippines under rather unusual circumstances. The United States was remitting military expenses to the Philippines every year to maintain its army and navy there. These military expenditures were first transferred in dollars to U.S. banks and then, as the dollars were deposited into the Philippine Gold Standard Fund, silver certificates (in pesos) were issued accordingly. It was due to the constant influx of U.S. military expenditures that the quantity of U.S. dollars in the Gold Standard Fund continuously increased in spite of a trade deficit before World War I. The amount of the transfer of U.S. army and navy expenditures in the Philippines varied year by year; between 1912 and 1921, the annual average was recorded as US$11,635,000, with a low of US$5 million in 1919, and a high of US$23 million in 1918.[29] This was a substantial amount when compared to the overall

Philippine economy before World War I—by comparison, total exports and imports in the Philippines averaged roughly US$50 million annually between 1911 and 1915. As a result, by the early 1910s the Philippine government secured an amount in the Gold Standard Fund equivalent to approximately 40 percent of the total amount of currency in circulation. (See Table 1).

Table 1. Status of the Gold Standard Fund, 1909–1912

| Year | (a) Fund in Manila | | (b) Fund in U.S. (1000 dollars) | (a) + (b) (1000 pesos) | (c) San Francisco Mint (1000 pesos) | (d) Net Balance in Fund (a + b + c) [2] (1000 pesos) | (e) Currency in Circulation (1000 pesos) | (d)÷(e) (%) |
|---|---|---|---|---|---|---|---|---|
| | Philippine Pesos (1000 pesos) | US dollars [1] (1000 dollars) | | | | | | |
| 31 July 1901 | 590 | 518 | 5,825 | 13,277 | 4,806 | 18,082 | 41,429 [3] | 43.6 |
| 30 June 1910 | 4,134 | -304 | 7,675 | 18,876 | 463 | 19,339 | 48,755 | 39.7 |
| 30 June 1911 | 2,479 | -782 | 9,619 | 20,153 | 442 | 20,595 | 48,156 | 42.8 |
| 30 June 1912 | 7,112 | -1,819 | 7,242 | 17,960 | 288 | 18,247 | 52,056 | 35.1 |

Source: Philippine Islands, Bureau of the Treasury, *Annual Report of the Treasurer of the Philippine Islands*, various years.

Notes: (1) A minus sign indicates an overdraft.
(2) Excluding the amount in the hands of disbursing agent.
(3) As of 30 June 1909.

With the Gold Standard Fund maintained at a sufficient level, certain provisions regarding the fund and the methods of deposit were revised several times.

First, in January 1908 a portion of the Gold Standard Fund was allowed to be deposited in commercial banks in Manila. Under this new regulation, a sum of 800,000 pesos from the Gold Standard Fund was deposited at the Manila branch of the Hongkong Shanghai Banking Corporation. The Manila branch of the Chartered Bank of India, Australia and China and the Bank of the Philippine Islands also received deposits from the fund. Total deposits from the fund at these three banks reached 1,702,000 pesos, which meant that 41 percent of the Gold Standard Fund of 4,134,000 pesos was held in Manila at that time.[30]

Second, by Act No. 2067 of July 1911, a portion of the Gold Standard Fund could be loaned to local governments (provinces or municipalities) for a repayment period of up to five years. This act also permitted using the fund to purchase interest-bearing first mortgage bonds of sugar mills, where those mills were established by sugarcane landowners as their stockholders, on the following conditions: (1) the bonds purchased could not exceed 70 percent of the value of the property offered as security; (2) the sugar mill had contracts with landowners (or stockholders) owning 3,000 hectares or more; and (3) the sugar mills maintained a sinking fund for the redemption of the bonds and the debt repaid within thirty years.[31]

Third, in December 1912, the following regulations were imposed by Act No. 2083: (1) the total amount of the Gold Standard Fund was fixed at a sum equal to 35 percent of the Philippine government money in circulation; (2) all the monies in the Gold Standard Fund in excess of the above provision were to be deposited to the credit of a general fund in the Bureau of Treasury in Manila; and (3) less than 50 percent of the Gold Standard Fund could be invested for periods not exceeding ten years in loans to provinces and municipalities, though up to half of this 50 percent could be invested as a construction fund for the Manila Railroad Company with the prior approval of the governor-general of the Philippines.[32]

As a result, as shown in Table 2, loans and investments allocated from the Gold Standard Fund increased year by year until they reached nearly 80 percent of the total Fund in 1916–1917. Utilizing the Gold Standard Fund in

Table 2. Loans and Investments of the Gold Standard Fund, 1912–1918

| Year | (1000 pesos) | |
|---|---|---|
| | Total Amount of Fund | Loans and Investments |
| 30 June 1912 | 18,272 | 2,214 (12.1) |
| 30 June 1913 | 18,369 | 5,714 (31.1) |
| 31 December 1913 | 18,402 | 7,647 (41.6) |
| 31 December 1914 | 18,456 | 8,443 (45.7) |
| 31 December 1915 | 18,519 | 9,942 (53.7) |
| 31 December 1916 | 13,391 | 10,608 (79.2) |
| 31 December 1917 | 13,474 | 10,741 (79.7) |
| 15 August 1918 | 14,497 | 10,466 (72.2) |

*Source*: Same as Table 1.

such a manner was a deviation from the original purpose of maintaining the parity of Philippine currency against fluctuations in the value of silver. This should have brought about a shortage in the currency reserve. Why did the Philippine government take such a risk?

The Philippines needed to promote the export of primary commodities in order to relieve its trade deficit, and for this purpose it took measures to vitalize agricultural investment for export. The currency system in the Philippines before World War I faced a dilemma. After the occupation of the Philippines, American businessmen came to the Philippines seeking new investment opportunities in various areas; however, until the mid-1910s, the Philippines did not export sufficient commodities to maintain a favorable balance of trade. Under such economic conditions, the Philippine government promoted investment not only in the construction of the infrastructure, such as railroads, by American enterprises, but also in the processing industries of primary commodities, such as sugar mills run by Filipino entrepreneurs. Under a self-supporting budgetary system, the Philippine government had to procure for itself all the funds needed for its expenditures. It was in response to these colonial circumstances that a preponderance of the Gold Standard Fund was appropriated for investments in public utilities and the processing industries for primary commodities.

The role of the Silver Certificate Reserve also changed during this period. With the establishment of the civil government in July 1901 and its announcement of the end of pacification one year later, the domestic economy of the Philippines gradually recovered, accompanied by an increase in the quantity of money in circulation, including silver certificates. However, such a situation made it unfavorable for the Philippine government to maintain a balance in the Silver Certificate Reserve equal to the issue of silver certificates, as required both by the Philippine Coinage Act and by the Philippine Gold Standard Act. Thus, in June 1906 new provisions were made: a maximum of 60 percent of the total amount of silver certificates outstanding could be held in U.S. gold coins, while silver certificates would be redeemable either in silver pesos or gold coins.[33] Under these provisions the government was not necessarily obliged to redeem silver certificates in silver coins. The silver certificates were transformed from the original "coin certificates" into "currency notes" by this measure.[34] In February 1916, the Philippine government made another provision that the Silver Certificate Reserve could be deposited in U.S. dollars in United States commercial banks designated as depositories of the Philippine government.³⁵ This measure created a new relation between the Silver Certificate Reserve and the Gold Standard Fund, as Luthringer explains:

> [W]hen the major part of the Silver Certificate Reserve became deposits in United States banks, held in exactly the same manner as the balance of the Gold Standard Fund maintained in that country, the Silver Certificate Reserve began to be used in such a way that it assumed in part the function of the Gold Standard Fund. Namely, instead of being used merely as a reserve for the maintenance of the parity of the silver certificates with the coined silver pesos which they represented, the Silver Certificate Reserve began to be used as a regulator fund for maintaining the parity of the silver certificates with the theoretical gold peso. Thus, silver certificates were issued directly against deposits in banks in the United States and were redeemed in drafts drawn on these deposits.³⁶

Interestingly enough, Luthringer suggested the possibility that "the U.S. army and navy transfers must have been affected by the direct issue of silver certificates in the Philippines against deposits in banks in the United States to the credit of the Silver Certificate Reserve."³⁷ Here it may be seen how important the role played by the transfer of U.S. army and navy expenditures must have been in maintaining the parity of the Philippine peso against the U.S. dollar.

In recognition of the fact that a significant portion of the Gold Standard Fund was already being appropriated for domestic investments, along with the transformation of the role of the Silver Certificate Reserve, the Philippine Legislature revised the currency law through Act No. 2776 in May 1918. This revision was made with the strong recommendation of the BIA, which had been considering reform of the Philippine currency system (in response to the shortfall in the Gold Standard Fund) since early in the decade.³⁸ Act No. 2776 revised some of the currency regulations in the Administration Code of 1917 (Act No. 2711), which reorganized the administrative system of the Philippine government under the Jones Law of 1916. Major revised provisions for the currency system in Act No. 2776 were as follows³⁹:

1. The designation "silver certificate" was changed to Treasury certificate (Sec. 1610).
2. The basic currency unit in the Philippine Islands was established as the gold peso; two gold pesos would be equal to one gold U.S. dollar (Sec. 1611).

3. The Governor-General was authorized to order the reduction of the weight and fineness of the Philippine coins, subject to the consent of the presiding officers of both houses of the Philippine legislature (Sec. 1612).
4. The parity between the Philippine silver peso and the legal gold coins of the United States would be kept at the rate of one dollar for two pesos as before (Sec. 1613).
5. The Insular Treasurer was authorized to deposit silver pesos or gold coin of the United States in the Bureau of the Treasury and to issue Treasury certificates (Sec. 1622).[40]
6. The Gold Standard Fund and the Silver Certificate Reserve were combined, to form a new Currency Reserve Fund. The Currency Reserve Fund would be deposited at member banks of the Federal Reserve System in the United States designated by the Governor-General of the Philippines. However, not more than 25 percent of the Currency Reserve Fund could be deposited with any single branch depository in the United States, except at branches of the Philippine National Bank in the United States (Sec. 1624).
7. The Currency Reserve Fund could not be less than the amount of Treasury certificates in circulation, plus 15 percent of the total money of the Philippine government in circulation, exclusive of the silver certificates in circulation protected by a gold reserve (Sec. 1624).

Moreover, three conditions were necessary to sustain the new currency system. First, the Bureau of the Treasury in the Philippines had to be responsible for maintaining the credibility of Treasury certificates as with silver certificates. Second, the U.S. government would have to keep its legal tender at par with the gold dollar. Third, the U.S. depository banks would have to remain solvent to redeem the deposit in gold coins.[41] However, the Philippine currency system under the revised law of 1918 remained unstable. After the consolidation of the two previously separate currency reserves, the newly created Currency Reserve Fund was appropriated for other purposes with even less restraint than the previous Gold Standard Fund had been; it was this that precipitated the financial crisis of 1919–1922 in the Philippines.

## FROM THE 1919–1922 FINANCIAL CRISIS TO THE 1930s: INTRODUCTION OF THE DOLLAR EXCHANGE STANDARD

Figure 1 shows the amount of the Philippine currencies in circulation from 1910 to 1940, including silver pesos, silver certificates (Treasury certificates after 1918), and bank notes. The total amount of Philippine currency in

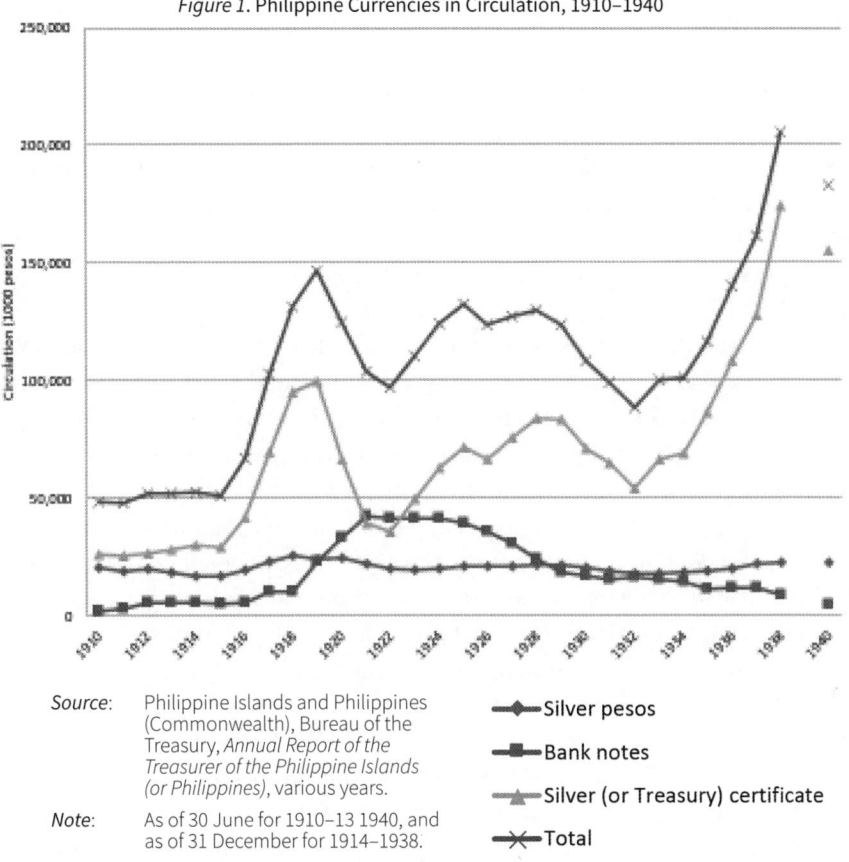

Figure 1. Philippine Currencies in Circulation, 1910–1940

Source: Philippine Islands and Philippines (Commonwealth), Bureau of the Treasury, *Annual Report of the Treasurer of the Philippine Islands (or Philippines)*, various years.

Note: As of 30 June for 1910–13 1940, and as of 31 December for 1914–1938.

◆ Silver pesos
■ Bank notes
▲ Silver (or Treasury) certificate
✕ Total

circulation stood at only 50 million pesos until 1916; however, it increased sharply to 100 million pesos as a result of the economic boom during World War I. In 1919 it swelled even further— to 150 million pesos— the outcome of the serious currency and credit inflation that brought about a shortage in currency reserves. Under measures to stabilize the currency imposed in 1922, circulation in the Philippines fluctuated at around 120 to 130 million pesos during the 1920s, and then dropped to less than 100 million pesos in the early 1930s due to the effects of the world depression. However, in the late 1930s it again increased sharply under yet another reform of the currency system.

It should also be noted that the composition of the Philippine currencies in circulation changed drastically between the 1910s and the 1930s. As shown in Figure 1, silver pesos made up over 30 percent of the total during the first half of the 1910s, and then fell to 20 percent or even less in the late 1910s. At the same time, the percentage of silver certificates and Treasury certificates increased sharply from approximately 50 percent in the first half of the 1910s to between 60 and 70 percent in the late 1910s. In the 1920s the number of Treasury certificates declined, while the number of bank notes rose dramatically, although it was still Treasury certificates that made up the greater part of the money in circulation. Figure 1 also traces the process of how silver certificates or Treasury certificates became the major currency issued after World War I.

What was the main cause of the serious currency and credit inflation after World War I? It was in fact very closely related to the drain of the Currency Reserve due to deposits in the New York agency of the Philippine National Bank. The Philippine National Bank had been established in 1916 as a semi-governmental bank with three major functions: (1) a loan business mainly for agriculture and the processing industries of agricultural commodities; (2) financing for commercial sectors; and (3) issuing bank notes.[42] From the time of its establishment, the Philippine National Bank sought to maintain links with the Federal Reserve System in the United States.

The Federal Reserve System was a central bank unique to the United States, created in December 1913 by the Federal Reserve Act. Under the administration of the Federal Reserve Board in Washington, established by the Act, twelve regionally based banks were put up to supervise and regulate the banking and financial activities, including national and state banks, in their respective regions.[43] However, under the Federal Reserve System, a bank based in the Philippines was deemed a foreign bank, not eligible for qualification under the system. Therefore, according to Section 14 of the Federal Reserve Act, the Federal Reserve Board authorized the designation of the Philippine National Bank as its foreign correspondent or agent in the Philippines.[44]

Before the Philippine National Bank was established, the Philippine government had deposited substantial portions of the Gold Standard Fund and the Silver Certificate Reserve at U.S. commercial banks designated as depositories of the Philippine government. However, most of these deposits were transferred to the New York agency of the Philippine National Bank when it was opened in 1917. By the end of 1916, US$12 million of the Silver Certificate Reserve and US$4 million of the Gold Standard Fund had been deposited in U.S. banks. Out of the US$16 million, US$7 million (44 percent) had been deposited at the Irving National Bank in New York City alone. By the end of 1917, the deposited amount of the Gold Standard Fund and the Silver Certificate Reserve combined in the United States shot up to 30 million dollars, two-thirds of which was held at the New York agency of the Philippine National Bank.[45]

After the consolidation of the two reserve funds, the amount of the Currency Reserve Fund deposited in the New York agency soared to US$ 38 million by the end of 1919. This figure represents 84 percent of the total amount of the funds deposited in the United States. It is indisputable that mismanagement of the Currency Reserve Fund underlay this huge deposit activity during 1918–1919. First, a large portion of the New York deposits of the Currency Reserve Fund was transferred to Manila by the purchase of drafts on Liberty Loan bonds that the United States sold after its declaration of war on Germany in April 1917 (resulting in the issue of more silver certificates in Manila).[46] Second, the National Bank began to appropriate funds transferred from New York, along with amounts from its domestic Currency Reserve Fund, to extend extravagant loans or credits to landowners, entrepreneurs, and exporters, positioning them to take advantage of price hikes in primary commodities during World War I. Inevitably, the haphazard sale of drafts and currency mismanagement during 1916–1919 precipitated currency and credit inflation on the enormous scale shown in Figure 1, making the Currency Reserve Fund essentially non-functional.[47]

Luthringer estimates that by 1919 the transfer of the Currency Reserve Fund from New York to Manila reached more than US$41 million.[48] In April 1919, the Philippine government sold US$10 million worth of short-term notes in the United States, and the Insular Treasury resumed the sale of dollars; however, the treasury continuously faced a serious shortage in its currency reserves.[49] In 1920, as the price of primary commodities declined sharply, currency and credit inflation resulting from the wartime economic boom plunged the Philippines into a severe monetary crisis. The Philippine government attempted to remove Treasury certificates from circulation by selling drafts from 1920 onwards, but the Philippine National Bank could not reclaim bank notes issued improperly by the appropriation of the Currency Reserve Fund. To demand full repayment of loans to landowners, entrepreneurs, or exporters would have meant the collapse of the Philippine economy, at a time when a deflation policy was needed to combat the depreciation of the peso due to the decline in prices of export commodities.

In January 1921, responding to the serious shortage in the currency reserve, the Philippine government implemented Act No. 2939 to revise some of the provisions in Section 1624 of the Currency Reserve Fund in Act No. 2776 of 1918. First, it was now required that the Currency Reserve Fund be maintained at a minimum of 60 percent of the nominal value of Treasury certificates in circulation, up to a total circulation of 120 million pesos, and 100 percent of pesos in excess of 120 million. Second, any surplus in the Currency Reserve Fund, and all its investment, was transferred to the general fund in the Bureau of the Treasury, and any surplus accumulated in excess of 25 percent of the minimum established could be transferred to the general fund entirely or in part.[50]

As shown in Figure 1, the total value of the Treasury certificates in circulation in the early 1920 was well below 120 million pesos, which dictated that the minimum level of the Currency Reserve Fund be set at 60 percent of certificates in circulation. This minimum requirement under Act No. 2939 was far lower than that of Act No. 2776. With this limited currency reserve, the Philippine government faced the difficulty of not being able to cope with the increased demand for drafts on New York, and was forced to suspend the sale of exchange until the end of 1922.[51]

In the midst of this situation, the Philippine government promulgated Act No. 3058 in June 1922, revising yet again the regulation of the currency reserve as follows:[52]

1. A Gold Standard Fund and a Treasury Certificate Fund were established as separate currency funds, by the abolition of the Currency Reserve Fund (Sec. 1622 and 1626).
2. The Gold Standard Fund was to be maintained at a level not less than 15 percent of the Treasury certificates and silver pesos in circulation (Sec. 1622).
3. The Gold Standard Fund would be deposited in Federal Reserve Banks in the United States to be designated by the Governor-General of the Philippines as the depositories of the Philippine government. No portion of the fund could be deposited in any domestic bank or any branch or agency of a foreign bank doing business in the Philippines. No more than 20 percent of the fund could be deposited with any single depository in the United States, except with the bank where the Insular Treasurer kept his deposits in a current account in connection with his exchange operations (Sec. 1623).
4. The Treasury Certificate Fund had to be equivalent to 100 percent of all Treasury certificates in circulation (Sec. 1626).

In addition, this Act also provided the issuance of additional bonds of US$ 23.5 million under the guarantee of the U.S. government.[53]

These measures to reform the currency reserve system were implemented in January 1923, after government bonds were issued with the guarantee of sufficient funding to do so.[54] Thus, the Philippine currency system reverted to the original gold exchange standard after five years' confusion resulting from the revision of the Act in 1918. However, under the reconstructed system, the Gold Standard Fund never recovered its role in maintaining the parity of the peso. With the new emphasis on the circulation of Treasury certificates, the importance of the Treasury Certificate Fund increased in comparison to the Gold Standard Fund.

*Table 3.* Annual Average Amount of the Gold Standard Fund and the Treasury Certificate Fund, 1923–1934

| Year | In Philippine Treasury | | In Authorized Depositories in U.S. (1000 dollars) | Total (1000 pesos) |
|---|---|---|---|---|
| | (1000 dollars) | (1000 pesos) | | |
| (1) Gold Standard Fund | | | | |
| 1923–25 | 2,692 | 807 | 4,720 | 15,630 |
| 1926–30 | 1,919 | 3,947 | 9,889 | 27,562 |
| 1931–34 | 2,272 | 8,406 | 15,119 | 43,188 |
| (2) Treasury Certificate Fund | | | | |
| 1923–25 | 617 | 19,523 | 28,476 | 77,707 |
| 1926–30 | 1,850 | 14,623 | 37,422 | 93,166 |
| 1931–34 | — | 13,095 | 37,414 | 87,922 |

*Source*:   Same as Table 1.

Table 3 shows the amounts of the Gold Standard Fund and the Treasury Certificate Fund during the 1920s and early 1930s. From 1923 to 1925 the annual average amount of the Treasury Certificate Fund was 77 million pesos, five times larger than that of the Gold Standard Fund. During 1931–1934, the annual average amount of the Gold Standard Fund grew to 43 million pesos, still smaller than the Treasury Certificate Fund of 88 million pesos. Treasury certificates (silver certificates before 1918), which had been the predominant currency since World War I, now acquired the status of "currency note," a change from the original status of "coin certificate." Reflecting the transformation in the nature of the Treasury certificate, the Treasury Certificate Fund came to play a much more significant role than that of the Gold Standard Fund in the structure of the currency reserve system.

With the establishment of this new Treasury certificate as the major currency in circulation, the currency system in the Philippines was no longer dependent on the stabilization of foreign exchange through the operation of the Gold Standard Fund, but rather on the maintenance of the parity of the peso against the U.S. dollar, a system fundamentally different from the gold exchange standard. Under the gold exchange standard, it had been the Gold Standard Fund that regulated foreign exchange and the currency system. With the implementation of Act No. 3058 in January 1923, it was the Treasury Certificate Fund that began to play the leading role in the currency reserve system of the Philippines. Because most of the Treasury Certificate Fund was deposited in U.S. banks, the stabilization of Philippine currency was now closely linked to the monetary and credit system of the United States.[55] In this context, it is clear that the reconstructed gold exchange standard was heavily dependent on the strength of the U.S. dollar in international exchange markets, and was actually a de facto dollar exchange standard. Accordingly, the Philippines enjoyed a relatively smooth path following the reform of the U.S. currency system during the Great Depression.

In April 1933 the United States withdrew from the gold standard by suspending the convertibility of paper currency, and in January 1934 the U.S. Congress enacted the Gold Reserve Act. By this act, the United States set a new parity for the dollar, and implemented a devaluation of 40 percent. This was the beginning of the managed currency system in the United States. Following these U.S. measures, the Philippine government also lowered the nominal value of the peso by about 40 percent, maintaining the official rate of one dollar for two pesos as before.[56] Then in March 1935, before the establishment of the Philippine Commonwealth, Act No. 4199 was implemented to reform the regulation of the currency system that had been in effect since the implementation of Act No. 3058 in January 1923. The major changes were as follows:[57]

1. The unit of monetary value in the Philippines would be the peso, and two pesos would be equal in value to one dollar, the dollar being defined as that used as legal tender in the United States (Sec. 1611).
2. For the purpose of maintaining the parity of the Philippine peso with the legal tender currency in the United States, a new Exchange Standard Fund was established (Sec. 1621).
3. The Exchange Standard Fund would be maintained at a level comprised by not less than 15 percent of all Treasury certificates and coins (Sec. 1622).
4. The Exchange Standard Fund would be held in the vaults of the Bureau of the Treasury in Manila, or a portion could be held in the U.S. Department of Treasury and/or with Federal Reserve Banks or member banks of the Federal Reserve System in the United States (Sec. 1623).
5. The Treasury Certificate Fund had at all times to be equivalent to 100 percent of Treasury certificates in circulation and had to be constituted entirely of silver coins. It was to be held in the vaults of the Bureau of the Treasury in Manila (Sec. 1626).

Evidently the new currency regulations did not set the value of the Philippine peso directly against gold. In order to exchange Philippine pesos with gold, they had first to be exchanged for U.S. dollars. For this purpose the Exchange Standard Fund was established, which was actually deposited mostly with the U.S. Department of the Treasury.[58] The Philippine peso had become a currency whose unit of value was determined according to the U.S. dollar, and its relation with gold was sustained only through the medium of the U.S. dollar. By this 1935 Act, the Philippine currency system had lost all vestiges of its original gold exchange standard, having gone over entirely to a dollar exchange standard.

To summarize, the currency systems introduced into various colonies during the early twentieth century were conditioned by a variety of factors, such as the trade structures between colonial masters and colonies, capital investments in these colonies by their masters, the economic interests of domestic landowners, entrepreneurs, or exporters, and the development of banking systems. These factors were in turn also influenced by the currency systems in the colonies. The Philippine currency system during the American colonial period underwent almost constant adjustment to maintain a good fit with its U.S.-dependent trade structure and the prominence of domestic capital in major export industries. In such a context, the gold exchange standard that evolved into the dollar exchange standard could be considered representative of the evolving export economy of the Philippines under U.S. rule. The linkage between the export economy and the banking sector in the Philippine colonial economy is discussed in the next chapter.

CHAPTER 2

# THE EMERGENCE OF MODERN BANKING IN THE PHILIPPINES

AS HAS BEEN WIDELY DISCUSSED, the export sector of the Philippine economy developed from the strengthening of the trade relationship between the Philippines and the United States, particularly after World War I. In comparison with export economies in other Southeast Asian countries, the Philippines experienced neither an overwhelming penetration of capital from its colonial master nor the decisive impact of overseas Chinese. It was rather Filipino and Spanish landowners or entrepreneurs who played the major role in developing the primary commodity industries in the Philippines. Under these circumstances, how did the modern banking sector emerge and expand in the Philippines with the rise of the export economy in the first half of the twentieth century? How did this emergence affect Philippine economic structure during the American colonial period?

This chapter first briefly surveys the Philippine foreign trade structure under U.S. rule and then examines the process by which various banking laws were enacted, with attention to these laws' characteristics. Next, it tracks the development of the modern banking sector from its beginning to its later stages. The chapter concludes with a critical consideration of some exemplary case studies which elucidate the roles of foreign exchange banks, commercial banks, and government banks in the Philippine export economy. In this process, as the interaction of modern banking business and the indigenous financial system in the Philippines is mapped and elaborated, the nature of the economic transformation of the Philippines during the American colonial period will come into focus.

## GENERAL FEATURES OF PHILIPPINE TRADE AND INVESTMENT UNDER U.S. RULE

The Philippine economy was integrated into the British-led world market in the late nineteenth century with the expansion of export crop production (e.g., Manila hemp [*abaca*], sugar, tobacco, coconut products) under Spanish rule. The rise of the export economy and the development of commercial agriculture brought about the formation of a landed elite, along with increasing tenancy and landlessness for most Filipinos. With the U.S. occupation the Americans aimed to delink their major colony from the British sphere in Asia and to integrate it into their own expanding overseas economy. The implementation of this U.S. policy wrought enormous changes in the Philippine economy, itself already undergoing transformation as a result of the end of Spanish rule.

The nature and direction of the U.S.-Philippine trade relationship is clearly discernible in two acts of the U.S. Congress—the Payne-Aldrich Tariff Act of 1909 and the Underwood-Simmons Tariff Act of 1913—by which the Philippine economy was effectively tethered to the United States under conditionalities of "mutual free trade." Trade between the two countries grew rapidly, especially with the opening of the Panama Canal in 1914, which dramatically shortened the distance of the sea lane between Asia and the eastern coast of the United States. The U.S.-Philippine preferential trade structure lasted until 1934 and the enactment of the Tydings-McDuffie Act in the wake of the Great Depression.[1] Thus, the Philippine economy was totally integrated into the U.S. economic sphere for three decades, becoming a major exporter of agricultural products to the United States and a dependent importer of U.S. industrial goods.[2]

Table 4 shows the total amounts of Philippine exports and imports and the share of major trading partners in Philippine foreign trade from 1903 to 1940. Philippine trade, both exports and imports, steadily increased from the early twentieth century to the end of the 1920s. Its aggregate amount swelled from 60 million pesos to 300 million pesos during this period, with a sharp increase after 1910. The average amount of exports and imports increased 1.5 times between the 1906–1910 and 1911–1915 periods, while it increased by 1.8 to 2.2 times between the 1911–1915 and 1916–1920 periods. With the economic boom spurred by World War I, the amount of trade after 1915 ballooned, not declining seriously until the 1930s with the global and lingering effects of the Great Depression.

During this early period there were also significant shifts in the Philippines' trading patterns with partners and among the foremost trade partners. Table 4 shows that before World War I the Philippines' major trade partners were Britain, France, and French Indochina. During this period, Philippine trade with Great Britain comprised 15–30 percent of its total exports and 10–20 percent of its total imports. Trade with France made up over 10 percent of total Philippine exports, while that with French Indochina chalked up a 10–20 percent share of total imports. After the war, however, the share of these three countries declined dramatically, while that of the United States increased sharply. Indeed, trade with the United States constituted over 60 percent of both Philippine exports and imports beginning in the late 1910s, with its share peaking at a high 70–80 percent of Philippine exports by the late 1920s. It is also noteworthy that Philippine trade with Japan increased from the late 1910s, approximating a 10 percent share of total Philippine imports.

The U.S. domination of Philippine foreign trade after World War I is also emphatically evidenced by the data on the major Philippine export products to the United States. Table 5 shows the amount of major export products and the share of the United States by product. The major export products of the Philippines were Manila hemp (*abaca*), sugar, and coconut products (copra, made by drying coconut meat, and coconut oil). The share of these major products, considered in terms of total exports, changed drastically over the period 1901–1940, as shown in the phenomenal rise of sugar and coconut oil exports, which were almost all solely to the United States by the end of the 1920s. Sugar, for example, comprised 40–50 percent of total exports in the 1930s, becoming the Philippines' top export product. Manila hemp, which had maintained the top position in Philippine exports from the late nineteenth century until the 1910s, began to decline in its share since the early 1920s, with income from its export falling below that of coconut products (copra and coconut oil) from the late 1920s onwards.

The shifts in the shares of these major export products were a clear reflection of the development of the processing sectors in primary commodities for Philippine exports. In the case of the sugar industry, the

Table 4. Shares in Philippine Foreign Trade by Region and Country, 1903–1940
(%, 1000 pesos)

| Year [1] | Yearly Average | Europe ||||| | America ||||
| --- | --- | --- | --- | --- | --- | --- | --- | --- | --- | --- | --- |
| | | Great Britain [2] | Spain | France | Germany | Others | Sub-total | United States | Canada | Hawaii & Guam [3] | Sub-total |
| 1. Exports |
| 1903–05 | 63,334 | 28.1 | 3.9 | 7.3 | 0.8 | 0.7 | 40.8 | 41.6 | 0.0 | | 41.6 |
| 1906–10 | 69,558 | 21.2 | 5.4 | 13.2 | 2.0 | 3.6 | 45.4 | 37.2 | 0.1 | 0.1 | 37.4 |
| 1911–15 | 100,014 | 16.6 | 4.8 | 12.8 | 2.3 | 3.7 | 40.2 | 42.9 | 0.1 | 0.2 | 43.2 |
| 1916–20 | 225,991 | 12.5 | 3.1 | 1.9 | 0.2 | 3.3 | 21.0 | 61.9 | | 0.3 | 62.2 |
| 1921–25 | 235,469 | 6.4 | 3.6 | 1.9 | 2.2 | 4.7 | 18.8 | 68.9 | | 0.4 | 69.3 |
| 1926–30 | 298,051 | 4.7 | 3.5 | 1.5 | 2.0 | 3.3 | 15.0 | 75.3 | | 0.4 | 75.7 |
| 1931–35 | 203,892 | 2.5 | 2.7 | 1.6 | 1.0 | 1.7 | 9.5 | 83.2 | | 0.4 | 83.6 |
| 1936–40 | 233,975 | 3.2 | 0.7 | 1.3 | 1.1 | 3.8 | 10.1 | 77.9 | | 0.5 | 78.4 |
| 2. Imports |
| 1903–05 | 62,293 | 15.1 | 6.4 | 3.3 | 5.0 | 3.2 | 33.0 | 15.5 | 0.0 | | 15.5 |
| 1906–10 | 66,739 | 17.9 | 4.6 | 2.8 | 5.6 | 4.0 | 34.9 | 24.7 | 0.1 | 0.0 | 24.8 |
| 1911–15 | 104,362 | 9.4 | 2.3 | 2.3 | 4.0 | 2.3 | 20.3 | 46.2 | 0.1 | 0.6 | 46.9 |
| 1916–20 | 191,188 | 3.3 | 0.8 | 1.2 | 0.2 | 1.1 | 6.6 | 60.1 | | 1.0 | 61.1 |
| 1921–25 | 204,512 | 4.7 | 0.6 | 1.0 | 1.5 | 2.2 | 10.0 | 59.1 | | 0.7 | 59.8 |
| 1926–30 | 256,024 | 4.3 | 0.7 | 1.1 | 3.3 | 3.2 | 12.6 | 62.1 | | 0.5 | 62.6 |
| 1931–35 | 166,026 | 2.9 | 0.5 | 1.0 | 3.9 | 3.9 | 12.2 | 64.0 | | 0.3 | 64.3 |
| 1936–40 | 214,927 | 2.3 | 0.1 | 0.7 | 3.0 | 5.2 | 11.3 | 66.1 | | 0.3 | 66.4 |

Sources: 1903–1920: Philippine Islands, Bureau of Commerce and Industry, *Statistical Bulletin No. 3: Philippine Islands 1920*, Manila: Bureau of Printing, 1921, pp. 125–135.
1921–1940: Philippine Islands and Philippines (Commonwealth), Bureau of Customs, *Annual Report of the Insular Collector of Customs*, Manila: Bureau of Printing, various years.

Notes:
(1) 1939 figures cover January–June only, and 1940 figures are for July 1939–June 1940.
(2) 1921–1940 figures include Ireland.
(3) 1903–1920 figures include Hawaii only.
(4) Japan-China.
(5) British colonies in Asia like Singapore.
(6) The sources state that this category may include trade involving Europe, the Americas and Asia.

| | | | | Asia | | | | | | |
|---|---|---|---|---|---|---|---|---|---|---|
| China | Hong Kong | Japan | Kwantung (4) | British East Indies (5) | French East Indies | Dutch East Indies | Thailand | Sub-total | Australia | Others (6) |
| 2.3 | 7.2 | 3.3 | | 2.1 | 0.0 | 0.1 | | 15.0 | 1.4 | 1.1 |
| 4.6 | 6.4 | 1.1 | | 2.4 | 0.1 | 0.1 | 0.0 | 14.7 | 1.4 | 1.1 |
| 2.4 | 4.5 | 5.5 | | 2.3 | 0.0 | 0.1 | 0.0 | 14.8 | 1.1 | 0.5 |
| 2.4 | 5.1 | 6.1 | 0.0 | 1.3 | 0.6 | 0.3 | 0.0 | 15.8 | 0.8 | 0.2 |
| 2.1 | 2.3 | 5.5 | 0.0 | 0.9 | 0.0 | 0.2 | 0.0 | 11.0 | 0.6 | 0.3 |
| 2.0 | 0.8 | 4.5 | 0.0 | 0.8 | 0.0 | 0.2 | 0.1 | 8.4 | 0.4 | 0.5 |
| 0.9 | 0.5 | 3.7 | 0.0 | 0.3 | 0.0 | 0.2 | 0.1 | 5.7 | 0.2 | 1.0 |
| 0.8 | 0.7 | 6.4 | 0.1 | 0.5 | 0.0 | 0.3 | 0.1 | 8.9 | 0.4 | 2.2 |
| 11.3 | 1.1 | 2.7 | | 7.2 | 21.3 | 0.2 | | 43.8 | 3.7 | 4.0 |
| 7.6 | 1.3 | 4.5 | | 3.5 | 14.9 | 0.8 | 0.4 | 33.0 | 6.5 | 0.8 |
| 4.2 | 1.0 | 6.3 | | 2.2 | 11.9 | 0.9 | 0.7 | 27.2 | 4.8 | 0.9 |
| 6.6 | 0.2 | 11.2 | 0.1 | 1.9 | 5.7 | 1.9 | 1.5 | 29.1 | 3.1 | 0.1 |
| 7.2 | 0.4 | 9.1 | 0.5 | 1.7 | 5.2 | 2.9 | 0.5 | 27.5 | 2.5 | 0.2 |
| 5.1 | 0.2 | 9.5 | 0.6 | 2.3 | 2.3 | 2.3 | 0.1 | 22.4 | 1.7 | 0.7 |
| 4.9 | 0.1 | 10.9 | 0.4 | 2.1 | 0.5 | 2.2 | 0.0 | 21.1 | 1.5 | 0.9 |
| 2.5 | 0.7 | 9.8 | 0.1 | 1.9 | 1.2 | 2.2 | 0.6 | 19.0 | 1.9 | 1.4 |

modernization of its manufacturing accelerated during the 1910s; large sugar mills with modern equipment, called "centrals," were established in sugar-producing areas, replacing the smaller mills that had operated since the late nineteenth century.[3] Copra, which had been for many years exported directly as a raw material for vegetable oil to be produced elsewhere, gave way to processing plants that produced coconut oil for direct export. The amount of and income from exports of coconut oil exceeded those of copra by the 1920s.[4]

The preferential tariff agreements with the United States indisputably stimulated the development of the processing sectors in primary Philippine commodities, bringing about the rise of entrepreneurs in the Philippines, a

Table 5. Shares of Major Export Products in Total Export of the Philippines and Shares of the United States in Major Philippine Export Products, 1901–1940

| Year (1) | Shares of Major Export Products in Total Export of the Philippines (%) | | | | | | Shares of the United States in Major Philippine Export Products (%) | | | | |
|---|---|---|---|---|---|---|---|---|---|---|---|
| | Manila Hemp | Sugar | Copra | Coconut oil | Tobacco | Total | Manila Hemp | Sugar | Copra | Coconut oil | Tobacco |
| 1901–05 | 67.5 | 11.6 | 8.9 | 0.0 | 7.5 | 95.5 | 50.4 | 26.5 | 0.2 | 0.0 | 0. |
| 1906–10 | 51.8 | 15.6 | 18.9 | 0.3 | 9.2 | 95.8 | 52.8 | 42.7 | 4.5 | 51.6 | 14. |
| 1911–15 | 39.2 | 20.2 | 22.4 | 2.6 | 8.8 | 93.2 | 49.2 | 63.8 | 14.3 | 98.8 | 31. |
| 1916–20 | 35.5 | 19.5 | 5.8 | 17.8 | 10.6 | 89.2 | 58.0 | 58.8 | 53.7 | 84.7 | 46. |
| 1921–25 | 20.4 | 29.2 | 13.5 | 14.7 | 8.2 | 86.0 | 50.3 | 84.5 | 60.1 | 95.9 | 44. |
| 1926–30 | 18.2 | 31.6 | 12.0 | 15.9 | 5.8 | 83.5 | 42.9 | 96.3 | 77.0 | 98.8 | 42. |
| 1931–35 | 8.1 | 53.2 | 8.4 | 10.1 | 6.0 | 85.8 | 30.5 | 100.0 | 65.5 | 95.0 | 49. |
| 1936–40 | 10.9 | 42.4 | 10.6 | 9.9 | 4.4 | 78.2 | 31.9 | 99.9 | 68.9 | 94.2 | 48. |

*Source*: Philippines (Commonwealth), Bureau of Customs, *Annual Report of the Bureau of Customs, 1940*, Manila: Bureau of Printing, 1941, pp. 101–111.

*Note*: (1) 1939 figures cover January–June only, and 1940 figures are for July 1939–June 1940.

development beyond the scope of the account here.[5] Table 6 shows the amount of investments in major export industries in 1935, providing a bird's eye view of capital outlays in the Philippine export sector. Unsurprisingly, U.S. investments assumed the dominant position in the development of mills and refineries (or factories) for the coconut industry; however, Filipino investments in the sugar industry, and Filipino or Spanish investments in the tobacco industry, overshadowed their American counterparts in those sectors. Particularly noteworthy was the Filipino share of nearly 50 percent in sugar mills investments, most of which were financed by the Philippine National Bank.[6] The considerable Spanish investments in sugar mills should not be counted as "foreign investments" because most of these could be traced back to the Spanish colonial period and had become indigenized, representing de facto domestic capital. In the tobacco industry, however, a major Spanish tobacco company named Compañía General de Tabacos de Filipinas (Tabacalera) held the prominent position in industrial investments; with its headquarters in Barcelona, Tabacalera could still therefore qualify as "foreign investment."[7]

In land and improvements (agricultural farms or plantations), Filipinos dominated investment across all of the major export industries. Because the

Table 6. Investment in Major Export Industries, as of 31 July 1935

| | Nationality | Land and Improvement million pesos (%) [1] | | Mills, Refineries, etc. million pesos (%) [1] | | Total million pesos [1] | |
|---|---|---|---|---|---|---|---|
| Sugar | Philippine | 340.9 | (94.0) | 79.7 | (47.4)[2] | 420.6 | (79.3) |
| | American | 10.9 | (3.0) | 44.9 | (26.7) | 55.7 | (10.5) |
| | Spanish | 7.3 | (2.0) | 40.0 | (23.8) | 47.3 | (8.9) |
| | Others | 3.6 | (1.0) | 3.6 | (2.1) | 7.2 | (1.4) |
| | Total | 362.6 | (100.0) | 168.1 | (100.0) | 530.7 | (100.0) |
| Coconuts | Philippine | 389.3 | (93.0) | 1.8 | (7.6) | 391.1 | (88.4) |
| | American | 16.8 | (4.0) | 11.1 | (46.6) | 27.8 | (6.3) |
| | Spanish | 8.4 | (2.0) | 1.1 | (4.6) | 9.4 | (2.1) |
| | British | — | | 7.0 | (29.4) | 7.0 | (1.6) |
| | Others | 4.2 | (1.0) | 2.9 | (12.2) | 7.0 | (1.6) |
| | Total | 418.6 | (100.0) | 23.8 | (100.0) | 442.4 | (100.0) |
| Manila Hemp | Philippine | 352.5 | (94.2) | 2.0 | (12.8) | 354.5 | (90.9) |
| | American | 11.0 | (2.9) | 7.9 | (50.6) | 18.9 | (4.8) |
| | Japanese | 7.3 | (2.0) | 1.5 | (9.6) | 8.8 | (2.3) |
| | British | — | | 2.8 | (17.9) | 2.8 | (0.7) |
| | Others | 3.7 | (1.0) | 1.4 | (9.0) | 5.1 | (1.3) |
| | Total | 374.5 | (100.0) | 15.6 | (100.0) | 390.1 | (100.0) |
| Tobacco | Philippine | 40.7 | (96.9) | 0.2 | (1.1) | 40.9 | (67.6) |
| | Spanish | 0.8 | (1.9) | 12.1 | (65.4) | 12.9 | (21.3) |
| | Others | 0.4 | (1.0) | 6.2 | (33.5) | 6.7 | (11.1) |
| | Total | 42.0 | (100.0) | 18.5 | (100.0) | 60.5 | (100.0) |

Source: Philippines (Commonwealth), Department of Agriculture and Commerce, *The Philippine Statistical Review*, vol. III, no. 4 (1936), p. 310.

Notes: (1) Due to rounding error, in some cases the total cannot be equal to the aggregate figures of the amount of each item.
(2) Including the investment of 37,700,000 pesos by the Philippine National Bank.

Philippines was the only Southeast Asian country where large estates (like *haciendas* or plantations) arose and developed, most of these investments came from its emergent *hacendero* class. These big landowners were generally Chinese or Spanish *mestizos* (mixed-blood Filipinos) and some of them became entrepreneurs in the processing industries of primary commodities, together with American and Spanish entrepreneurs. In the Philippines,

Chinese or Spanish *mestizo* families formed the upper-class stratum of society, the product of strategic intermarriages during the Spanish colonial period and, because of their economic activities, becoming instrumental in Philippine capital formation during the American colonial period.[8] In this context, we might characterize the Philippine export economy under U.S. rule as landlord class-initiated, with domestic capital investment predominating.

How did the U.S.-dependent foreign trade structure and the landlord class-initiated export economy relate to the emergence and development of the modern banking sector in the Philippines? To address this question, it is necessary at the outset to discuss the enactment of banking laws by the Philippine government.

**ENACTMENT OF BANKING LAWS**

As has been briefly noted in chapter 1, at the onset of the U.S. occupation it was the Philippine Commission that governed the islands under temporary military rule. The Philippine Commission organized the administrative institutions by establishing various bureaus, including the Bureau of the Treasury which took charge of currency and banking matters. In November 1900, the Philippine Commission promulgated Act No. 52, providing for the supervision of bank operations in the Philippine and stipulating that: (1) the Insular Treasurer would supervise banking operations and submit every six months its report to the Philippine Commission and to the U.S. Comptroller of the Currency; and (2) each bank or each branch of a foreign bank would submit its report of operations to the Insular Treasurer in January, April, July, and October, following the regulations of the U.S. National Bank Act.[9] After the transition to civil government in July 1901, four administrative departments were set up: the Department of Interior, the Department of Commerce and Police, the Department of Finance and Justice, and the Department of Public Instruction. Along with other bureaus, the Bureau of Treasury was placed under the jurisdiction of the Department of Finance and Justice. This administrative structure was confirmed by the Philippine Organic Act of July 1902 and, after further revisions in 1905, 1908, and 1910, such a structure had put Philippine governance on a firm footing by 1912.[10]

In the year following the U.S. Congress passage of the Jones Act of 1916, which sought to prepare the Philippines for eventual independence, the Philippine Administration Code of 1917 (Act No. 2711) was enforced. This act split the Department of Finance and Justice into two, with the Bureau of the Treasury integrated into the Finance Department for currency control and the supervision of banking operations.[11] In February 1929, Act No. 3519 reorganized the system of supervision for banking institutions, creating the Bureau of Banking and placing it under the Department of Finance to discharge supervisory authority over banking institutions, a mandate formerly held by the Bureau of the Treasury. A banking commissioner was granted the power to issue regulations regarding banking operations and was obligated to review and examine them at least once a year.[12] The Bureau of Banking continued to function in the same capacity after the Philippine Commonwealth was inaugurated in 1935 to prepare Filipinos for independence within a ten-year transitional period from that date.

The first Philippine banking law under U.S. rule was the Corporation Law (Act No. 1459) of March 1906,[13] eventually amended several times until its final revision as Act No. 3610 in November 1929.[14] A Banking Law (Act No. 3154) was enacted in March 1924, while a law for the regulation of foreign banking business was created in February 1929 as Act No. 3520.

The Banking Law of 1924 (Act No. 3154) contained the following major stipulations:

1. Banks allowed to operate were required to guarantee a minimum subscribed capital of 500,000 pesos or more, at least 50 percent of which must be paid in cash (Sec. 1).
2. Banks organized under this Act enjoyed powers to carry on such banking business as: discounting and negotiating of promissory notes, drafts, and bills of exchange; receipt and stewardship of deposits; buying and selling of exchange; and issuance of loans on personal security or real estate. Additionally, such banks were disallowed from investing more than 60 percent of their paid-up capital and 50 percent of the money received for deposits in loans on real estate, with the further specification that no loan would be given a grace period longer than one year (Sec. 2).
3. Said banks were authorized to purchase or discount promissory notes, drafts, and bills of exchange, issued or drawn for agricultural, industrial, or commercial purposes and to make available loans on, or discount notes secured by, harvested and stored crops, provided no loans on the security of harvested and stored crops would exceed 60 percent of the market value; in like manner, they could make loans to agriculturalists on standing crops such as rice, copra, sugar, tobacco, and corn, provided these do not exceed 50 percent of the estimated value of crops (Sec. 3).[15]

The revised Corporation Law of 1929 (Act No. 3610) classified banking institutions into four categories (savings and mortgage bank, commercial banking corporation, trust corporation, and building and loan association), and drew up regulations pertinent to each category. The savings and mortgage bank was organized for the purpose of accumulating the small savings of depositors and investing them, together with its capital, in bonds or in loans secured by bonds, bullion, or real estate mortgages. The commercial banking corporation was authorized to receive money on deposit and use it, together with its own capital, for the purpose of making loans, the maintenance of a note circulation, and the purchase, sale, or collection of bills of exchange. The trust corporation was tasked with administering any trusts, or holding property in trust or on deposit, for the use, benefit, or on behalf of others. The building and loan association was dedicated to accumulating the savings of its stockholders, encouraging home building among its stockholders, and loaning its funds to them.[16]

The law regulating foreign banking business of 1929 (Act No. 3520) laid down the following regulations for the branches or agencies of foreign banks:

1. Foreign banks were permitted to conduct business in the Philippines on the condition that they kept at least 90 percent of the deposits payable within the Philippines (Sec. 1).
2. The total liabilities to a branch of a foreign bank doing business in the Philippines could not exceed an amount of 5 percent of its average deposits payable within the Philippine Islands during the preceding calendar year, plus 15 percent of the amount due from such branch to the home office and branches outside the Philippines, after deducting from such amount sums due such branch from the home office and outside branches; furthermore, the discount of bills of exchange or commercial and business papers could not be considered as money borrowed as explained in this section (Sec. 2).
3. If a foreign bank has more than one branch or agency in the Philippines, the accounts of all branches or agencies would be consolidated (Sec. 3).[17]

In sum, the noteworthy features and effects of banking regulations in the Philippines, specifically Act No. 3154, Act No. 3610, and Act No. 3520 may be considered in three ways.

First, while the Banking Law (Act No. 3154) signaled the importance conferred on agricultural loans given its detailed regulations, Act No. 3610 put a premium on commercial loans as well, indicating the primary importance of the business of the savings and mortgage bank and the commercial banking corporation, with some regulations concerning loans on real estate (as collateral) even without specification of agricultural loans on the security of harvested and stored crops. However, as will be discussed later in this chapter, this does not mean that commercial banks did not provide agricultural loans. The major producing activity in the 1920s and 1930s in the Philippines was agriculture, with special emphasis on sugar, coconut products, and Manila hemp for export. In all probability, therefore, major commercial banks provided loans for export agriculture and foreign trading business on the securities of real estates, shipping papers, or warehouse certificates of export products, while the branches and agencies of foreign banks offered loan services to foreign traders.

Second, Act No. 3154 ruled that the maximum period of loans on the securities of real estate would be one year, while Act No. 3160 declared that the saving and mortgage bank could give loans from five to ten years, and the commercial banking corporation for five years. This relatively shorter period for loans that private banks could make available presented some difficulties to local entrepreneurs committed to larger industrial investments because of the dependence on loans from private banks that it implied. The industrial investments in primary commodities, particularly in sugar manufacturing, needed longer lending terms of ten to twenty years. But the private banks themselves could not offer such longer-term loans to local entrepreneurs or investors due to the aforementioned legal constraints imposed by the Philippine government. Borrowers now needed to seek loan services suited to their requirements from other financial institutions able to offer them preferable or better options.

Third, Act No. 3610 recognized the building and loan association, giving this type of banking the official standing it required to count among the financial institutions allowed to operate in the Philippines. Modeled after the mutual building and loan association that developed as a non-banking financial institution in the United States (which had originated in Britain), its main activity was the provision of loans for housing to the urban population, and thus its relevance was to the construction business, not to agriculture or agro-related industries.[18] The building and loan association is therefore excluded from the discussion of the development of the banking sector in the Philippines that follows.

## THE DEVELOPMENT OF THE MODERN BANKING SECTOR

The Bureau of Banking published annual reports replete with various data on the regulations that were laid down for the banking industry, providing valuable information on the development of the banking sector from 1929 to 1940. Such information is not available for the period before 1928. The Insular Treasurer's annually submitted reports can be culled for banking-related information for this earlier period, but given the varieties of items that the Insular Treasurer was required to account for, data on the banking sector were not systematically reported. Using the limited data available from government publications, supplemented by information from other contemporary reports, this section considers the changing trends in banking operations in particular, and the rise and fall of banking institutions in general, during the American colonial period.

Figure 2 shows the changing amounts in assets, loan/discounts/overdrafts, and deposits for the years 1909–1938, taken from the *Annual Report of the Bank Commissioner of the Philippine Islands, 1938*. It should first be noted that the method of compilation of the statistical information was different between the periods before and after 1929. After 1929, banking institutions consisted of savings and mortgage banks, commercial banks, trust companies, and branches of foreign banks. Before 1929, together with these four types of banking institutions, building and loan associations were included (during the 1910s, insurance companies were also possibly added).[19] Certain trends are immediately discernible from the statistical data compiled in Figure 2. Each amount for the three items (assets, loans/discounts/overdrafts, and deposits) reflected no change before 1915. After 1916, all three items increased dramatically, reaching a peak in 1918–1920. Then, in 1921–1922, they declined sharply, stabilizing only after 1925–1926, and increasing again in the late 1930s. Why did they fluctuate in this manner?

First, it is important to interpret such statistical data in relation to the development of foreign trade in general. The rapid increase of banking assets, deposits, and loans/discounts/overdrafts in the late 1910s amply testified to the development of a Philippine foreign trade largely dependent on the U.S. market. Second, as has been discussed in chapter 1, Philippine currency policy, as first established in 1903, was based on the gold exchange standard with two currency reserves; however, the two currency reserve funds were combined into a single Currency Reserve Fund in 1918. The increase

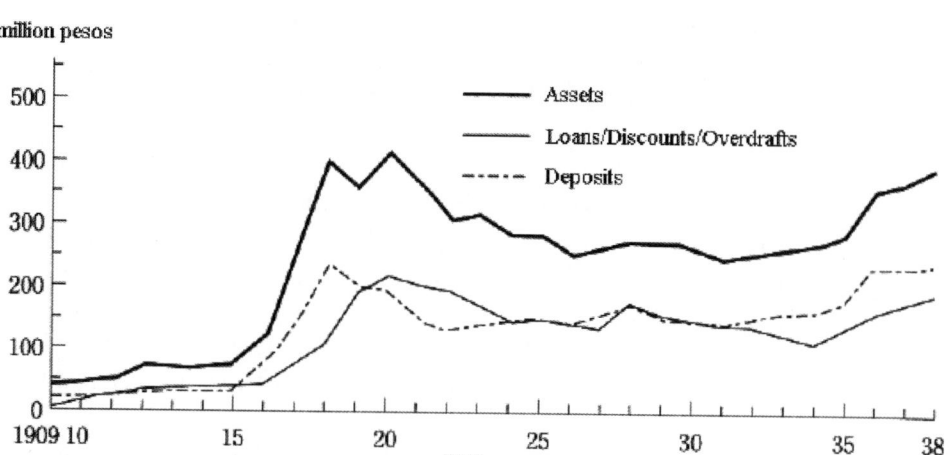

Figure 2. Aggregate Amount of Assets, Loans/Discounts/Overdrafts and Deposits in Banks of the Philippines, 1909–1938

Source:   Philippine (Commonwealth), Bureau of Banking, *Annual Report of the Bank Commissioners of the Philippine Islands, 1938*, Manila: Bureau of Banking, 1939, p.16.

in banking assets, loans/discounts/overdrafts, and deposits for the years 1918–1921 manifests the series of mistaken policies on currency management adopted by the Philippine Treasury and by the Philippine National Bank. Third, the gradual increase in banking assets by the late 1930s might be understood as the result of the recovery from the depression in general, and the 1937 gold mining boom in particular.[20]

Needless to say, the time series data in Figure 2 merely index the general trend of banking activities. To understand such a trend more precisely, it is important to examine when and how banking institutions were established during the American colonial period. Table 7 enumerates the thirty-three banks established in the Philippines from the late nineteenth century to the early 1940s, listing their years of establishment, the nationalities of capital, and their institutional types. Two banks are not listed here, however; one of these was approved for operation but information as to when it actually operated is unavailable, and the other one is recorded as "reopening" in the 1920s but the year of its establishment is unknown.[21] Thus, banks established in the Philippines from the late nineteenth century to the early 1940s give a total count of thirty-five, eighteen of which were still in business in 1940.[22]

These banks may be classified by type of institution: four of them were government-affiliated banks, thirteen commercial banks, two trust companies, two savings and mortgage banks, and twelve foreign banks. Of these, three government-affiliated banks, five commercial banks, two trust companies, two savings and mortgage banks, and six foreign banks operated until the end of the 1930s. Commercial banks and foreign banks composed the majority of those established, approximately half of which eventually closed or merged. Notably, out of five banks established at the end of the Spanish colonial period (two of them were British banks), four served as major banks and continued their operations throughout the American period.[23] During the period 1901–1908, ten banks were established one after the other, but nine of them ceased operations through shutdowns or mergers. These were American, Filipino, Chinese, or Japanese banks with relatively small capital and were poorly managed.

As shown in Table 7, while the period 1901–1908 represents the first phase of the establishing of banks in the American colonial period, the period from the late 1910s to the end of 1920s might be classified as its second phase. During the latter period, eleven new banks were established, five of these subsequently closed, but the remaining six maintained their position as major banks throughout the American period, together with four other banks that date back to the Spanish era. The period from the late 1910s to the end of the 1920s was the most important for the establishment of banks under the Americans, as this was the decade or so when the Philippine export economy became dependent on U.S. markets. The late 1930s might be understood as the third phase, when four smaller private banks were opened by Filipinos, Manila-based Spaniards, and Chinese, along with the opening of one government-affiliated bank.[24] As a new phenomenon, foreign banks in Taiwan (then under Japanese control) and the Netherlands East Indies also opened their branches in Manila, while a Chinese bank incorporated a local bank as its subsidiary. This regional banking expansion reflected the increasing importance of Asian markets like Japan for Philippine foreign trade in the late 1930s.

Table 8 shows the business activities of sixteen banks in 1940, based on the data from the *Annual Report of the Bank Commissioner of the Philippine Islands, 1940*. As shown in Table 8, eighteen banks operated in 1940. (Two government-affiliated banks—the Postal Savings Bank and the Agricultural and Industrial Bank—are excluded from Table 8).[25]

Table 7. Process of the Establishment of Banks in the Philippines, 1851–1940

| Name of the Bank | Year of Establishment | Nationality | Type [1] | Other Remarks (the number indicates the number of the bank in the table) |
|---|---|---|---|---|
| **The End of Spanish Period** | | | | |
| 1. Banco Español de Isabel II (Bank of the Philippine Islands, BPI) | 1851 | Spanish (in Philippines) [3] | C | |
| 2. Chartered Bank of India, Australia and China (Manila branch) | 1873 | British | F | |
| 3. Hongkong and Shanghai Banking Corporation | 1875 | British (in Hongkong) | F | |
| 4. Monte de Piedad y Caja de Ahorros de Manila (Monte de Piedad and Savings Bank) | 1882 | Spanish (in Philippines) [3] | S | |
| 5. Banco Peninsular Ultramarino de Madrid (Manila branch) | 1883 | Spanish | F | Closed in 1887 |
| **First Phase of American Period** | | | | |
| 6. American Bank | 1901 | American | C | Locally incorporated, closed in 1905 |
| 7. International Banking Corporation (Manila branch) | 1902 | American | F | Closed in 1930, merged in (26) |
| 8. Guaranty Trust Co. (Manila branch) | 1902 | American | F | Closed in 1930, merged in (7) |
| 9. Wai Hung Bank | 1902 | Chinese (in Philippines) | C | Closed in 1905 |
| 10. Abreu, Newberry and Reyes Bank | 1902 | Filipino | C | Closed in 1902 |
| 11. Bank of Pangasinan | (1902, 04, 05) [2] | Filipino | C | Closed in 1905, reopened in 1917, closed again in 1919 |
| 12. Bank of Zamboanga | (1902, 04, 05) [2] | Filipino | C | Closed in 1908–1909 |
| 13. Postal Savings Bank | 1906 | Filipino | G | Excluded from the supervision of the Bureau of Banking in 1930 |
| 14. S. Misaka Bank | 1906 | Japanese (in Philippines) | C | Ordered to be closed in 1906 |
| 15. Agricultural Bank of the Philippine Government | 1908 | Filipino | G | Merged with (16) in 1916 |
| **Second Phase of American Period** | | | | |
| 16. Philippine National Bank | 1916 | Filipino | G | |
| 17. Philippine Trust Co. | 1916 | Filipino [3] | T | |

*Table 7*, cont'd.

| | | | | | |
|---|---|---|---|---|---|
| 18. | Yokohama Specie Bank (Manila branch) | 1918 | Japanese | F | |
| 19. | Asia Banking Corporation (Manila branch) | 1919 | American | F | Closed in 1924, merged with (7) |
| 20. | American Foreign Banking Corporation (Manila branch) | 1920 | American | F | Closed in 1920, merged with (22) |
| 21. | China Banking Corporation | 1920 | Chinese (in Philippines) | C | |
| 22. | Chinese-American Bank of Commerce of Peking (Manila branch) | 1920 | Chinese (in U.S.) | F | Closed in 1924, merged with (7) |
| 23. | Cabanatuan Bank | 1923 | Filipino | C | Short-lived |
| 24. | Mercantile Bank of China | 1924 | Chinese (in Philippines) | C | Ordered to be closed in 1931 |
| 25. | Peoples Bank of Trust Co. | 1926 | American | T | Locally incorporated |
| 26. | National City of Bank of New York (Manila branch) | 1930 | American | F | |
| **Third Phase of American Period** | | | | | |
| 27. | Savings Bank of the Commonwealth | 1937 | Filipino | C | Became the Bank of Commonwealth in 1939 |
| 28. | Nederlandsch Indische Handelsbank, N.V. (Manila branch) | 1937 | Dutch (in Netherlands East Indies) | F | |
| 29 | Philippine Bank of Commerce | 1938 | Filipino | C | |
| 30. | Bank of Taiwan (Manila branch) | 1938 | Japanese (in Taiwan) | F | |
| 31. | Philippine Bank of Communications | 1939 | China | C | Locally incorporated by the Chinese Bank of Communications |
| 32. | Agricultural and Indistrual Bank | 1939 | Filipino | G | |
| 33. | Banco Hipotecario de Filipinas | 1940 | Spanish & Filipino (in Philippines) | S | Andres Soriano y Roxas was the chairman |

Sources: H. P. Vibal, "Philippine Banking History," *Banking, Finance and Investments Annual & Directory 1959*, Manila: [Insurance & Finance Pub.] 1960, pp. 52–53; Seiichi Nawata, *Firipin no Tsuka oyobi Kinyu* [Philippine Currency and Finace], Tokyo: Toa Kenkyujo, 1943, pp. 101-104; Mary Grace A. Tirona, "Financial Entrepreneurship and Monopoly Capitalism," *Journal of History*, vols. 32–33 (1987–1988), pp. 34–64; Philippines Islands, Bureau of Banking, *Annual Report of the Bank Commissioner of the Philippine Islands, 1929–1934*, Manila: Bureau of Banking, 1930–1935; Philippines (Commonwealth), Bureau of Banking, *Annual Report of the Bank Commissioner of the Philippines*, 1935–1940, Manila: Bureau of Printing, 1936–1941.

Notes:
(1) G: Government-affiliated bank; C: Commercial bank; T: Trust company; S: Savings & mortgage bank; F: Foreign bank.
(2) Year of establishment varies in different sources.
(3) Major stockholder of the bank around 1940 was the Archbishop of Manila. See Maria Teresa Colayco, *Tradition of Leadership of the Philippine Islands*, Manila: Bank of the Philippine Islands, 1984, pp. 116, 127.

With a head office in Manila and 58 branches, including local agencies and a foreign agency in New York, the Philippine National Bank was the most prominent bank in 1940. It was, indeed, the biggest bank in the Philippines in terms of both size and assets, or the amount of loans and discounts, paid-up capital, and deposit (private or commercial) it held. Other major domestic banks (established locally either by Filipino, Spanish or other foreign investors) were commercial banks such as the Bank of the Philippine Islands and the China Banking Corporation; the Philippine Trust Company and the Peoples Bank and Trust Company were also preeminent. The Monte de Piedad and Savings Bank was the sole savings and mortgage bank until the Banco Hipotecario de Filipinas opened in 1940.

The Bank of the Philippine Islands was the first commercial bank established in the Philippines. Authorized to issue bank notes both during the Spanish and the American colonial periods, it opened branches in Iloilo in 1897, in Zamboanga in 1912, and in Cebu in 1924, eventually expanding its operations to include foreign exchange and discounting notes. Its assets, amount of loans, discounts and overdrafts, paid-up capital, and deposits ranked at the top of commercial banks and trust companies in 1940.[26] The China Banking Corporation was incorporated in 1920 by Manila-based Chinese merchants. It opened its overseas branches in Amoy in 1925 and Shanghai in 1929, and almost monopolized the trade and remittance business with China.[27]

The Philippine Trust Company was established in 1916 by Manila-based Americans for trust business and started its operations in commercial banking by 1920. In the early 1940s, the president of the company was an American, but the major stockholders were Filipinos.[28] The Peoples Bank and Trust Company commenced its business under American capital in 1926. In 1940, it opened branches in the provinces of Pampanga, Laguna, and Tarlac, as well as in Baguio where it specialized in the business of giving out loans for the export of gold to the United States.[29] The Monte de Piedad and Savings Bank was established in 1881, with its initial capitalization drawn from the commutation of some trust funds (*obras*) by the Archbishop of Manila. First created to provide for the charity needs of the poor, it later developed into a savings and mortgage bank with pawnshop operations.[30]

Among the six foreign banks listed in Table 8, two were British, one was American, two were Japanese, and one was Dutch. The major banks among them were the Chartered Bank of India, Australia and China, the Hongkong

Table 8. Number of Branches and Several Items of Balance Sheet of Banks in the Philippines, as of 30 June 1940

| Name of Bank | Total Number of Head Office and Branches | Assets 1000 pesos (%) | Loans & Discounts 1000 pesos (%) | Overdrafts 1000 pesos (%) | Paid-up capital 1000 pesos (%) | Deposits (commercial) 1000 pesos (%) |
|---|---|---|---|---|---|---|
| A. Government-affiliated Bank | | | | | | |
| 1. Philippine National Bank | 59[1] | 144,114 (37.2) | 72,479 (59.3) | 10,918 (11.7) | 10,000 (35.2) | 35,386 (21.5) |
| B. Commercial Banks and Trust Companies | | | | | | |
| 2. Bank of the Philippine Islands | 4 | 38,442 (9.9) | 7,177 (5.9) | 16,733 (17.9) | 6,750 (23.7) | 24,187 (14.7) |
| 3. Philippine Trust Company | 5[2] | 11,176 (2.9) | 4,821 (3.9) | 2,371 (2.5) | 1,000 (3.5) | 9,338 (5.7) |
| 4. China Banking Corporation | 3[3] | 33,480 (8.6) | 4,778 (3.9) | 2,826 (3.0) | 5,713 (20.1) | 14,459 (8.8) |
| 5. Peoples Bank and Trust Company | 5 | 11,316 (2.9) | 2,513 (2.1) | 3,021 (3.2) | 1,000 (3.5) | 9,572 (5.8) |
| 6. Philippine Bank of Commerce | 1 | 3,637 (0.9) | 1,002 (0.8) | 628 (0.7) | 612 (2.2) | 2,705 (1.6) |
| 7. Philippine Bank of Communications | 1 | 8,076 (2.1) | 560 (0.5) | 151 (0.2) | 2,000 (7.0) | 4,996 (3.0) |
| 8. Bank of the Commonwealth | 1 | 904 (0.2) | 277 (0.2) | 436 (0.5) | 500 (1.8) | 374 (0.2) |
| C. Savings & Mortgage Banks | | | | | | |
| 9. Monte de Piedad and Savings Bank | 1 | 10,764 (2.8) | 5,586 (4.6) | — | — | 8,899 (5.4) |
| 10. Banco Hipotecario de Filipinas | 1 | 873 (0.2) | 670 (0.5) | — | 853 (3.0) | 16 (0.0) |
| D. Foreign Banks | | | | | | |
| 11. Chartered Bank of India, Australia and China | 3 | 23,292 (6.0) | 695 (0.6) | 10,977 (11.7) | —[4] | 12,032 (7.3) |
| 12. Hongkong and Shanghai Banking Corporation | 2 | 47,962 (12.4) | 4,200 (3.4) | 35,615 (38.0) | —[4] | 13,724 (8.3) |
| 13. National City Bank of New York | 1 | 36,509 (9.4) | 11,083 (9.1) | 5,932 (6.3) | — | 24,663 (15.0) |
| 14. Yokohama Specie Bank | 1 | 10,250 (2.6) | 3,732 (3.1) | 3,761 (4.0) | —[5] | 2,915 (1.8) |
| 15. Nederlandsch Indische Handelsbank, N.V. | 1 | 4,780 (1.2) | 1,740 (1.4) | 189 (0.2) | —[5] | 970 (0.6) |
| 16. Bank of Taiwan | 1 | 1,639 (0.4) | 945 (0.8) | 60 (0.1) | — | 294 (0.2) |
| Total | 90 | 387,214 (100.0) | 122,258 (100.0) | 93,618 (100.0) | 28,428 (100.0) | 164,530 (100.0) |

Source: Philippines (Commonwealth), Bureau of Banking, *Annual Report of the Bank Commissioner of the Philippines, 1940*, Manila: Bureau of Printing, 1941, pp. 9, 42–57.

Notes:
(1) Including 47 agencies and one foreign branch.
(2) Including 4 agencies.
(3) Including 2 foreign branches.
(4) Capital account amounted at one one million pesos.
(5) Capital assigned amounted at a half million pesos.

and Shanghai Banking Corporation (both British), and the National City Bank of New York (American). As is widely known, the Chartered Bank was the second British bank to establish a branch in Asia in 1853, with extensive operations in India and the Malay Peninsula. It also opened a branch in Manila in 1873, while agencies were opened in Iloilo in 1883 (closed once in 1885 and reopened in 1911), in Cebu in 1900, and in Zamboanga in 1923 (closed in 1938).[31] The Hongkong and Shanghai Banking Corporation, incorporated in Hongkong in 1867, opened a branch in Manila in 1875 and an agency in Iloilo in 1883.[32] As shown in Table 8, its assets and overdrafts in 1940 reached nearly 48 million pesos and 36 million pesos, respectively, thus holding the top position among foreign banks.

The National City Bank of New York came to Manila only in 1930, when it absorbed a Manila branch of the International Banking Corporation. The National City Bank had served as a mother company of the International Banking Corporation in the United States since 1915. With the Manila merger, and the dollars it brought from the United States, it aggressively made inroads into the foreign exchange business in the Philippines previously dominated by the British banks (Chartered, Hongkong & Shanghai).[33] In 1930, along with a Manila branch, an agency was opened in Cebu, which was turned into a branch in 1931 but which closed by 1934.[34] The other foreign exchange banks that were opened in this period included the Yokohama Specie Bank, the Bank of Taiwan (both Japanese), and the Nederlandsch Indiche Handelsbank, N.V.[35] These banks proved instrumental in expanding Philippine trade with East and Southeast Asian countries.[36]

**THE BANKING BUSINESS AND THE EXPORT ECONOMY**

In what specific ways did the business activities of major banks relate to export-oriented agricultural production? Figure 3 shows the different roles played by foreign banks, commercial banks, and government-affiliated banks in the export sector through their loan business. It also suggests that while the branches of foreign banks and the domestic major banks expanded their nationwide financial networks during this period, Filipino or Chinese merchants and usurers established their own regional or local counterparts. No linkage between the nationwide networks of major banks and the regional networks of Filipino or Chinese local merchants and usurers seems to have existed; from all indications, they seem to have been completely distinct from each other.[37] It is obvious then that Philippine finance during this period possessed a dual structure, similar to counterparts in other Southeast Asian countries under colonial rule.

In what follows, while considering the general characteristics of the Philippine financial structure, we illustrate the relationship between the banking business and export economy by way of comparative case study of three different kinds of banks: the Hongkong and Shanghai Bank (for foreign banks), the Bank of the Philippine Islands (for domestic banks), and the Philippine National Bank (for government-affiliated banks).

### Hongkong and Shanghai Banking Corporation

This British bank occupied the paramount position in the Philippine banking sector in the early period of U.S. colonial rule. In 1906–1908, the

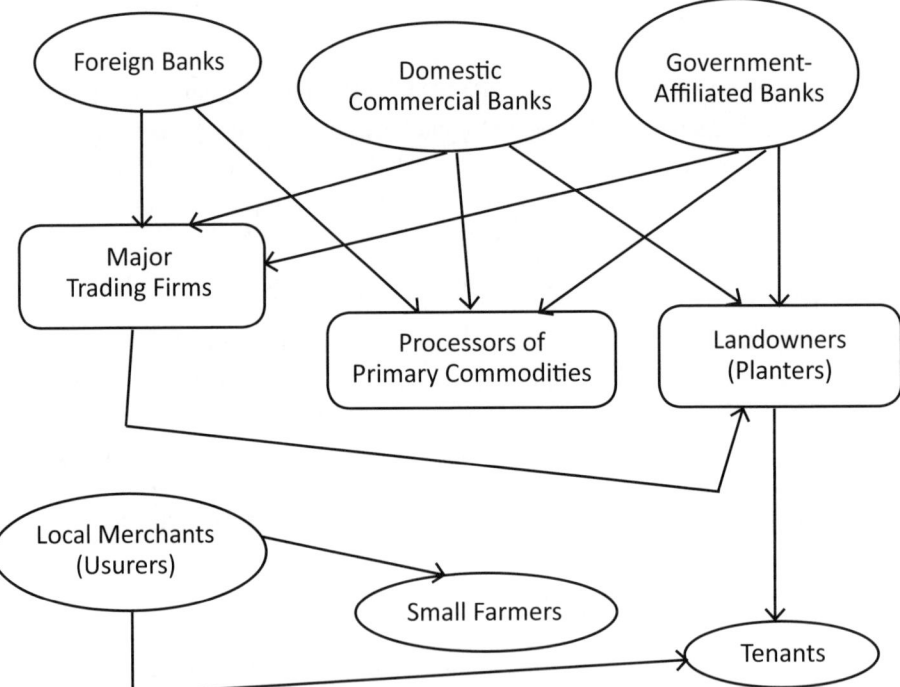

Figure 3. Relations Between Major Banks, Traders and Producers

assets of the Bank's Manila and Iloilo branches constituted 40 percent of the total resources in Philippine banking, although this percentage share declined to around 10 percent in 1916–1918 with the subsequent boom in the establishment of various banks and the expansion of their respective operations.[38] The Hongkong and Shanghai Banking Corporation, however, continued its domination of the field until the outbreak of World War II. It was designated as government depository at the onset of the U.S. rule in the Philippines, along with the Chartered Bank. The International Banking Corporation and the Guaranty Trust Company also became government depositories when they opened Philippine branches in 1902. This designation ended with the institution of the Philippine National Bank in 1916.[39] The major business activities of the Hongkong Bank branches in the first half of the twentieth century were foreign exchange and loan business with foreign trading firms, which had been its emphases toward the end of the Spanish colonial period.

During the late nineteenth century, the funding for foreign trade in the Philippines was mostly sourced from Hongkong. In the 1880s and 1890s, the Hongkong Bank granted credits by commodities and the discounting of promissory notes, while also providing loans with agricultural crops as collateral to foreign trading firms (agency houses), or larger domestic merchants who dealt in the trading of export crops like sugar, Manila hemp, copra, tobacco, and coffee.[40] In the early 1900s the most important trading firms to which the banks made loans were Warner, Barnes & Co., Smith, Bell & Co., Macleod & Co. (British firms all), Aldecoa & Co., and Compañía Maritima. These five companies alone are credited with 83 percent of the bank's outstanding loans and overdrafts in 1904. The Bank's loan portfolio comprised 42 percent of its entire assets in 1904, demonstrating the importance of the lending business to the bank's operations, but this concentration on the credit facility that characterized its activities throughout the American period in fact earned the bank a great deal of criticism.[41]

Needless to say, the Hongkong Bank further expanded its scope of operations through other activities such as deposit-taking and transactions in bills of exchange. Among its major clients were the American construction company Atlantic Gulf & Pacific Co., the Spanish trading firm Ynchausti & Co., and the Spanish tobacco company Compañía General de Tabacos de Filipinas (Tabacalera). It also invested in the Manila-Dagupan Railway in 1906.[42] From the 1900s to the early 1910s, it mostly made loans available to those in the abaca trading business. However, from about 1920 on, its lending services increased for the sugar and copra exporting businesses, as well as for rice milling. For instance, the bank offered loans to the Luzon Rice Mills and the Philippine Vegetable Oil Co. at this time. Much of the Iloilo branch business was connected to sugar exporting, and, as in Manila, the major clients of this Iloilo branch were Warner, Barnes & Co., Smith, Bell & Co., and Ynchausti & Co., together with local traders like Levy Hermanos, Lizarraga Hermanos, Gregorio Montinola, Jose Araneta, and Tabacalera. The operation of the Iloilo branch was limited, accounting for about 10 percent of the Manila total; however, it laid down the Bank's crucial linkages with the sugar industry in Negros Island, the sugarland of the Philippines.[43]

### Bank of the Philippine Islands

This bank was established as Banco Español Filipino de Isabel II in 1851 with the approval of the Spanish colonial government, more than twenty years after the King of Spain promulgated a decree establishing a public bank in 1828. Originally organized as a limited stock company, it had a charter provision for a renewable twenty-five-year term as well as the exclusive privilege of issuing notes up to the total amount equivalent to three-fourths of its paid-in capital. The charter also required that the bank should maintain cash at least one-third the value of the notes in circulation. Banking operations began with *obras pías*, or charitable foundations, providing the main sources for the Bank's capital funds.[44] A royal decree in 1854 approved the bank's by-laws, and authorization to engage in drafts and bills of exchange was granted in 1858. In 1869 the Spanish governor-general ordered that the Bank be renamed the Banco Español Filipino, deleting "Isabel II" (given the political change in Spain). Then, with two royal decrees (of 1876 and 1896), the bank gained a twenty-five-year extension on its franchise.[45]

Thus, the Banco Español Filipino was the only bank that had authority to issue notes under the royal decree of the Spanish government at the time the United States annexed the Philippines. Under the new colonial master, there were various discussions of the Banco Español Filipino's right to issue notes. However, with strong backing from the Archbishop of Manila as guardian of the *obras pías* and from William H. Taft, the first American governor-general (and who later became U.S. Secretary of War and President of the United States), the Bank was reorganized under Act No. 1790 in 1907, which granted the Bank the franchise to conduct business as a commercial bank

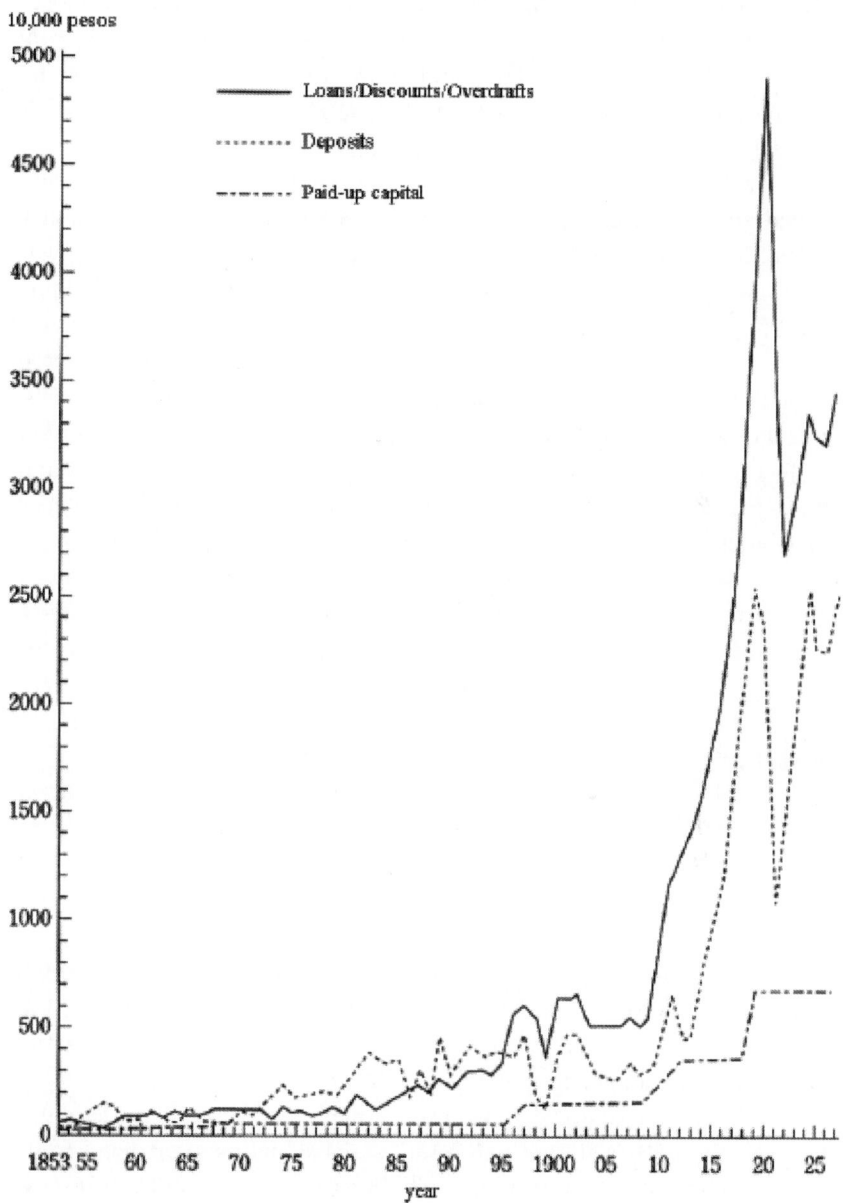

Figure 4. Paid-up Capital, Loans/Discounts/Overdrafts, Deposits of the Bank of the Philippine Islands, 1853–1927

Source: Banco de las Islas Filipinas, LXXV Aniversario, Remembratorio del primer banco establecide en el Extremo Oriente, [Manila]: [1928], drawn from graphs at the end of the book.

and invested it with the right to issue notes. In 1912 the Bank became officially known as the Bank of the Philippine Islands (BPI).[46] Figure 4 discloses paid-up capital, deposits, and loans/discounts/overdrafts of the Bank from the early 1850s to the mid-1920s, and shows the sharp expansion in the bank's business, mirroring the spike in the exporting of primary commodities under the U.S.-Philippine special trade agreement.

Major clients of the Banco Español Filipino in the late nineteenth century included American agency houses like Russell & Sturgis and Peele, Hubbell & Co., the Spanish tobacco firm Tabacalera, and the Compañía de los Tranvias de Filipinas, a railway company that had been set up by Spaniards residing in the Philippines.[47] In Negros or Panay islands, the bank made crop loans available to the landowners or planters of sugarcane farms, after the large sugar mills called centrals were established between the late 1910s and 1920s. Later, after it became the Bank of the Philippine Islands, it extended credit assistance to Victorias Milling Co., Inc., North Negros Sugar Co., Inc., and Asturias Sugar Central, Inc.[48] It can be inferred from the fact of the bank's establishment of its first branch in Iloilo in 1897 that loans provided to sugar producers accounted for a considerable portion of its business. However, the Great Depression adversely affected the Bank of the Philippine Islands; in 1937, for example, sugar and rice harvests in Negros and Panay islands declined, reducing the Iloilo branch's transactions. In Zamboanga, copra prices dropped and had an equally negative impact on the bank's business, even as it extended its operations to Cebu for copra and Manila hemp transactions involving the direct shipment of these export crops to the United States from this port city.[49]

### Philippine National Bank

This government-affiliated bank proved to be the biggest player in financing the export sector of the Philippine economy. As the rise and fall and the rehabilitation of the bank constitute the foci of chapters 4–7, the general features of the bank are just quickly discussed here to complete the comparison with Hongkong & Shanghai and BPI.

The Philippine National Bank was formally established in May 1916 under Act No. 2611 (National Bank Act), superseding its short-lived forerunner, the Agricultural Bank of the Philippine Government (1908–1916) (the details concerning this antecedent bank are taken up at length in chapter 3). Authorized capital for this bank was set at 20 million pesos, 50.5 percent of which was to be raised by the Philippine government. The government stock subscription to the Bank was made in two forms: first, by the transfer of the assets of the Agricultural Bank to it; and second, by subscription of actual cash to the capital stock. The initial subscription of the bank was 1 million pesos and, with the net assets of the Agricultural Bank, the total paid-up capital amounted to 3 million pesos. Afterward the paid-up capital of the bank rose rapidly, reaching 35 million pesos in 1922–1923 under what later turned out to be slipshod management that reduced it to 10 million pesos.[50]

The task of the Philippine National Bank was threefold: first, a development bank providing loans for the production of primary commodities; second, a commercial bank accepting deposits, conducting foreign exchange transactions, discounting notes, and so forth; and third, as an official bank for the depositing of government funds and for the issuance of bank notes. As shown in Table 8 and Figure 3, with the biggest nationwide network and resources among the banks in the Philippines, it directly provided loans to big landowners, mill owners, and traders engaged in the production and exportation of primary commodities like sugar, coconut products, and Manila hemp. The Bank's lending business was of such scale as to dwarf that of the other major foreign and domestic banks. It is therefore no exaggeration to say that the Philippine National Bank served as the pillar of the modern banking sector in the Philippine export economy from the late 1910s to the early 1940s.

From the foregoing discussion, the characteristics of the structure of the Philippine banking sector during the American colonial period may now be synthesized in three ways. First, among the banks that lasted throughout the American colonial period, the Philippine National Bank was the largest in terms of its size and the range of its business activities. As local commercial banks, the Bank of the Philippine Islands and the China Banking Corporation undoubtedly played significant roles, while as foreign banks, the Chartered Bank, the Hongkong and Shanghai Banking Corporation, and the National City Bank of New York were equally preeminent. It is noteworthy here that among the six banks discussed above for their importance in Philippine finance development, there was only one American bank, indicating the weakness of U.S. banking interest in the Philippines. In comparison with other colonies in Asia, a distinctive feature of the Philippine banking system during the American colonial period was that its colonial master showed little interest, and only maintained a token presence, in the banking sector of its colony.

Second, despite the penetration of foreign banks into Philippine capital markets, none of them could establish a monopoly over the financial activities of the burgeoning export economy. Domestic banks such as the Philippine National Bank or the Bank of the Philippine Islands dominated the financing of the export business not only by subsidizing trading firms but also by providing loans to local producers. Third, modern banking institutions provided loans or advances only to major trading firms, larger planters, or mill owners dealing in agricultural products for export. Small farmers or tenants were still forced to rely on usury in local areas.[51] The financial system in the Philippines developed a dual structure, segmenting into a nationwide network among major modern banking institutions and the locally marginalized network of the usury system.

This dual structure of the financial system was typical of Southeast Asian economies during the colonial period. What was peculiar to the Philippines was the absence of the monopolistic control of the financial sector by its colonial master. This is because the financial system developed according to the structure of the production system in the Philippines. It was the local landowners or planters who mainly controlled the export sectors, and only minor investment by U.S. capital could be observed in the agricultural sector. It seemed then that U.S. banking capital was rather hesitant to invest in the Philippines on this account and, once the modern banking sector was established in this way in the Philippines, it could only influence the production system of primary commodities by promoting its fossilization through disinvestment. Herein lies the importance of analyzing the nature of the Philippine National Bank throughout this book so as to understand how it constituted the bedrock of Philippine political economy under the American rule. The next chapter takes up the case of the Agricultural Bank of the Philippine Government as the Philippine National Bank's forerunner.

*Illustration 1.* Escolta, Manila, the then "Wall Street of the Philippines" in the bustling District of Sta. Cruz in Manila, 1916. (U.S. National Archives, RG350-P-E-11-2-3)

*Illustration 2.* The Masonic Temple at Escolta on the Pasig River, the first Manila skyline in the late 1910s. The Manila office of the Philippine National Bank was located on the first floor. (U.S. Library of Congress, Prints and Photographs Division, Foreign Geographical File:46215)

*Illustration 3.* The members of the Board of Directors of the Philippine National Bank at its establishment. From left to right: Leon Rosenthal, V. Singson Encarnacion, Venancio Concepcion, H. Parker Willis, Samuel Ferguson, William H. Anderson, and Charles C. Robinson. (*Bankers Magazine* 95, no. 2 [Aug. 1917])

*Illustration 4.* Staff of the Manila office of the Philippine National Bank (*Bankers Magazine* 95, no. 2 [Aug. 1917])

Illustration 5. H. Parker Willis, first president of the Philippine National Bank. (*Bankers Magazine* 95, no. 2 [Aug. 1917])

Illustration 6. Venancio Concepcion, third president of the Philippine National Bank. (*Far Eastern Review*, Sept. 1923))

*Illustration 7.* Silver certificate, ten pesos, series of 1912, issued 1916–1918. (Author's collection)

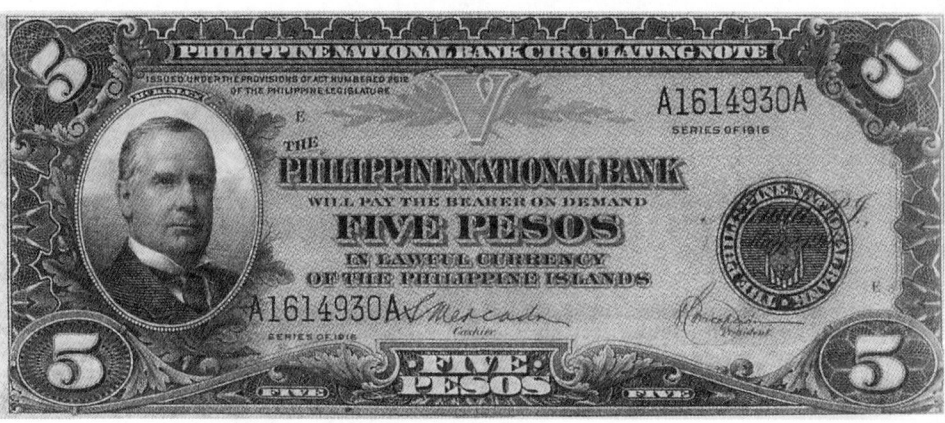

*Illustration 8.* Philippine National Bank note, five pesos, series of 1916, issued 1920–1921. (Author's collection)

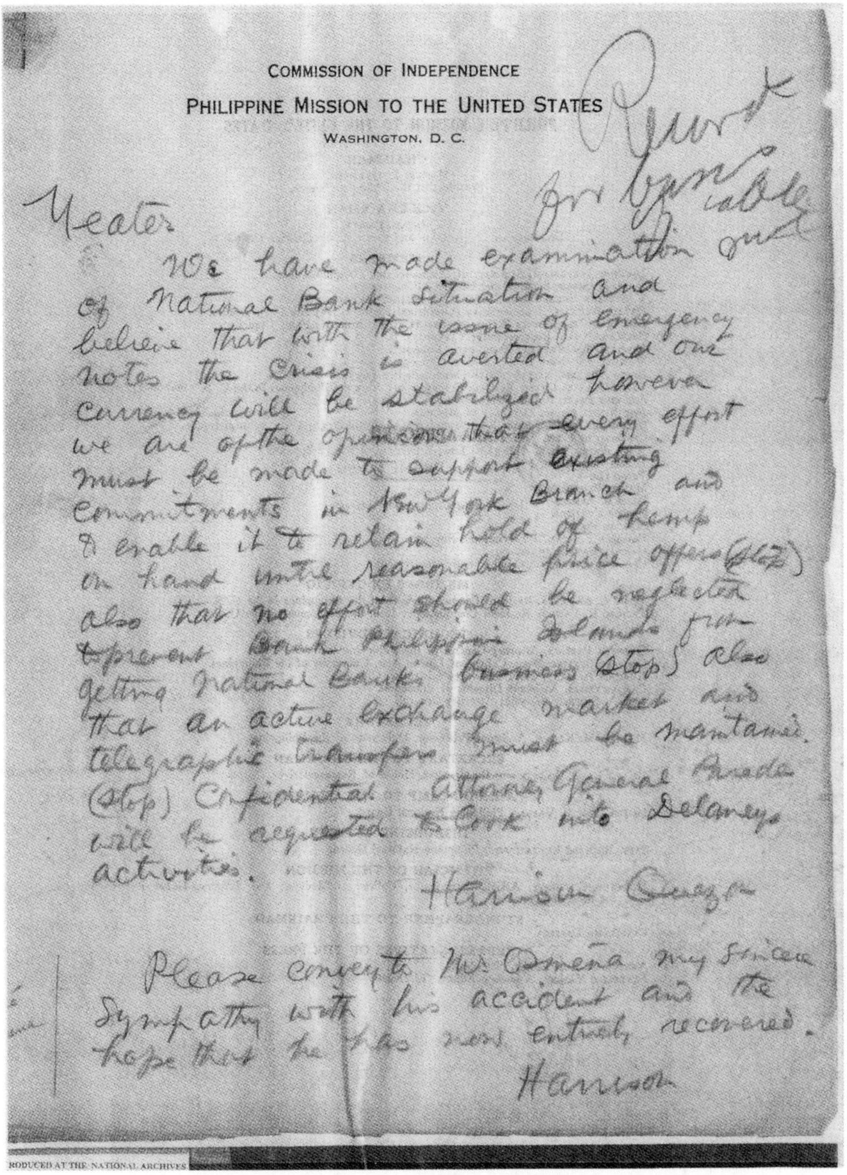

COMMISSION OF INDEPENDENCE
PHILIPPINE MISSION TO THE UNITED STATES
WASHINGTON, D. C.

Yeater

We have made examination out of National Bank situation and believe that with the issue of emergency notes the crisis is averted and our currency will be stabilized however we are of the opinion that every effort must be made to support existing commitments in New York Branch and to enable it to retain hold of hemp on hand until reasonable price offers (stop) also that no effort should be neglected to prevent Bank Philippine Islands from getting National Bank's business (stop) also that an active exchange market and telegraphic transfers must be maintained. (stop) Confidential Attorney General Araneta will be requested to look into Delaney's activities.

Harrison Quezon

Please convey to Mr Osmeña my sincere sympathy with his accident and the hope that he has now entirely recovered.

Harrison

*Illustration 9.* Manuscript of the telegram drafted by Governor-General Francis Burton Harrison jointly with Senate President Manuel L. Quezon in Washington and sent to Vice Governor-General Charles E. Yeater in Manila on 7 April 1919. (U.S. National Archives, BIA 6769-207after)

*Illustration 10.* New York agency of the Philippine National Bank in Manhattan's financial district. (*Bankers Magazine* 95, no. 2 [Aug. 1917])

*Illustration 11.* The Bank of the Philippine Islands, 10 Plaza Cervantes, Manila in the late 1910s. (*Bankers Magazine* 96, no. 3 [Mar. 1918])

*Illustration 12.* Sergio Osmeña, House Speaker (left), Francis Burton Harrison, Governor-General (center), and Manuel L. Quezon, Senate President (right). (*The Philippine Review* 2 no. 12 [Dec. 1917])

# PART II
# START-UP

CHAPTER 3

# THE AGRICULTURAL BANK OF THE PHILIPPINE GOVERNMENT

IN THE FIELD of Philippine political history, several studies have characterized Philippine colonial politics during the American period in terms of various forms of "colonial democracy." In his edited volume, Norman Owen (1971) uses the term "*compadre* colonialism" to illustrate the nature of the relations between the United States and the Philippines. It was understood that the relations between the two countries were similar to the *compadrazgo* system, casting the U.S. colonial administration in the role of "godparent" to Filipino elites under its rule.[1] Peter W. Stanley, in *Reappraising American Empire: New Perspectives on Philippine-American History* (1984), not only emphasizes the importance of the interactions among American colonial officers and the Filipino elite but also attempts to show how the Filipino elite responded to U. S. policy toward the Philippines. Stanley sees the reaction of the Filipino elite as the key factor that forced U.S. rule in the Philippines to deviate from what had been initially attempted.[2] Ruby Paredes (1989a) stresses a "colonial democracy" founded on the grant of autonomy to the Filipino elite, effected by interwoven relationships among Filipino politicians and American government officials in Manila.[3] Michael Cullinane (2003) gives us a more detailed and nuanced study of the Filipino elite reaction to U.S. rule in the early years of the colony.[4] Frank H. Golay's monumental work, *Face of Empire: United States-Philippine Relations, 1898–1946*

(1997) places Philippine politics in the broader context of U.S. colonial policy toward the Philippines, dynamically describing the nature of the colony's political economy.[5]

It was Bonifacio S. Salamanca who first proposed a full-fledged "revisionist" approach to the history of the Philippines under U.S. rule—that the period could not be understood until we appreciated how the demands of the Filipino elite shaped U.S. colonial policy. As Salamanca aptly put it in his book:

> The outbreak of the Filipino-American War on February 4, 1899, was the immediate Filipino response to the American decision to acquire the Philippines. It was the response of the people desiring recognition as a nation, and made all the more brutal by the feeling that the United States had betrayed an earlier trust
> . . . .
> The result was the formation of a policy calculated to reconcile the Filipinos to American rule as quickly as possible and to win back their confidence without promising them independence. This could be accomplished only by meeting some of their demands. From the outset, therefore, Filipino aspirations became important determinants of American policy.[6]

The Filipino demands that the American occupiers sought to accept were not those of the general populace but those of the elites, the *ilustrados* who strongly aspired to political power as a continuation of the economic prosperity they had enjoyed during the last decades of the nineteenth century.

The *ilustrados* belonged primarily to the landed families who had accumulated wealth during the expansion of the export economy toward the end of the Spanish colonial period. In the 1880s they had demanded that the Spanish colonial government establish financial institutions to provide them loans. However, with the outbreak of the Philippine Revolution in 1896, and during the war against the United States that ensued, landowners were forced to rely on usury due to the scarcity of lending institutions.[7] Later, in 1907–1909, when the Philippine Assembly discussed the issue of tariff reduction in U.S. trade, the Filipino elite worked for the establishment of lending institutions for agriculture. When the tariff on U.S. Trade was reduced, the landlords increased their exports of agricultural products such as sugar, Manila hemp (*abaca*), coconuts, and tobacco products. Therefore, it was not a coincidence that, one year before the enactment of the Payne-Aldrich Tariff Act of 1909 in the United States, the Agricultural Bank of the Philippine

Government was established as the government-affiliated lending institution for agriculture.[8]

In general, the period between 1901 and 1927, that is, from the time of the establishment of the civil government to the time of its stabilization, can be divided into three periods. In the Taft era (1901–1913), the United States built up the foundation of colonial policy in the Philippines, keeping the demands of the Filipino elite under tight control;[9] in the Harrison era (1913–1921), "Filipinization" in political and economic institutions was promoted, offering the Filipino elite greater liberty and autonomy in decision-making; in the Wood era (1921–1927), this autonomy became restricted. The workings of "*compadre* colonialism" or "colonial democracy" in the relations between American colonial officials and the Filipino elite are apparent in administrative institutions, nationwide elections, local politics, economic policies, and economic institutions in all three periods. However, because most of the research in this field has been conducted by political historians, we know more about the politics and the bureaucracy of the colony than we do about economic institutions such as banks. Peter Stanley's work (1974) is a partial exception, as it provides a brief discussion of the formation of such government banking institutions as the Agricultural Bank of the Philippine Government and the Philippine National Bank.[10]

Many questions remain. How did American policymakers regard the existing agricultural credit systems in the Philippines? How did the Americans meet the needs of the Filipino elite and formulate appropriate banking policy? What was the response of the Filipino elite to American banking policy? And after its establishment, did the Agricultural Bank only serve the landed elite, or did it have other functions? For what purposes did larger landowners use bank credit? Why did the Agricultural Bank survive only a short period before it was dissolved and merged into the Philippine National Bank in 1916?

This chapter examines the dynamics of the collaboration between American colonists and the Filipino elite through an analysis of the Agricultural Bank of the Philippine Government. First it traces the emergence of a movement for the establishment of a Philippine agricultural bank within both the U.S. and the Philippine governments, paying attention to the petitions and reactions of the Filipino elite on this issue. Second, it examines the evolution of U.S. banking policy toward the Philippines and specifically, Edwin Walter Kemmerer's proposal for the establishment of an agricultural bank in 1905, and the subsequent enactment of the Philippine Agricultural Bank Act (Public Act No. 243) by the U.S. Congress in 1907. Third, it discusses the Agricultural Bank Act (Act No. 1865) passed by the Philippine Legislature in 1908, delineating the role of the Agricultural Bank in the extension of agricultural credit. Fourth, it shows how the Bank's major agricultural loans were offered to landowners who exploited economic opportunities for exporting agricultural products to the United States under preferential tariff agreements in the 1910s.

## PROLOGUE TO THE ESTABLISHMENT OF AN AGRICULTURAL BANK, 1901–1904

An examination of the reports of the Philippine Commissions that initially controlled the legislative and administrative powers in the islands at the onset of U.S. rule reveals the rationale behind the establishment of a new banking regime there. For example, in its report of January 1900 the First Philippine Commission suggested that it was desirable to establish U.S. banks in the Philippines, as no U.S. banks operated in the islands at that time. Three banks controlled the Philippine monetary and exchange business, two of them British (the Hongkong and Shanghai Banking Corporation and the Chartered Bank of India, Australia and China), and the third Spanish (Banco Español-Filipino).[11] The first report of the Second Philippine Commission (1901), contained a concrete request to establish U.S. banks in the Philippines, and apply the U.S. national banking system to the islands. In the report, the Commission stated that the deposit of Philippine government funds in foreign banks was detrimental to U.S. interests, and moreover, if U.S. banks came to the Philippines, they would make a great contribution to the progress of Philippine industry and commerce.[12]

The First and Second Philippine Commissions did not refer directly to the incorporation of an agricultural bank, as their main concern was to reduce and potentially eliminate the British domination of Philippine financial markets. In July 1901, Elihu Root, U.S. Secretary of War, asked Charles A. Conant to investigate financial conditions in the islands and to prepare a reform plan incorporating a new monetary and banking system. As has been discussed in chapter 1, Conant served as a financial expert for the U.S. government. He presented his report in November of the same year,[13] proposing a new monetary system for the Philippines based on the minting of new silver pesos and the introduction of a modified gold standard. In the area of banking reform, he suggested the extension of the U.S. banking system to the Philippines and the establishment of a mortgage banking system.[14]

In drafting his recommendations, Conant took into consideration the desire of American businessmen in the Philippines to secure legislation promoting the establishment of U.S. banks, and the strong demand expressed by the U.S. Army and Navy and Philippine government officials for the creation of an institution to handle remittances from the United States.[15] With these points in mind, and with the support of the Philippine Commission, Conant suggested that the Philippine government be given full powers to regulate the banking business in the islands, using the law relating to national banking associations in the United States. He suggested in addition that the Philippine government should allow mortgage banks to extend credit to real estate and agriculture, and that the U.S. Treasury should be authorized to receive deposits and engage in other transactions with the treasury of the Philippine government.[16]

As indicated above, Conant's report suggested establishing two different types of banks: (1) a bank to serve as the legal depository of the Philippine government which issued circulating notes; and (2) a mortgage banking system that would extend credit to real estate and other local interests. Conant wrote that, when he visited various towns and provinces during his tour of the islands, the desire to create mortgage banks for agricultural loans had been vigorously expressed by local officials as well as by the Philippine Commission.[17] In the report, he explained in detail why he believed the establishment of mortgage banks was necessary. The main point of his argument can be summarized as follows:

> First Civil Governor William H. Taft is especially solicitous that some provisions be made for loans for the benefit of agriculture, and at his request I conferred with Señor Jose Ruis Luzuriaga, recently made governor of Occidental Negros and now a member of the Philippine Commission, in regard to existing conditions and their remedy. He states that interest rates for agricultural loans in Negros are now excessively high. Small money lenders as well as commercial houses charge interest running as high as 25 percent a year, and in some cases it reaches at the incredible limit of 40 percent. Not only in Negros but in the rest of the Philippines the interest rates are generally high due to the risk involved in the loans. In the Philippines, the titles to lands are not always perfectly clear and there is the risk that loans are not repaid due to the failure of crops. However, like in the fertile sugarland in Negros, the security seems to be adequate for the loans

at lower rates of interest. It is obvious that the loans of American capital at lower rates will greatly relieve the present condition of borrowers, while American banks can get more profits than those which are usually earned at home.[18]

The logic of Conant's argument was faulty. While claiming that it was profitable for U. S. banks to offer agricultural loans to Philippine producers at a low rate, he also anticipated that local agriculturalists would default on their loans.[19] Nevertheless, as early as 1901, William H. Taft, the First Civil Governor of the Philippines, was already well aware of the plight of landowners in the island of Negros or other provinces who suffered the scarcity of credit facilities, and considered it imperative to overcome factors detrimental to the production of export crops, and to find ways to respond to the difficulties faced by local elites.

The second report of the Philippine Commission (1901) proposed the introduction of the U.S. national banking system to the Philippines and that mortgage banks be created.[20] However, regarding the second point, a slight difference can be observed between Conant's recommendations and those of the Philippine Commission. Although the Commission acknowledged the need to create banking institutions to provide agricultural loans, its members knew that the financial difficulties faced by the government made it difficult to establish mortgage banks for this purpose. Thus, the Commission recommended that the U.S. Congress pass legislation allowing it to create mortgage banks, thereby encouraging U.S. commercial banks to enter the mortgage business in the Philippines. The capitalization of mortgage banks should not be less than 250,000 dollars and, in the case of a larger commercial bank whose capital was 1 million dollars or more, 25 percent of the total capital could be loaned against mortgages. In the absence of independent mortgage banks in the Philippines, the Commission recommended that the authority to conduct mortgage business should be granted to commercial banks, subject to certain limitations.[21] At this stage, the Philippine Commission showed a very positive attitude toward the creation of agricultural credit facilities by U.S. private investors to serve the needs of local elites. However, local elites wanted banks predominantly offering agricultural credits.

In 1902 the Filipino elite, recognizing that the creation of an agricultural bank was under discussion, began to state their petition more clearly. The first Filipino to submit a concrete plan for an agricultural bank to the Philippine Commission was Emilio Aguinaldo, the leader of the Philippine Revolution. On 23 November 1902, Aguinaldo presented a petition to create an agricultural bank to the Philippine Commission. Governor Taft sent the petition to Secretary Root, who forwarded it to the President of the U.S. Senate and the Speaker of the U.S. House of Representatives on 20 January 1903.[22] The petition, originally written in Spanish, can be outlined as follows:

> It is proposed that the Philippine Commission would obtain from the U.S. National Treasury a loan of US$20 million and a credit of US$80 million from other sources. When the loan and the credit are granted, a bank will be opened, which might be named "The United States Agricultural Protection Bank in the Philippines," under the inspection and control of the insular government. It will loan money to the agriculturalists at a maximum rate of interest of four percent a year, payable every six months. If the bank works well and Filipinos are interested in acquiring the bank, the government would grant them rights, by means of requiring them to pay the expenses made for the establishment of the bank, or such expense as would be deemed necessary.[23]

The background of Aguinaldo's petition is unknown, but it might be surmised that he presented it on behalf of the landlords facing a shortage of funds for agriculture in the aftermath of the war.[24]

In October 1904, Pascual H. Poblete, who issued daily newspapers in Manila like *Ang Kapatid ng Bayan* and *El Grito del Pueblo*, sent a petition to Governor Taft seeking to create a Banco Hipotecario Territorial y Agricola, along with a letter to U.S. President Theodore Roosevelt calling his attention to the issue.[25] The petition was accompanied by a newspaper clipping from *El Mercantil* of 27 October 1904, which offered some observations on the need for an agricultural bank. The major part of this Spanish article can be summarized as follows:

> The creation of Banco Hipotecario Territorial y Agricola with a capital of no less than 30 million pesos will greatly contribute to remedy the country's agricultural crisis. First, it will develop the country's economy, eradicating the high interest rate which prevails in agriculture, industry and commerce. If many Filipino entrepreneurs have intention to invest in industry, commerce and agriculture, they have to borrow money at the annual interest rate ranging from 25 percent to 300 percent. Second, the creation of the bank will make it possible to import agricultural and industrial machineries from North America and Europe and to strengthen the international competitiveness of the country's economy. The property of North America has been brought by the machineries which increased agricultural and industrial products. In the Philippines, on the other

hand, agriculture still depends on ploughs or *carabaos* (water buffalos) which are already obsolete. If bank loans are available in the Philippines, it will be possible to establish the mills for daily necessities such as paper, textile, glasses and ceramics. Agriculturalists or *hacenderos* (landlords) should unite together and demand the government to establish the bank. Unity is might.[26]

This editorial exaggerated the needs of the Filipino elite, which was composed for the most part of landed gentry rather than industrial entrepreneurs, but the establishment of an agricultural and mortgage bank would clearly help restore the agricultural economy and expand the export of agricultural products by making funds available for farm management or loans to tenant farmers.

In 1905 the Filipino petitions to create agricultural loan banks received strong support from American officials in the colonial government,[27] and the executive committee of the Filipino Chamber of Commerce met on 29 June 1905 to take the first step toward the establishment of a real estate loan and agricultural bank. The committee advocated that the proposed bank be founded with private capital, with the assistance of the Philippine government insofar as this could be given within constitutional limits; for example, the Philippine government might guarantee a certain rate of interest on capital invested in the bank. The Insular Collector of Customs, W. Morgan Shuster,[28] commented that the insular government was quite interested in the establishment of an agricultural bank, but was prevented by law from taking direct action; in the United States, however, there was much capital available for such a scheme. The committee agreed that the creation of a private bank for agricultural loans should be encouraged and that a committee should be named for the preliminary work of organization, such as drafting of laws, holding conferences with authorities, and obtaining public and private information for the matter.[29] Thus, at this point it appears that American officials and local elites were in agreement concerning the need to create an agricultural mortgage bank, and that the Philippine Commission was ready to take concrete action for that purpose.

The Filipino elite continued pressing its demand for the creation of the bank. In August 1905, public hearing on the reduction of tariffs on Philippine sugar and tobacco were held in Manila, Iloilo, and Bacolod. At the hearing in Manila on 8 August 1905, Francisco Liongson, a sugar planter from Bacolor in the province of Pampanga, submitted a paper on the petition to establish an agricultural mortgage bank and tariff reduction. He said that the purpose of establishing the bank was to make money available to planters wishing to conduct farming operations, and that they would mortgage their lands to get advances from the bank. He added that there was a great need for the Philippine government to relieve planters of the current depressed condition of agriculture by establishing such a bank, in spite of the fact that under the present law, the government was not permitted to invest funds in private businesses.[30]

Liongson's petition was only one of a number submitted by local landowners, but its presentation at a public hearing for the reduction of tariffs on sugar and tobacco, two major export products in the Philippines, is highly symbolic. The establishment of an agricultural mortgage bank would greatly benefit the interests of landlords who had suffered decreases in production due to wartime devastation, and would particularly aid planters who wished to expand their production for export to the U.S. market. As a reduction of tariffs on export products was already on the agenda in 1905, it was natural for local elites to speak out for the creation of a new bank to meet their needs. Thus, the U.S. government had to approach the issue more seriously than before.

## THE AGRICULTURAL BANK AND THE U.S. CONGRESS, 1905–1907

What concrete proposals did the U.S. and Philippine governments make regarding the incorporation of an agricultural bank? As far as the Philippine Commission is concerned, we cannot answer this question on the basis of its third, fourth, and fifth reports (in 1902, 1903, and 1904).[31] However, from other documents it is possible to locate a direct commitment on the part of the Philippine Commission as early as mid-1904, when Edwin W. Kemmerer formulated the guidelines for the establishment of an agricultural bank.

In October 1903, with the enactment of the Philippine Gold Standard Act (Act No. 938), a Division of Currency was created within the Bureau of the Treasury in Manila and Edwin W. Kemmerer became its head.[32] Kemmerer had been appointed financial advisor to the Philippine Commission in June 1903, and he arrived in Manila in August of the same year to draft the new currency act.[33] In June 1904, under the direction of the Insular Treasurer, he began to prepare a plan to establish an agricultural bank. Kemmerer argued in the report he submitted to the Insular Treasurer in February 1905[34] that an agricultural bank was indispensable for the development of agriculture in the Philippines. The lack of agricultural credit facilities was detrimental to agriculture, and without funds the fertile and rich agricultural resources of the islands would be misused. He attached particular importance to the fact that 24 out of 28 provincial treasurers who responded to his inquiries regarding the need for an agricultural bank replied in the affirmative.[35]

Kemmerer outlined four types of agricultural bank: (1) a private entity; (2) a purely governmental institution, financed by the government and administered by governmental agencies; (3) a type of cooperative association common in Europe, where farmers from one or more communities deposited funds and managed the institution themselves; and (4) a private institution under government control such as the Agricultural Bank of Egypt.[36] After discussing the matter with local experts, he concluded that a bank organized along the lines of the Agricultural Bank of Egypt would be most suitable for the Philippines.

While private enterprise lacked the resources to shoulder the problems of agricultural facilities entirely, Kemmerer considered a purely governmental institution in the Philippines undesirable because (1) it would tend to encourage the population to depend on the government for financial assistance; (2) government officials were not in a position to assume the responsibility entailed by such a task; (3) the rigid enforcement of loan contracts would be difficult for the government and would cause it to acquire many hectares of land as a result of foreclosures. Cooperative associations, the third category, had been successful in European countries such as Austria, Belgium, and Italy, although they had to be run through the initiative of farmers' associations, and Kemmerer felt that Filipino farmers were not yet ready to organize such institutions.[37]

As a model for the Philippines, Kemmerer described the operations of the Agricultural Bank of Egypt, quoting annual reports by Lord Cromer, the British Consul-General to Egypt. The Egyptian government had first provided small loans to the *fellaheen* (farmers) around 1895, and a newly created National Bank of Egypt began making advances for agriculture in 1899. To satisfy the need for an agricultural credit facility, the Agricultural Bank of Egypt had been organized in June 1902, under the auspices of the National Bank of Egypt. According to Kemmerer, this bank was "in all respect a private enterprise." Private capital was invested in the bank, while the government held the authority to guarantee a certain interest rate on the invested capital, to keep a certain quantity of bank stocks, and to join the board of directors for supervising its operations. He added that it "has so far proven a remarkable success, both from the standpoint of the stockholders and of the Egyptian fellaheen...."[38] Based on the above analysis, Kemmerer proposed a plan to establish an agricultural bank of the Egyptian type in the Philippines, with an authorized capital of 10 million pesos.[39]

In addition, Kemmerer submitted a report on the Agricultural Bank of Egypt both to the U.S. Secretary of War and to the Philippine Commission in June 1906.[40] This report was written after Kemmerer had served as special commissioner to Egypt on his way home from the Philippines following the abolition of the Division of Currency in the Philippine government in January 1906.[41] In this later report, which described the organization and management of the bank, Kemmerer pointed out three factors that had contributed to its success: (1) the bank's top personnel consisted of British staff members who strictly supervised operations; (2) by utilizing the services of civil servants, the government was able to collect loan payments and land tax at the same time; (3) by using the government's land valuations for tax assessment, farmers were able to obtain loans from the bank without land titles.[42] Kemmerer's two-week stay in Egypt reaffirmed his conviction that an agricultural bank of the Egyptian type was the best arrangement for the Philippines. He argued that, although only small areas had been brought under the Land Registration Act in the Philippines, the availability of loans from the bank at low rates of interest would provide a stimulus to land registration by farmers.[43]

In its sixth report, the Philippine Commission recommended in 1905 that the U.S. Congress authorize the establishment of an agricultural bank funded by private capital, based on Kemmerer's plan, with principal guaranteed by the Philippine government, and an interest rate of no more than four percent a year to private investors. The total amount which the government would be called upon to pay in a year should not exceed 200,000 dollars, and the maximum rate of interest charged for loans should be 10 percent. The difference between the interest charged for loans and the interest paid for principal would be utilized for the payment of operational expenses under government supervision.[44] Thus, the Philippine Commission took a firm step to push the U.S. Congress to establish an agricultural bank in the Philippines.

In October 1905, major newspapers in Manila published reports of Kemmerer's plan to establish an agricultural bank, and suggested that the U.S. Congress would probably act on the proposal at its next session.[45] True enough, between December 1905 and May 1906, an agricultural bank bill was drafted in Washington.⁴⁶ Senator Henry Cabot Lodge introduced a bill on 22 May 1906, acting at the request of William H. Taft, now the U.S. Secretary of War.⁴⁷

Landowners in the provinces of Ilocos, Bulacan, and Negros Occidental immediately sent petitions to the governor-general and to the U.S. Congress, supporting the bill and urging prompt action.⁴⁸ By contrast the issue generated heated debate in the United States in both houses of Congress.⁴⁹ In the House of Representatives, Henry A. Cooper of Wisconsin, Chairman of the Committee on Insular Affairs, presented a series of bills in January 1907, each with slightly different contents, and as a result the issue became extremely confused.⁵⁰ Meanwhile, Philippine interests intensified their efforts in support of the bill. In February 1907, the provincial governor of Negros Occidental informed Secretary Taft that more than 1,500 landowners there had requested the establishment of an agricultural bank.⁵¹ Taft clearly wished to promote the economic interests of larger landowners in the Philippines and said in a letter to Senator Eugene Hale that the maximum figure of 5,000 dollars for each loan included in Lodge's bill should be dropped, suggesting that if some limitation was considered necessary, it should be 50,000 dollars.⁵² However, this opinion was not widely shared in the U.S. Congress; the bill passed on 4 March 1907, with only slight modification to the original bill. The main points of the Philippine Agricultural Bank Act (Public Act No. 243) were as follows:⁵³

> *Section 1:* For the purpose of establishing an agricultural bank, the Philippine government was authorized to guarantee an income of no more than four percent a year on the capital invested by individuals or corporations in such an agricultural bank. The guaranty would be granted by an act of the Philippine Commission which would contain the following provisions: (1) the guaranty would be made to a company organized under the laws of the Philippines; (2) the bank would grant loans only for the purpose of being engaged in agriculture; (3) no loans exceeding 5,000 dollars would be made except upon the permission of the Secretary of Finance and Justice of the Philippine government; (4) interest on loans would not exceed 10 percent a year and the total annual liability of the bank under the government guaranty would not exceed 200,000 dollars and such guaranty would not continue for more than twenty-five years.
>
> *Section 2:* The guaranty made by the insular government would be a liability of the bank to the government and would be paid from the annual net profits of the bank. The stockholders had the right to receive four percent dividends a year

upon the bank's paid-up capital. No dividends above four percent would be paid until the bank fully repaid the cash advances from the government. The above guaranty would not be deemed a guaranty of the government to the paid-up capital of stockholders if the bank should go into liquidation.

*Section 3:* The bank would not be permitted to hold real estate other than for business purposes. In the case where it acquired land as a result of foreclosure or for some other reason, such land would be sold within ten years from the date of acquisition.

The Agricultural Bank Act passed by the U.S. Congress closely resembled Kemmerer's plan of 1905. However, when the Philippine Legislature passed an Agricultural Act in June 1908, it diverged significantly from this framework. The original concept of a bank based on private capital with a government guarantee was replaced by a bank created at the government's initiative and using government funds.

## THE AGRICULTURAL BANK IN PRACTICE

Why did the Philippine Legislature abandon the scheme envisaged by the U.S. Congress? After the passage of the Agricultural Bank Act in March 1907, both the U.S. and Philippine governments alerted private banks and corporations to the opportunity to invest in an agricultural bank for the Philippines. In March the representatives of the major banks operating in the Philippines took part in a conference to discuss the matter, and three banks (the Hongkong and Shanghai Banking Corporation, the International Banking Corporation, and the Chartered Bank of India, Australia and China) said that the matter was under consideration by their home offices, and local branches had not enough information to define intentions. A fourth bank, the Banco Español Filipino, stated that the business of an agricultural bank was too large for it to handle.[54] In the United States, the Bureau of Insular Affairs (BIA) of the War Department contacted Speyer and Co. and the International Banking Corporation, both located in New York, as well as a syndicate of bankers in Kansas City, to encourage them to invest in an agricultural bank in the Philippines. These efforts proved fruitless. The reason the banks gave for declining to take part varied; Speyer and Co. stated that it was not familiar with the Philippines; the International Banking Corporation said that it would be preferable for the Philippine government to take a major interest in stock and debentures; the syndicate of bankers in Kansas City showed considerable interest but wanted special privileges, including a twenty-five-year government guarantee for their invested capital.[55] In the end, the attempt to establish an agricultural bank using private capital proved unsuccessful.

There were underlying reasons for this reluctance to invest in an agricultural bank. First, the business of the bank would be restricted to agricultural loans. It could not engage in the foreign exchange business that produced great profits for the commercial economy of the late nineteenth century by providing loans to agency houses which purchased agricultural crops for export. Commercial banks were well placed to expand their positions in export economies without taking the risk that investment in an agricultural bank would entail.[56]

While this stalemate remained unresolved, the Insular Treasurer recommended in a letter dated 25 October 1907 that the Philippine Legislature should appropriate one million pesos from the general fund of the Philippine government for the establishment of a government agricultural bank. His reasoning was that the annual revenues of the insular government were expected to exceed general expenses by at least 3 million pesos in the future, and by drawing on the services of provincial treasures, the Insular Treasurer would be able to manage the bank successfully.[57] The move seemed timely, for in September of the same year, the Philippine Commission enacted Act No. 1730, which authorized the government to appropriate funds for paying the annual interest of four percent on the capital invested in an agricultural bank, as regulated by the Agricultural Bank Act passed by the U.S. Congress in March 1907.[58]

However, the demand for establishing a government agricultural bank continued to grow in strength in the Philippines. In February 1908, the Philippine Assembly, acting jointly with the Philippine Commission, passed a resolution to appoint a committee that would study plans to establish an agricultural bank.[59] However, much of the initiative to establish a government agricultural bank came from Secretary Taft. In March 1908 Governor-General Smith informed Taft that the committee, which included representatives of the Philippine Assembly, commercial houses, the agricultural interest, and all banking institutions, strongly supported his recommendation for legislation establishing a government agricultural bank with capital of no less than 2 million dollars.[60] At almost the same time, Taft asked the U.S. attorney general whether the Philippine legislature could enact a law to establish a government agricultural bank without authorization from the U.S.

Congress,[61] and received an affirmative reply. The decision of the attorney general spurred the government to act, and on 18 June 1908, the Philippine legislature passed the Agricultural Bank Act (Act No. 1865).

The Agricultural Bank Act of 1908 contained twenty sections. Its main points may be summarized as follows:[62]

1. An agricultural banking corporation named "the Agricultural Bank of the Philippine Government" shall be established, with a principal office located in Manila (Sec. 1).
2. For the capital of the bank, one million pesos shall be appropriated out of the general funds of the Insular Treasurer (Sec. 2).
3. The bank is authorized to receive deposits of funds of provinces, municipalities, the Postal Savings Bank, societies, corporations, and private persons. Interest on deposits paid by the bank shall not exceed 4 percent a year (Sec. 3).
4. A board of directors shall be composed of the Secretary of Finance and Justice, the Insular Treasurer, and three Filipinos or American residents in the Philippines appointed by the governor-general (Sec. 4). The Insular Treasurer shall be the manager of the bank (Sec. 5).
5. With the approval of the Governor-General, the Insular Treasurer is authorized to nominate provincial and municipal treasurers as agents of the bank (Sec. 6).
6. The Attorney General shall be the legal adviser of the bank (Sec. 7).
7. The board of directors is empowered to adopt by-laws not in conflict with this act (Sec. 8).
8. The bank shall provide loans only for the payment or satisfaction of encumbrances on agricultural lands, for the construction of drainage and irrigation works, and for the purchase of fertilizers, agricultural seeds, machinery, implements, and animals. No loan shall be made for non-agricultural purposes (Sec. 10).
9. Each loan shall be set at an amount between 50 pesos and 25,000 pesos, and 50 percent of the bank's capital shall be set aside for loans of no more than 5,000 pesos each (Sec. 11).
10. All loans shall be provided upon the security of real estate or chattel mortgages. Upon the security of real estate, no loans shall be made to exceed 40 percent of the value of a first mortgage on unencumbered, improved urban property or agricultural land; upon the security of chattel mortgages, no loans shall be made to exceed 40 percent of the market value of crops harvested, gathered, and stored on the date of loan (Sec. 12).
11. All mortgages shall be registered with the register of deeds in the respective

jurisdiction. The expenses of registration shall be paid by the borrower (Sec. 13).
12. Interest rate for loans shall not exceed 10 percent a year (Sec. 14) and loans shall not be made for a period exceeding ten years (Sec. 15).
13. No commission shall be received by any official of the bank for loan service (Sec. 16).

On 22 September 1908, by-laws of the Agricultural Bank of the Philippine Government were approved. These described the major functions of the board of directors as well as the president, manager, agents, and secretary, and set down regulations for the banking business covering loans, deposits and withdrawals, mortgage insurances, appraisal of property, and personnel. Section 17 stipulated that loans between 10,000 pesos and 19,999 pesos required the approval of four directors of the board, and loans greater than 20,000 pesos needed the agreement of all members of the board.[63]

Thus, on 20 October 1908, three and a half years after Kemmerer submitted his plan to establish an agricultural bank of the Egyptian type, the Agricultural Bank was formally incorporated, being wholly owned and managed by the Philippine government.[64] The Bank approved relatively few loans in its first few years of operation, and those for only small amounts. During the nine months between its establishment and the end of its fiscal year (FY) in June 1909, the Bank received 417 loan applications, amounting to a total of 804,000 pesos. Only twenty-three of these applications were approved, amounting to 55,450 pesos (about five percent of the bank's capital); eleven were withdrawn, nineteen were returned because of incomplete documentation, and 150 remained under consideration by the provincial boards of various provinces. The remaining 214 were rejected, primarily because of bad titles for the land offered as security.[65] During FY1910 (July 1909–June 1910), however, the number and amount of loans approved showed a significant increase. Out of 148 applications, eighty-nine were granted, covering loans amounting to 229,000 pesos, bringing the total amount lent out to 284,450 pesos, or 28.5 percent of the bank's capital at the end of FY1910.[66] (See Table 9 for the number of applications and number of loans approved in FY1909–FY1915.[67])

These numbers disappointed the Bank's backers — both the Insular Treasurer and the Philippine Commission were discouraged by the low level of business carried out by the Agricultural Bank. During FY1910, the Bank's manager sent letters to provincial treasurers asking why local people did not

Table 9. Application and Approval of Loans in the Agricultural Bank of the Philippine Government, FY1909–FY1915

| Fiscal Year | 1909 | 1910 | 1911 | 1912 | 1913 | Late 1913[1] | 1914 | 1915 | Total |
|---|---|---|---|---|---|---|---|---|---|
| Application | | | | | | | | | |
| Number | 417 | 148 | 123 | 170 | 369 | 172 | 350 | 441 | 2,190 |
| Amount (1000 pesos) | 804 | 495 | 482 | 711 | 3,068 | 1,516 | 2,752 | 3,772 | 13,600 |
| Approval | | | | | | | | | |
| Number | 23 | 89 | 61 | 68 | 148 | 138 | 185 | 247 | 959 |
| Amount (1000 pesos) | 55 | 224 | 230 | 221 | 1,029 | 1,148 | 1,396 | 1,122 | 5,425 |
| Percentage of the Amount of Approval (%) | 6.8 | 45.3 | 47.7 | 31.1 | 33.5 | 75.7 | 50.7 | 29.7 | 39.9 |

Source: Philippine Islands, Bureau of Treasury, *Annual Report of the Treasurer of the Philippine Islands, FY1915*, Manila: Bureau of Printing, 1915, pp. 52–55.
Note: (1) For the period of July–Dec. 1913.

possess land titles (either those issued during Spanish times or Torrens titles from the American period). In reality, the procedures for securing a Torrens title were too complicated and too expensive for people to be induced to register land in order to apply for bank loans.[68]

In an attempt to stimulate both the registration of land titles and loan applications, the board of directors of the Bank passed a resolution that interest should be reduced from 10 to 8 percent a year for loans guaranteed by Torrens titles, and that this reduction should also apply to previous loans.[69] To expand its local networks, the Bank also established agencies in areas where no commercial banks were located. The first agency opened in Zamboanga in 1909, and by January 1912 there were twelve agencies operating throughout the country.[70]

The Agricultural Bank's efforts to attract loan applications by these means produced results in FY1913 (July 1912–June 1913). As a result of widespread publicity concerning the bank's services, and even with the slow process of land registration following enactment of the Cadastral Act of 1913 (see chapter 4), total loans granted during FY1913 amounted to 1,028,650 pesos, exceeding the aggregate amount of loans made since the Bank's establishment by 297,047 pesos. At the end of FY1913, repayment of principal amounted to 137,603 pesos, leaving a balance of 1,622,650 pesos in outstanding loans.[71]

Table 10 shows the distribution of approved loans by amount during FY1909–FY1913. Most loans made during FY1911–FY1912 were for sums of less than 5,000 pesos. In FY1913, however, of 148 loans provided, thirty-three were in the range of 5,001–10,000 pesos, and forty-six in range of 10,001–35,000 pesos.[72] Loans in excess of 5,000 pesos made up more than half of the total. Looking at the distribution of loans by province in Table 11, it is apparent that the average amount for loans in Negros Occidental was extremely large. Loans in this province made up about half the total amount of loans throughout the Philippines, exceeding the aggregate amount of loans in Tarlac, Nueva Ecija, Pampanga, Iloilo, and Tayabas, although all of these provinces were larger. In FY1913, fifty-two loans were approved in Negros Occidental, with an average of approximately 9,900 pesos. In terms of the average amount of each loan, Pampanga followed Negros Occidental, averaging 7,300 pesos in FY1913 and 8,500 pesos in FY1914. Negros Occidental and Pampanga were the country's two major sugar-producing provinces, and these loans were made in connection with a big push to export sugar to the United States under the preferential tariff act. Thus, the Agricultural Bank took positive action to provide large loans to landowners in these two provinces at a time when they each demanded agricultural credit facilities. It is

Table 10. Number of Loans by the Range of Amount in the Agricultural Bank of the Philippine Government, FY1909–FY1913

| Amount of Loans (pesos) | 1909–1911 | 1912 | 1913 |
|---|---|---|---|
| – 1,000 | 80 | 17 | 25 |
| 1,001 – 5,000 | 76 | 35 | 44 |
| 5,001 – 10,000 | 8 | 15 | 33 |
| 10,001 – 20,000 | 6 | 1 | 32 |
| 20,001 – 25,000 | 3 | 1 | 0 |
| 25,001 – 35,000 | 0 | 0 | 14 |
| Total | 173 | 69[(1)] | 148 |

Source: Philippine Islands, Bureau of Treasury, *Annual Report of Treasurer of the Philippine Islands, FY1911*, Manila: Bureau of Printing, 1911, p. 15; idem, *Annual Report of the Treasurer of the Philippine Islands, FY1912*, Manila: Bureau of Printing, 1912, p. 23; idem, *Annual Report of the Treasurer of the Philippine Islands, FY1913*, Manila: Bureau of Printing, 1913, p. 46.

Note: (1) The number differs from that of Table 9, due to the difference of sources.

Table 11. Number and Amount of Loans in the Agricultural Bank of
the Philippine Government by Province, FY1909–FY1915

(a) Number of loans; (b) Amount of loans (1000 pesos)

| Fiscal Year | | 1909 | 1910 | 1911 | 1912 | 1913 | Late 1913[1] | 1914 | 1915 | Total[2] | % |
|---|---|---|---|---|---|---|---|---|---|---|---|
| Iloilo | (a) | – | 2 | – | 2 | 10 | 3 | 16 | 7 | 40 | 4.2 |
| | (b) | – | 11 | – | 3 | 67 | 47 | 270 | 17 | 414 | 7.6 |
| Negros Occ. | (a) | – | 25 | 7 | 4 | 52 | 56 | 47 | 37 | 228 | 23.8 |
| | (b) | – | 97 | 68 | 18 | 515 | 774 | 612 | 457 | 2,540 | 46.8 |
| Nueva Ecija | (a) | 2 | 5 | 3 | 8 | 16 | 12 | 18 | 30 | 94 | 9.8 |
| | (b) | 4 | 33 | 29 | 24 | 98 | 91 | 64 | 87 | 429 | 7.9 |
| Pampanga | (a) | 1 | 5 | 3 | 3 | 9 | 8 | 9 | 17 | 55 | 5.7 |
| | (b) | 10 | 9 | 10 | 12 | 66 | 36 | 77 | 101 | 321 | 5.9 |
| Tarlac | (a) | 2 | 21 | 15 | 13 | 14 | 6 | 9 | 39 | 119 | 12.4 |
| | (b) | 5 | 20 | 30 | 36 | 41 | 17 | 49 | 114 | 312 | 5.8 |
| Tayabas | (a) | – | 1 | 2 | 6 | 8 | 15 | 32 | 25 | 89 | 9.3 |
| | (b) | – | 4 | 5 | 25 | 33 | 39 | 142 | 82 | 329 | 6.1 |
| Philippines | (a) | 23 | 89 | 61 | 68 | 148 | 138 | 185 | 247 | 959 | 100.0 |
| | (b) | 55 | 224 | 230 | 221 | 1,029 | 1,148 | 1,396 | 1,122 | 5,425 | 100.0 |

Source: Philippine Islands, Bureau of Treasury, *Annual Report of the Treasurer of the Philippine Islands, FY1915*, Manila: Bureau of Printing, 1916, pp. 52–55.

Notes: (1) For the period of July–Dec. 1913.
(2) The aggregation of the number and amount of each year may differ to the total due to rounding off.

to be noted, however, that in granting loans to larger landowners rather than to small farmers, the Bank deviated from the original regulation which stipulated that 50 percent of the bank's capital should be set aside for loans of no more than 5,000 pesos each (Sec. 11, Act No. 1865). Furthermore, there is ample evidence that the Agricultural Bank inflated real estate appraisals, and that landowners spent money raised through loans for personal expenditures rather than for the purpose specified.[73]

How was it possible for the Agricultural Bank to operate in this way? And who made the decision to change the character of the Bank? The answers lie in the Agricultural Bank Act's provision by which the Insular Treasurer was authorized to nominate provincial (or municipal) treasurers to act as agents of the Bank (Section 6)—a provision of which the provincial treasurers (mostly

Americans at this stage) took full advantage. With regard to the loan business of the Bank, provincial treasurers clearly responded to the strong demand for funds among local landowners, and neglected the interests of small farmers. Provincial treasurers were appointed by the Philippine Commission, and later by the governor-general with the consent of the Commission and were responsible for provincial and municipal funds. Although some Filipinos began to be appointed to this position as early as 1907, Americans remained dominant through the end of the Taft Era in 1913 (at which time they still outnumbered Filipinos by eighteen to thirteen).[74] Overall, the granting of these loans is a phenomenon that reflects the position of the U.S. colonial administration generally, in that it had to convince local elites that their interests would be served under U.S. rule while at the same time trying to strike a balance between elite demands and other social needs.[75]

### THE COLONIAL GOVERNMENT'S RESPONSE TO THE LANDLORD-ORIENTED LOAN BUSINESS

By 1913, the Philippine government had become aware that the Agricultural Bank was seriously overlending. Its response was to allow the Agricultural Bank to receive deposits of provincial government funds—a change accomplished by a revision of the Agricultural Bank Act in 1913. There had already been some relatively minor adjustments: in 1909, the Bank was allowed to make loans for the cost of purchasing agricultural land, bringing land under cultivation, and managing farms[76] and in January 1911 another revision increased the maximum sum that could be loaned from 40 percent to 60 percent of the value of the mortgaged property.[77] However, the new law passed in 1913, substantially transformed the nature of the Agricultural Bank.

Early in 1913, faced with a scarcity of funds to make loans, the manager of the Agricultural Bank presented three options to the board of directors: (1) to raise capital by obtaining a grant from the legislature of an appropriation from the general funds of the government; (2) to issue debenture bonds or obligations secured by the bank's mortgage loans; (3) to accept deposits of government funds and use a limited portion of this capital to make agricultural loans. The first measure was rejected due to the scarcity of the government funds while the second measure was also abandoned because the Attorney General of the Philippine Islands issued an opinion that the Agricultural Bank Act did not authorize the issue of bonds and that the Philippine Legislature did not have the power to authorize the bank to do so. The third measure was adopted by the board of directors, which decided that only funds deposited by provincial governments should be used for loans, and that loans should not exceed 50 percent of the minimum level these deposits had reached during the preceding six years. At the suggestion of the Governor-General, this was provisionally reduced to 20 percent until the authorities in Washington could make a decision on what percentage was appropriate.[78]

The Insular Treasurer had already sent a letter to provincial treasurers on 5 December 1912, designating the Agricultural Bank as an approved depository for all provincial governments, and Act No. 2214 of February 1913 had authorized the Agricultural Bank to receive deposits from the Philippine government as well as provincial and municipal governments (Sec. 3). At the same time, the government increased the maximum amount of property that could be used to secure a mortgage, provided that a loan did not exceed 60 percent of the value of the securities (Sec. 12).[79]

Prior to this change, most provincial funds had been deposited at the Manila branch of the International Banking Corporation.[80] In June 1913, the International Banking Corporation and the Agricultural Bank negotiated an agreement concerning the transfer of these deposits,[81] and in December the manager of the Agricultural Bank informed the Philippine government that the Bank was now accepting time and current deposits from provincial treasurers under the same terms and conditions as the International Banking Corporation.[82] Provincial treasurers received a circular stating that the Agricultural Bank had become the sole depository for provincial government funds, and instructing them to make their deposits accordingly.[83] As shown in Table 12, following this change the deposits of government funds increased dramatically and became the basis for agricultural loans.

Table 12. Deposits of Provincial Government Funds in the Agricultural Bank of the Philippine Government, FY1913–FY1915[(1)]

| Fiscal Year | Amount of Deposits (1000 pesos) |
| --- | --- |
| 1913 | 2,338 |
| 1914 | 7,323 |
| 1915 | 7,292 |

Source: Philippine Islands, Bureau of Treasury, *Annual Report of the Treasurer of the Philippine Islands*, various years.

Note: (1) The financial statement of the bank shows that provincial funds were not deposited in FY1909–FY1912.

However, even though the bank could draw on government funds to make agricultural loans, it continued to face a chronic shortage of funds, since the value of outstanding loans increased steadily. In FY1914, new long-term mortgage loans of 1,330,230 pesos were approved, making the total loans outstanding 4,073,200 pesos at the end of the fiscal year.[84] In the following fiscal year, the bank made new loans worth 1,121,570 pesos, which increased the total outstanding to 5,082,560 pesos by June 1915.[85] The Agricultural Bank could not sustain the continuous growth of loans outstanding without increasing its capitalization of 1 million pesos.

Earlier, on 7 March 1914, the *Philippine Free Press* had reported that Assemblyman Fidel A. Reyes of Batangas province submitted a resolution to the Philippine Legislature asking for a bond issue to increase the capital of the Agricultural Bank to 20 million pesos. Governor-General Francis Burton Harrison appointed a committee to study this proposal, and the committee endorsed a bond issue of 10 million pesos, disregarding the opinion of the Attorney General that the Agricultural Bank lacked authority to take this step.[86] Although the plan was not approved by the Philippine legislature, this can be understood as a calculated move by the Filipino elite to establish a new bank to service the needs of local elites in the development of export economy. And in fact, in 1916 the Philippine National Bank was established for this purpose and the Agricultural Bank of the Philippine Government was merged with it and ceased operations.

CHAPTER 4

# THE PHILIPPINE NATIONAL BANK AND LENDING IN AGRICULTURE

THE PHILIPPINE NATIONAL BANK was officially incorporated on 2 May 1916 under the National Bank Act of the Philippine Legislature, and its full-scale operations began on 24 July 1916. Its authorized capital was 20 million pesos, or about 10 million dollars.

Why was the Philippine National Bank established? It is interesting to follow the consequences of an alignment in the demands of the emergent Filipino elite for such a bank and the interests of the U.S. Bureau of Insular Affairs (BIA) in Washington as well as those of Manila-based American merchants. The first move toward the establishment of a larger agricultural bank was initiated by the Filipino elite in the early 1910s, at a time when it became apparent that the Agricultural Bank of the Philippine Government would be unable to provide enough credit to landowners seeking profits in the expansion of export agriculture. In October 1911, Governor-General W. Cameron Forbes gave a hearing to a proposal of Benito Legarda, a Filipino member of the Philippine Commission, that a private mortgage bank backed by French capital (and bearing the name of Crédit Foncier de Philippines) be established. In early 1913, a Negros Occidental assemblyman by the name of Montilla submitted a bill to the Third Philippine Legislature seeking to increase the capitalization of the Agricultural Bank of the Philippine Government by appropriating 1 million pesos from the Philippine Treasury fund.[1]

The possibility of establishing an agricultural bank under private capital had been repeatedly discussed in exchanges between the American officials in Washington and in Manila, but the major obstacle lay in the lack of interest among American capitalist investors. Accordingly, Chief Frank McIntyre of the BIA wrote Governor-General Forbes in Manila in May 1913 proposing a government bank, rather than private banks, as provider of agricultural loans to Philippine cash crop producers.[2] By this time it was not only the Filipino elite who demanded an agricultural bank; Manila Americans now saw the need for such a bank to service their business activities. It was under these circumstances that, in the middle of 1915, Vice Governor-General Henderson Martin drafted a bill seeking to establish an insular bank as a government credit bank not only for agriculture but also for industry and commerce. In October of the same year, Governor-General Francis Burton Harrison recommended the institution of a multi-purpose national bank to provide support for the total development of the Philippine economy.[3]

Initially, McIntyre disagreed with Harrison's recommendation. He was of the opinion that the insular government should not further involve itself in the lending business. After receiving information that the International Banking Corporation had merged with the National City Bank of New York in 1915, McIntyre recommended to Harrison that the Philippine government should totally withdraw from the banking business and devolve its investing commitments to the National City Bank. Although opinions in the Philippine Chamber of Commerce in Manila were divided regarding the involvement of the Philippine government in banking, members were in basic agreement on a standing proposal or advocacy for a fourfold increase of the capital investments in the proposed bank, in whatever guise it would emerge.[4]

In the Philippine Assembly, the leaders of the Nacionalista Party recognized the importance of establishing a government credit bank as proposed by Martin. For them, it was important that the bank should be not an American bank but a bank of the insular government. Manuel L. Quezon even asked the revaluation of the Martin bill by H. Parker Willis, secretary of the Board of the Governors of the newly formed U.S. Federal Reserve Board in Washington. Willis himself drafted a bill for the Philippines with the intent of establishing a government bank that would shoulder larger tasks relating to investment in private sectors, currency control, and the administration of colonial government funds. In December 1915, the Willis bill was sent to Manila with the support of Quezon. It was repackaged as a new bill, after being combined with the Martin bill, and passed as Act No. 2612 (An Act Creating the Philippine National Bank) by the Philippine Legislature on 4 February 1916.[5]

### ENACTMENT AND REVISION OF THE PHILIPPINE NATIONAL BANK ACT

Act No. 2612 led to the organization and operation of the Philippine National Bank. Now known as the Philippine National Bank Act of 1916, it was revised twice by Act No. 2747 in 1918 and Act No. 2938 in 1921. One can limn the salient characteristics of the operation and organization of the National Bank by examining these acts and their amendments to the original bill.

**Operation**: Major sections of Act No. 2612 concerning the operation of the Bank include the following:[6]

1. The capitalization of the National Bank was pegged at 20 million pesos, divided into 200,000 shares of the value at par of 100 pesos each. The Philippine government would purchase 101,000 shares by the end of January 1917, while the remaining 99,000 shares were to be offered to the public (Secs. 3 and 4).
2. All the assets and liabilities of the Agricultural Bank of the Philippine Government would be transferred to the National Bank. Such a transfer of the Agricultural Bank's assets would be deemed partial payment of the shares of the National Bank subscribed by the Philippine Government (Sec. 6).
3. The National Bank was authorized to lend amounts not to exceed 50 percent of its capital and surplus and all amounts realized from the sale of real estate bonds on notes secured by real estate mortgages. Payment of such notes would be secured by first mortgages on farm lands in the Philippine Islands. Such loans were to be barred from exceeding 60 percent of the actual value of farm lands. The due date of the mortgages would not be less than one year and not more than thirty years. Loans of this kind were to be offered for the purpose of promoting agriculture (Sec. 10).
4. The National Bank was authorized to loan amounts not exceeding 30 percent of its capital and surplus and the full amount of circulating notes on promissory notes, drafts, and bills of exchange issued or drawn for agriculture, industrial or commercial purposes (Sec. 11).
5. The National Bank was authorized to issue loans in amounts not to exceed 20 percent of its capital and surplus, 70 percent of its deposits subject to check, and 85 percent of its time deposits (Sec. 12). Preference was given to the loans specified in Sections 11 and 12. The National Bank was authorized to make loans on harvested and stored crops, with such loans not exceeding

70 percent of the market value of the crops (Sec. 14). The National Bank was authorized to make loans to the producers on standing crops of rice, hemp, copra, sugar, tobacco, and others. For the grant of such loans, the National Bank might require additional security in the nature of mortgages on real estate or upon livestock, machinery, or agricultural implements (Sec. 14).

6. The National Bank was authorized to issue its notes (known as circulating notes) in any amount not exceeding 75 percent of the securities held by the Bank. In addition, the National Bank would have the authority to issue its circulating notes against the gold coin of the United States (Sec. 18).

7. The National Bank was authorized to receive deposits of funds from the insular, provincial, and municipal governments, as well as from the Postal Savings Bank, associations, corporations, and private persons. It was obligatory for the insular, provincial, and municipal governments to make their deposits with the Bank (Sec. 19).

8. The National Bank would be permitted to establish up to two branches or agencies in the United States. The said branches or agencies were to receive, transmit, and disburse any funds of the insular or U.S. governments or private corporations or individuals and to engage in business with the Federal Reserve Bank of the district in which the said branches or agencies might be located (Sec. 33).

9. The National Bank would be permitted to establish branches in the provincial capitals or other municipalities. The officers or substituted agents of these branches would be appointed by the Board of Directors of the National Bank. With the authorization of the Governor-General, the Board could appoint the provincial or municipal treasurers themselves as agents, cashiers, or tellers of these branches (Sec. 34).

The Philippine National Bank was thus established as a multi-purpose bank (or a large-scale credit institution), responsible for issuing bank notes and controlling the currency reserve. It was designed to serve the dual function of depository of Philippine government funds and Philippine agency of the U.S. Federal Reserve Board.[7] It was a de facto government bank, intended to maintain only a minimum investment of private capital.[8] As a lending bank, the National Bank now had great latitude in extending agricultural loans, although mostly short-term loans on harvested or standing crops. Its authorized capital was ten times bigger than that of the Agricultural Bank, its forerunner.

Some sections of Act No. 2612 were subsequently revised in February 1918 by Act No. 2747, to wit:[9]

Sections 11, 12, and 13 of Act No. 2612 were deleted. A revision of Section 14 determined the major business of the National Bank to consist in (a) the purchase or discounting of promissory notes, drafts, and bills of exchange; (b) the extension of loans on, or the discount of, notes secured by harvested and stored crops; (c) the making of agricultural loans on standing crops; (d) the provision of loans for the provincial and municipal governments or branches of the insular government on promissory notes guaranteed by the insular government or the purchase of bonds issued by the provincial and municipal governments or branches of the insular government; and (e) the issuance of advances or discount paper for agricultural, manufacturing, industrial, or commercial purposes (new Sec. 11). A revision of Section 18 stipulated that the National Bank could only issue circulating notes not exceeding the amount of the paid-up capital and surplus of the bank and the amount of gold coin of the United States (new Sec.15). An amendment to Section 37 lifted the limitation on the amount of any real estate mortgage loan of 50,000 pesos and any other loan of 300,000 pesos (new Sec. 34).

Immediately notable about the revised National Bank Act of 1918 was its emphasis not only on agricultural loans but also on loans for manufacturing, industrial, and commercial purposes. In addition, not only were the restrictions on the amount of loans imposed by Sections 10–12 in the Act of 1916 lifted (except for real estate mortgage loans), but also the limitation on the amount of loans was abolished. In doing so, the Act made it possible for the National Bank to provide larger loans or discount paper for various business sectors.

In January 1921, Act No. 2938 was enacted as a further revision of the National Bank Act, with the following revisions to the original legislation:[10]

1. The National Bank was authorized to increase its capital from 20 million pesos to 50 million pesos and to a new issue of 300,000 shares of stock to be denominated the second issue, at the par value of 100 pesos each. By 30 June 1921, the Philippine government would purchase all the remaining shares of the first issue and par of the second issue of no less than 153,000 shares. The remaining shares could then be offered to the provincial and municipal governments or to the public (Secs. 3 and 4).
2. Any loan or credit account transferred to the National Bank by the Agricultural Bank which had been found to be uncollectible were subject to foreclosure by the National Bank (Sec. 7).
3. The National Bank was authorized to issue loans for agricultural purposes in amounts not to exceed 60 percent of its capital and surplus and all amounts realized from the sale of real estate bonds (Sec. 9).

The most drastic revision of the 1921 Act was the large increase (by 250 percent) in the Bank's paid-up capital. By this provision provincial and municipal governments were encouraged to purchase National Bank shares themselves. Also noteworthy was the expansion of the total amount available for loans (given the increase in the Bank's capitalization), including the jump in the percentage of the amount of loans against paid-up capital and surplus. Thus within five years from its establishment, the Philippine National Bank had emerged as a giant multi-purpose governmental bank with a strong focus on loans or credit accessible to business sectors.

**Organization**: The major regulations concerning the organization of the National Bank were stated in Act No. 2612 as follows:

1. The Bank was to be managed by a Board of Directors consisting of a President, a Vice President, and five other members. The President of the Bank was vested with the power to make loans on commercial paper for maximum periods of four months and in maximum sums of 50,000 pesos (Sec. 20).
2. The President and Vice President were to be appointed by the Governor-General but with the assent of the Upper House of the Philippine Legislature. The other five members of the Board of Directors were to occupy elective positions, in accordance with the provision for it by the Corporation Law (Act No. 1459) (Sec. 21).
3. The Attorney-General of the Philippine Islands was designated as the attorney of the Bank (Sec. 25).
4. The Bank was to be subject to inspection by the Insular Treasurer (Sec. 27).
5. The President and Vice President of the Bank could expect appointments for a term of six years. The other five members of the Board of Directors were to hold office for one year (Sec. 30).
6. The stockholders had the responsibility to meet in March of each year to elect the five directors or members of the Board (Sec. 31).

The above regulations were not changed by Act No. 2747 of 1918, but were revised by Act No. 2938 of 1921 in the following specific ways:[11]

1. The number of the members of the Board of Directors was increased from seven to nine (Sec. 16).
2. The stockholders would meet in March of each year to elect the members of the Board of Directors. The directors of the Board would elect a President

and a Vice President from among themselves, once the terms of incumbents end (Sec. 17).
3. The orders and resolutions of the Board of Directors were to be carried out by a general manager who would be chief executive of the Bank, with the help of an assistant general manager (Sec. 18).
4. The Board was granted the power to fix the rate of interest, discount, or exchange to be charged by the Bank and to fix different rates of interest on loans, along with the authorization to establish branches or agencies in the United States (Sec. 19).
5. The general manager of the Bank was vested with the power to make loans on commercial paper for maximum periods of four months and in maximum sums of 50,000 pesos (Sec. 20).

A conspicuous feature of the revised act of 1921 was that it designated the Board of Directors as the overseeing authority in the management of the National Bank, and it turned the general manager into the Bank's officer in charge. Even more striking was that the power to make loans now devolved from the Board of Directors to the general manager.

In addition to such modifications, the revised Acts of 1918 and 1921 also brought about significant changes in the Bank's organizational structure. Section 31 of the 1916 Act (retained its original formulation in Section 28 of the revised Act of 1918) had determined for each stockholder or his authorized proxy the right to vote in accordance with the number of registered shares of stock. However, in the revised Act of 1918 the following important provision was added to Section 4: "The voting power of all the stock of the National Bank owned and controlled by the Philippine government shall be vested exclusively in a committee consisting of the Governor-General, the President of the Senate and the Speaker of the House of the Representatives."[12] Section 4 of the revised Act of 1921 clarified this stipulation as follows: "The voting power of all the stock of the National Bank owned and controlled by the Government of the Philippine Islands shall be vested exclusively in a board, the short title of which shall be 'Board of Control,' composed of the Governor-General, the President of the Senate, and the Speaker of the House of the Representatives."[13]

The "Board of Control" that first appeared under this designation in the revised Act of 1921 now seemed to function as the umbrella organization for the bank's management, as might be affirmed in the following provisions of that Act[14]:

1. The Bank was authorized to invest a sum not exceeding 10 percent of its paid-up capital in the purchase of shares of stock of any bank in the United States. With the approval of the Board of Control, the Bank might incorporate any of its foreign agencies (Sec. 10).
2. In case of emergency, under the approval of the Board of Control, the Secretary of Finance might authorize the Bank to rediscount commercial paper of not over six months maturity, secured by exports or imports, and might issue against said commercial paper circulating notes for sums not to exceed 75 percent of the value (Sec. 14).
3. The general manager would be appointed by the Board of Directors, with the advice and consent of the Board of Control (Sec. 18).
4. The general manager of the Bank would have the duty to furnish any information regarding the operation of the Bank upon request of the Secretary of Finance, Governor-General, or Board of Control (Sec. 20).
5. The Insular Auditor would be *ex officio* auditor of the Bank and would, with the advice and consent of the Board of Control, appoint a representative who would be chief of the auditing department of the Bank. The representative of the Insular Auditor would make a quarterly report on the condition of the Bank to the Governor-General, the Secretary of Finance, the Board of Control, the Insular Auditor, and the Board of Directors (Sec. 22).
6. Whenever the President or Vice President, by order of the Board of Directors, assumed extra duties, they would be granted additional compensation only with the written approval of the member of the Board of Control (Sec. 23).
7. The Bank would at all times keep in its vaults or with the Insular Treasury a sum in lawful money either of the Philippines or of the United States. If the amount kept in the Bank fell below the amount prescribed, the Bank could restrict the business of making loans or discounts. However, the Secretary of Finance, at the request of the Board of Directors and with the approval of the Board of Control, would be authorized to suspend this requirement of maintaining the proportion of reserve specified in the Act (Sec. 44).
8. With the approval of the Board of Control, the Bank was authorized to guarantee the principal and interest of bonds issued by corporations for the erection of industrial plants (Sec. 45).

To sum up, with the insertion of various regulations regarding the Board of Control in the revised Act of 1921, this Board came to exercise authority over the management of the National Bank. The intervention of the colonial state and its political power in the management of the National Bank effectively received affirmation and legitimation.

## COMMENCEMENT OF BANKING
## OPERATIONS AND AGRICULTURAL LOANS

The first president of the Philippine National Bank was H. Parker Willis, an influential American economist.[15] A specialist in banking and finance, Willis had been appointed secretary of the U.S. Federal Reserve Board in 1914. He took a one-year leave from this lofty position to assume the presidency of the Philippine National Bank, serving from May 1916 until his resignation in February 1917 (although he left Manila and returned to the United States in September 1916). His role in the incorporation of the National Bank was highly significant because, as has been discussed earlier, it had been Willis himself who drafted the bill seeking the Bank's establishment. Upon his return from his Manila posting, Willis accepted an appointment as professor of banking at Columbia University in 1917, a role in which he wielded enormous influence over U.S. foreign policy until his death in 1937.[16]

After serving as the National Bank's president, Willis published a short but very informative article on the beginnings of the Philippine National Bank in 1917.[17] According to him, the first step in the bank's operations involved a careful examination of the assets of the Agricultural Bank of the Philippine Government. This resulted in the assumption of all the earlier bank's liabilities and the transfer of all of its assets, but excepting mortgages valued at approximately 900,000 pesos that were either in default or deemed bad.[18] Table 13 shows the balance sheet of the National Bank as of 25 May 1916, showing the paid-up capital of the bank at approximately 2.4 million pesos, composed of the assets transferred from the Agricultural Bank as well as the initial subscription of 1 million pesos by the insular government.[19] Loans and discounts amounted to nearly 5.5 million pesos, most of which seem to be agricultural loans transferred from the Agricultural Bank. The deposits of over 9 million pesos most likely represent the government funds that were received by the National Bank under its regulations.

With these assets the National Bank began operating, but the immediate problem it had to address was the recruitment of competent staff. The former Agricultural Bank came with a staff of about fifteen persons, three or four of whom worked as inspectors of the agricultural lands that were used as collateral for loans. The National Bank found these inspectors incompetent and did not rehire them, but the other staffers of the Agricultural Bank were retained to form a nucleus for an agricultural division of the new National Bank. During May, June, and July of 1916, the Bank conducted a

*Table 13.* Balance Sheet of the Philippine National Bank, as of 25 May 1916

(1000 pesos, %)

| Resources | | | Liabilities | | |
|---|---|---|---|---|---|
| Loans and discounts | 5,460.6 | (46.1) | Capital (paid-up) | 2,385.7 | (20.2) |
| Interest accrued receivable | 238.5 | (2.0) | Undivided profits | 54.0 | (0.5) |
| Cash: with Insular Treasurer and in banks | 5,571.5 | (47.1) | Deposits | 9,184.2 | (77.6) |
| Due from agencies | 562.8 | (4.8) | Interest accrued receivable | 106.9 | (0.9) |
| Other assets | 4.3 | (0.0) | | 107.0 | (0.9) |
| Total | 11,837.7 | (100.0) | Total[(1)] | 11,837.7 | (100.0) |

*Source:* H. Parker Willis, "The Philippine National Bank," *The Journal of Political Economy* vol .25, no. 5 (May 1917), p. 419.

*Note:* (1) Due to rounding off, this differs to the aggregation of the amount of each item.

special training course for the benefit of approximately fifty new staffers. This training program, along with an initial shortage of facilities and equipment, incurred a delay of several months before the Bank's physical plant was in working order.[20]

Once the Bank's business commenced operations, all went smoothly, and even those in Manila's business circles who had initially regarded it with suspicion soon welcomed the possibilities it represented and began to deposit some portion of their funds with the new Bank. Table 14 shows the Bank's balance sheet as of 31 December 1916. A comparison of Tables 13 and 14 reveals that the amount of the Bank's paid-up capital and that of its loans and discounts doubled, while the total amount of deposits increased more than fourfold in only six months. Table 14 includes the unmatured foreign bills or the exchange for future delivery among the items of assets that were not included in Table 13. Strikingly, the amount of the unmatured foreign bills accounted for six percent of the total assets, showing the larger weight of foreign trade-related business in the Bank's operations. There is not enough data to itemize the loans and discounts that make up 25 percent of the assets; however, it is apparent that loans constitute a large portion of it. On the liability side, deposits constituted 83 percent of the total, distributed

Table 14. Balance Sheet of the Philippine National Bank, as of 31 December 1916

(1000 pesos, %)

| Assets | | | Liabilities | | |
|---|---|---|---|---|---|
| Loans and discounts | 13,012.6 | (25.6) | Capital (paid in) | 4,364.4 | (8.6) |
| Unmatured foreign bill | 2,965.3 | (5.8) | Profit and loss | 359.3 | (0.7) |
| Provincial overdrafts | 30.4 | (0.1) | Unearned discount | 62.5 | (0.1) |
| U.S. government bonds | 500.0 | (1.0) | Reserved for taxes and fidelity bonds | 11.0 | (0.0) |
| Philippine government bonds | 286.0 | (0.6) | Circulation | 520.0 | (1.0) |
| Furniture and fixtures | 70.7 | (0.1) | Deposits[2] | 42,341.1 | (83.4) |
| Interest accured receivable | 421.3 | (0.8) | Acceptance | 4.3 | (0.0) |
| Exchange for future delivery | 800.1 | (1.6) | Interest accrued payable | 146.9 | (0.3) |
| Cash (due from branches, other banks, with Insular Treasurer) | 30,142.1 | (59.4) | Exchange contracts | 800.1 | (1.6) |
| Customers liability L/C | 2,558.0 | (5.0) | Letter of credit | 2,176.8 | (4.3) |
| Total[1] | 50,786.5 | (100.0) | Total | 50,786.5 | (100.0) |

Source: Same as Table 13, p. 423.
Notes: (1) Due to rounding off, this differs to the aggregation of the amount of each item.
(2) Insular government (2.67 million pesos), individual accounts (4.5 million pesos), and fixed deposits (107.7 million pesos).

as Philippine government shares, 63 percent; individual accounts, 10 percent; and fixed deposits, 25 percent.

Among the most important initial operations of the National Bank was the provision of agricultural loans for export crop production. As a public institution, with the majority of its stock owned by the government, and a large percentage of its liabilities consisting of public deposits, the Philippine National Bank was expected to entertain all legitimate demands for agricultural loans in a fairly expeditious fashion. But with the enormous expansion of export demand during World War I, the sheer magnitude of agricultural credit required proved to be beyond the capacity even of the new bank and necessitated highly selective consideration of loan applications. The interest rate for agricultural loans was set at 8 percent per year for the mortgages secured by land having a Torrens title, and at 10 percent for mortgages with a Spanish title. The loan applications varied in amount from a few pesos to the hundreds of thousands.[21]

The most crucial problem at this time stemmed from the absence of proper titles for many of the agricultural landholdings in the Philippines, and even where the landholdings were presumably titled under the Spanish system there were many cases in which the Spanish title certificates could not be procured. Needless to say, the process in issuing Torrens titles was very slow. Although the Philippine government had enacted a Land Registration Act (1902) and a Public Land Act (1903) — and then the Cadastral Act (1913) to systematize and modernize the land titling system — as late as 1918 out of nearly 2 million farms only 70,000 (or 4 percent) could be shown to hold Torrens titles and only 230,000 (12 percent) could be determined to have proper Spanish titles.[22] This limited land titling significantly reduced the volume of successful agricultural loan applications to the National Bank, invalidating many that might have otherwise merited serious attention.[23]

Section 10 of Act No. 2612 (1916), as has been discussed, stipulated that the total amount of loans that the National Bank could provide should not exceed one half of the Bank's capital and surplus and all its proceeds from the sale of real estate bonds. At the onset of the Bank's operations, no such bonds had been sold, so the actual sums available for agricultural loans were only one half of the Bank's capital and surplus.[24] As is clear from Table 13, the total amount of loans and discounts of the National Bank reached a level of 2.3 times the paid-up capital as of May 1916, and most of these were residual mortgages carried over from the old Agricultural Bank. This situation restricted the National Bank to a provision of loans in amounts less than those prescribed by law. To ensure that it functioned as a lending bank in accord with its mandate, more practical measures were taken by the inclusion of mortgages from the Agricultural Bank (in a limited amount of loans provided), and more new loans were made available by the bank authorities. Consequently, by the end of 1916, the total amount of loans and discounts reached 13 million pesos, almost three times the paid-up capital (Table 14).

Within a month after its formal opening the Bank began examining loan applications and deciding on their approval or rejection. According to Willis, in its capacity as a semi-governmental bank the Bank had to closely scrutinize the documentation presented by applicants so as to "insure safety and conservatism."[25] To obtain an agricultural loan, an applicant was required to submit two reports from independent sources with a reference to the assessment of the actual value of the land offered as collateral. One of the reports had to be obtained from "a traveling agent in the employ of the Bank, who should visit the land and personally inspect it and decide upon its income-producing powers, the honesty of the proprietor, and other essential questions."[26] At the time, it was not easy to deploy assessors who could make such value determinations, and thus, in most cases, the provincial tax assessors themselves had to shoulder the crucial task. The reports prepared by the provincial assessors were further checked by the provincial treasurer, and when he deemed it necessary he included additional data for the evaluation of the proposed loan.[27]

One feature of the agricultural loan operation of the Philippine National Bank requires special attention. As stated by Willis, before the establishment of the Philippine National Bank the Philippine government had deposited revenues in the sum of 2.5 million pesos for crop loans— loans on the standing sugar crop mainly in Negros and Panay Islands— in the Agricultural Bank. After the organization of the National Bank, the issue as to whether the National Bank should take over the task of providing crop loans or allow private banks to administer them was resolved with a special act of the Philippine Legislature permitting government funds to be transferred to the National Bank and allowing the Bank to provide "traditional" crop loans in large amounts.[28] Crop loans were secured not by real estate but by standing crops, a form of lending considered unworthy under the modern banking system.

In July 1916, Willis, together with two directors of the Bank, visited Iloilo city on Panay Island and found various anomalies attendant to such crop loans. In many cases the planters who filed applications for crop loans already carried first mortgages, mostly under the former Agricultural Bank. Some of the planters had outstanding second mortgages in favor of some local moneylender or some other bank, and in extreme cases even held third mortgages. In many instances planters had taken special mortgages on personal property, such as automobiles or machinery, so that it was often the situation that the only remaining security they could offer was the actual standing crop.[29]

Given this scenario, Willis oversaw a set of guidelines designed to impose restrictions on crop loans administered by the National Bank. These guidelines called for: (1) the rejection of any loan application where the titling to the land was unclear; (2) the refusal of loans even if the title was clear, unless reasonable value could be found in the land; (3) the payment of loans by monthly installment to meet the actual needs of the planter for necessary expenses; (4) the signing of documents waiving all rights to the crops by mortgagers who held a prior lien on the land, as a precondition for the release of loans; (5) the requirement of one reliable guarantor for each loan (where the members of a family were joint owners of the land, all of them were to be deemed responsible for the whole loan on the land); (6) the treatment of additional mortgages upon any other property, that any borrower could obtain, as collateral; and (7) the payment of the loan as soon as the sugar was produced and sold in the market.[30]

Many applications were rejected due to insufficiency of documentation, although there were also not a few cases of loans being extended despite the inability of sugar planters (or landowners) to comply with the conditions. During 1916 applications for loans totaled 2.2 million pesos, and three-fourths of them received approval from the committee. Some of these loan proceeds were not released after approval on account of failures of certain planters to meet requirements, such that in the end less than two-thirds of the applications for loans were actually paid out. These strict measures by the National Bank discouraged many landowners in the sugar-producing region, even provoking serious complaints from some that the Bank should provide crop loans without any security at all.

Some knowledge of the economics of local sugar production at the time is helpful in understanding this situation. At this period in the Philippines, *muscovado* sugar (brown sugar with low polarization) was produced at small sugar mills installed in sugar plantations (or *haciendas*). As a result of the inefficiency of this process, local producers did not usually earn the substantial profits they expected. The average cost of sugar production under these circumstances was 4 or 5 pesos per picul (63.25kg), while the selling price of the same was about 5 pesos at the port of Iloilo. Many planters, having no choice but to rely on crop loans, incurred significant indebtedness, a predicament made worse by the absence of any prospects for modernizing their sugar manufacturing operations. Recognizing this situation, Willis, seeking to help planters realize higher returns on their capital outlays, argued for investing in the construction of modern sugar mills or centrals that could produce centrifugal sugar of higher quality with a far higher market price than *muscovado*. He perceived that providing loans to planters under the current uneconomical practice of sugar production could prove hazardous to the continued viability of the new bank.[31]

### THE 1918 DISPUTE OVER LENDING IN AGRICULTURE

However, the guidelines inhibiting the Bank's crop loan operations were short-lived. Samuel Ferguson, who had served as Willis's vice president, replaced Willis as the Bank's second president, but resigned in March 1918 after only six months in office. The third president of the Bank — and a major driver of subsequent developments — was Venancio Concepcion, the first Filipino to serve in this capacity. As Peter Stanley points out, Concepcion's management style proved to be the exact of opposite of the first president's. Whereas Willis tried to manage the Bank according to the structures of modern banking, Concepcion relied on personal connections to secure and support the economic interests of privileged clients. Concepcion worked tirelessly to promote expansion in the provision of agricultural loans to the export sector, particularly sugar production.[32] By mid-1918, criticism from one of the Bank's American directors, Archibald Harrison, led to a fractious internal dispute that eventually led to Harrison's resignation.

Archibald Harrison was the brother of Governor-General Harrison, and served as secretary of the Board of Directors of the National Bank.[33] Observing a lot of anomalies or violations of the regulations governing the Bank's agricultural loans, he felt compelled, by May 1918, to ask the Bank's Executive Committee to conduct an investigation. A committee was subsequently organized for this purpose, with four appointed committee members: Archibald Harrison himself, Vicente Madrigal from the Executive Committee, Vicente Singson Encarnacion, and Fred N. Berry from the Bank's Agricultural Committee. Although this committee as a group was supposed to investigate loans extended by the Bank's Agricultural Department, it was Harrison himself who conducted the investigation.[34] His unpublished reports, now housed at the U.S. National Archives and among the Harrison Papers at the Library of Congress in Washington,[35] greatly enhance an understanding of the actual conditions of the National Bank's lending in a number of sugar-producing provinces, including Pampanga and Bulacan in Central Luzon, Iloilo on Panay Island, and Negros Occidental.

A few examples will suffice. One report, based on Harrison's field trip to Iloilo and Bacolod in July 1918, reveals that the Bank's Iloilo branch extended enormous crop loans to landowners in the provinces of Capiz and

Iloilo and in both provinces of Negros.[36] Agricultural loans in even larger amounts, based on real estate as collateral, as well as crop loans, that is, loans secured by the standing sugar crop, were made available to Negrense sugarcane planters. Because of persistent low prices of *muscovado* sugar on the market, along with an epidemic of disease among farm animals and unfavorable weather conditions over the last three years, many sugar planters had become massively indebted to the National Bank.[37]

One 1917 memorandum by the manager of the Bank's Iloilo branch, which Harrison cites, shows that in crop year 1916–1917, this branch had twelve outstanding crop loans amounting to 59,728 pesos. In crop year 1917–1918 the outstanding crop loans of this branch alone numbered seventy-two, with an aggregate amount of 909,840 pesos. During the next crop year 1918–1919, the Bank's Board of Directors approved 154 loans totaling 2,103,375 pesos. However, of these only eighty-five loans were actually released, in the total amount of 241,164 pesos, apparently due to a policy adopted by the Bank at that time not to grant any new loans or, rather, not to process new loan applications from the same parties until their previous accounts had been settled. An inspector at Iloilo had visited farms where loans had been provided at least twice.[38]

Data are unavailable regarding many details of the long-term agricultural loans processed by the Iloilo branch. Before a sub-agency was opened at Bacolod in Negros Occidental, most long-term loans to large-scale sugar growers in that province had been offered by the Iloilo branch. As many of these planters had outstanding liabilities, the manager of the Iloilo branch asked the Agricultural Department in the Manila office to furnish him full information from their records on such liabilities.[39] There were quite a few cases in which Negros Occidental sugar planters received approval not only for long-term agricultural and crop loans but also for commercial loans.

After visiting haciendas in various parts of Negros Occidental, Harrison compiled information for a number of case reports. Eight of them are summarized below.

**Hijos de I. de la Rama.** This firm, managed by Esteban de la Rama, incurred a total obligation of 1,294,000 pesos to the Bank, which included 794,000 pesos of outstanding crop loans over a three-year period, and 500,000 pesos in commercial loans. The collateral for these loans included: seven haciendas with a total area of 2,700 hectares; sugar centrals located in the municipality of Bago; 85,000 piculs of centrifugal sugar; and 7,613 piculs of *muscovado* sugar. This firm owned three additional haciendas with a total area of 1,000 hectares and another small central in the municipality of Talisay, but these three haciendas had apparently already been mortgaged to the Bank of the Philippine Islands. Two more small sugar centrals were deemed to be mismanaged. Finally, de la Rama had bad relations with other sugar planters in the area, a factor that prevented his centrals from operating at full capacity.[40]

**Araneta Family.** This family controlled 12,000 hectares of land, stretching from the coast to the mountains at Bago, with the ownership divided among family members. The Bank held crop and long-term loans in the aggregate amount of 800,000 pesos. It was found to be this family's practice for one member to mortgage his property share so as to liquidate the amortization payments of another member's. With what was deemed mismanagement of the plantations, the family faced difficulties in paying back the loans incurred with the Bank.[41]

**Gomez Brothers.** Located near the municipality of La Castellana, a hacienda of 600 hectares and a sugar central, both operated by the Gomez brothers, were each valued at 240,000 pesos. This family's indebtedness totaled 491,000 pesos, exceeding the assessed value of the collateral upon which its loans were based. These loans included a long-term loan (288,000 pesos), a loan for crop year 1917–1918 (36,000 pesos), and a debt against Germann & Co. (167,000 pesos). Yet another loan for crop year 1918–1919 (67,000 pesos) had just been approved for this family at the time of Harrison's investigation.[42]

**Esperidion Guanco and Victoriano Siguenza.** Guanco and his father-in-law, Victoriano Siguenza, both had outstanding loans from the National Bank and from the Bank of the Philippine Islands. Siguenza's loan for crop year 1917–1918 from Germann & Co. was already overdue, with the *muscovado* sugar he offered as security being determined to be insufficient to cover the obligation. He had also been extended a loan of 35,000 pesos from the old Agricultural Bank, based on one of four haciendas he owned as collateral. This loan was supposedly intended for the purchase of animals and machinery, but the money had instead been used to help Guanco in his first payment for the construction of his sugar central.[43] Guanco himself took a loan from Germann & Co. with four haciendas of 679 hectares as its collateral. Of these four haciendas, the larger two belonged to Siguenza, with the remaining two listed under Guanco's name. The Bank also approved a crop loan of 100,000 pesos for crop year 1917–1918 against some 4,000 piculs of centrifugal sugar in Guanco's favor. Additionally, Guanco had applied for a crop loan of about 160,000 pesos for crop year 1918–1919. As a result of his visit and inspection of the property and inventories, Bank President Venancio Concepcion assessed the value of these four haciendas and a sugar mill at 1,350,000 pesos; but based on current market prices, the properties were in fact only worth 685,000 pesos.[44]

**Isabela Sugar Factory.** A group of sugar planters headed by Gil Montilla built this sugar central in the municipality of Isabela. Together, these planters successfully applied for a loan of 1.5 million pesos from the Bank with 6,000 hectares of their haciendas as security. This loan was approved by the Bank's Executive Committee but the initial procedure was deemed irregular because the committee had previously agreed to a separate loan for the purchase of machinery. Archibald Harrison voted in favor of the loan proper of 1.5 million pesos but on the precondition that the cost of machinery be included in it. About one third of the 6,000 hectarage was devoted to rice and its value was assessed at 1.2 million pesos (200 pesos per hectare), a fairly higher estimate than would otherwise be the case, yet lower than the loan approved. The Bank's investment in this sugar central through this loan was only the beginning, and further financing would be required before the factory actually operated.[45]

**Properties Owned by the Heirs of Remigio Montilla.** Members of this family included the widow of Remigio Montilla, seven daughters, and one son, Emilio Montilla. Their seven farms, all located a few miles away from the proposed site of the Isabela Sugar Factory, totaled 731 hectares in area. These farmlands were separate from the 6,000 hectares that were pledged as security for the Isabela factory loan, and could not be included in that hectarage as this family was already heavily indebted, with an outstanding long-term loan of 115,000 pesos from the old Agricultural Bank as well as an unpaid crop loan of 27,000 pesos. On Harrison's visit to Emilio Montilla, this family's financial position was determined to be quite tenuous, ostensibly made so by one practice of the Bank's Agricultural Department of issuing either a new long-term loan or a crop loan to nearly-defaulting debtors to help them cover the overdue interest.[46]

**Yulo Brothers.** This family owned six haciendas totaling 1,859 hectares in area in the municipality of Binalbagan. Five of these were mortgaged to the Bank as the collateral for a loan of 485,000 pesos. This loan was made available to the Yulo family to save their property from foreclosure by Ynchausti & Co. But it was unlikely that the Yulos would be able to deliver on their obligation, owing to their wasteful and unbusinesslike methods of farm management. Under the manager's name, the family qualified for a loan of 45,000 pesos for crop year 1917–1918, 34,000 pesos of which remained unpaid. This loan was not secured by any sugar, but by mortgages on real estate in Iloilo province that could not be utilized as collateral on a crop loan. Bank President Concepcion nonetheless extended a crop loan, with the understanding that its proceeds were to be used to pay interest charges due Ynchausti & Co. in the prior year. President Concepcion estimated the value of the Yulo agricultural assets at 1,336,250 pesos. Harrison believed the properties to be overvalued, with his own assessment of its worth at 630,000 pesos.[47]

**Salvador Serra.** Serra's hacienda, along with its sugar central, was located near the municipality of Ilog. The Bank had provided him a long-term loan of 160,000 pesos and a crop loan of 150,000 pesos for crop year 1918–1919. The proceeds of the long-term loan were used to cancel the obligations incurred in the purchase of machinery for the central, and the crop loan was intended for machinery and labor. Serra represented a sound example of successful plantation management. His properties included 280 hectares of sugarcane land (valued at 140,000 pesos); 220 hectares of wood land convertible into agricultural land (worth 22,000 pesos); and machinery at the central and storage facilities (200,000 pesos in total value).[48]

Most of the cases outlined above involved sugar planters who built relatively smaller centrifugal mills or centrals in their respective haciendas, and they might not represent general examples of sugar planters in Negros Occidental. Harrison later visited other municipalities like Himamaylan, Pontevedra, and La Carlota to investigate the state and status of long-term loans or crop loans made by the Bank to borrowers in these areas. He discovered that, generally speaking, the long-term loans were provided there on a fairly sound basis, while crop loans were practically, without exception, excessively given. The trouble was that planters in these areas usually applied for their loans based on overestimations of sugar production for the coming year, even as most of the loans approved by the Bank were slightly reduced in amounts against the declared figures of production.[49]

George Seaver, Harrison's research assistant, supplemented Harrison's investigation. In a letter dated 9 August 1918, he described a similar glut of problematic crop loans he had uncovered since mid-July in his survey of a wide range of plantations in the less fertile parts of Negros Occidental, from Escalante in the north to Cauayan in the south. The 230 cases of agricultural loans he investigated in sixteen municipalities covered a total of 49,695 hectares of land used as collateral for loans totaling 3,461,370 pesos. He also examined 127 cases of crop loans unpaid since 1916 in the total sum of 2,209,311 pesos and found that, in many cases, loans were offered in sums exceeding the market value of the lands used by debtors as collaterals. Loans were even provided to help nearly-defaulting borrowers make due payments, in installments, of the principal or the interest of previous loans. Seaver cited some striking examples demonstrating the great risks faced by the Bank in loaning money on lands backed by Spanish titles. In one case, where the Bank's mortgage was for 248 hectares bearing a Spanish title, the cadastral survey yielded an actual landholding of less than 137 hectares. In some instances, the money obtained from the Bank for agricultural purposes was in fact diverted into commercial or industrial investments, or occasionally even loaned out by the borrower to other farmers at the rate of 25 percent a year. In some extreme examples, an influential man like the Justice of the Peace would induce a landowner to apply for a loan, acting as agent in the preparation of documents, and then, upon approval of the loan, would take 50 percent of the proceeds as a commission.[50]

In another letter, dated 12 August 1918, Seaver reported that of the 230 agricultural loans inspected in Negros Occidental, forty were found not complying with the required conditions, and recommended that corrective measures be taken on a case-by-case basis. Among them Seaver described loans in amounts of less than 10,000 pesos (twenty-two cases), loans ranging in amount from 10,000 to 19,999 pesos (seven cases), loans in amounts between 20,000 and 29,999 pesos (five cases), and one loan of 30,000 pesos. Irregularities found included the following variations or patterns: (1) loans were not used for the original purpose such as clearing lands, the purchase of *carabaos* (water buffaloes) or the payment in installments for the equipment of small sugar centrals; (2) new loans that were approved for the payment of outstanding loans were not used for this original purpose; and (3) only a small part of the land presented as collateral was actually cultivated or used for sugarcane agriculture, in violation of the requirement that loans were offered to these haciendas on the understanding that the land was under cultivation and not so near to mountainous areas as to be considered poor agricultural land.[51] Two examples are described below.

**Ricardo Nolan.** Nolan received three loans from the old Agricultural Bank: 9,600 pesos on land lying southwest of Escalante, hectarage unknown; 1,600 pesos on 184 hectares of land situated northwest of Sagay; and 12,000 pesos on approximately 194 hectares located northwest of La Carlota. All of these lands were found to be unimproved and uncultivated. Nolan had another landholding of 216 hectares, and a mortgage of 4,000 pesos had been fixed on this land by the Agricultural Bank in the name of Francisco Ferrer, but this also remained uncultivated.[52]

**Jose E. Domingo.** Domingo obtained a loan of 13,000 pesos from the National Bank on a 500-hectare property northwest of Murcia. Only about sixty hectares was planted: about eighteen or twenty hectares to sugarcane (found to be poorly cultivated), and forty hectares to upland rice. Moreover, practically all of this land was of such an elevation that it could not, under normal circumstances, be considered good agricultural land.[53]

In a memorandum dated 17 August 1918, which examines certain applications for crop loans, Archibald Harrison observed that major sugar planters like Javellana and Ledesma, as well as the Spanish tobacco company Tabacalera had obtained 1917 crop loans that presumably remained unpaid, and, were they to secure 1918 crop loans from the National Bank, these could conceivably be used to settle previous and outstanding loans. He opined that this situation was absolutely improper, and new loans should not be approved if they were going to be applied toward such questionable ends.[54]

When Concepcion understood that his management style had been put into question by these investigative findings, he sent a confidential report dated 18 August 1918 to Manuel L. Quezon, President of the Philippine Senate, strongly contesting Harrison's report and claiming that it was marred by falsehoods and many mistakes.[55] In self-defense, Harrison called the Bank's investigation committee into session, and sent other documents to Concepcion supporting his findings. A resolution was also adopted by the committee requesting formal comments or rejoinders from Concepcion.[56] Concepcion's response was to dismiss George Seaver and another staffer on 1 September 1918.[57] To make matters worse for Harrison, Concepcion's decision was supported by three Filipino members of the Bank's Agricultural Division: Vicente Singson Encarnacion, Vicente Madrigal, and R. J. Fernandez.[58] In turn, given this escalating conflict with Concepcion, Harrison sent a letter to Concepcion filing his resignation from his post as secretary of the Bank's Board of Directors effective 13 September 1918.[59] The upshot was that, despite Harrison's careful and revealing investigation, his efforts did not succeed in returning the National Bank to its aspiration to regulate agricultural loans and subject them to strict terms. In a halfway measure declared in 1921, the National Bank imposed a regulation permitting the foreclosure of securities on irrecoverable loans, but it was limited in its applicability only to loans transferred from the old Agricultural Bank.[60]

## DECODING THE MEANINGS OF
## THE DUAL STRUCTURE OF LENDING IN AGRICULTURE

Ostensibly, the confrontation between Venancio Concepcion and Archibald Harrison over banking policy on agricultural loans, particularly in relation to crop loans, can be seen as merely indicating antagonism between a Filipino bank president and an American director of the bank, or manifesting the near-impossibility of imposing modern banking regulations in an entrenched culture of favoritism inclined toward the interests of the planters involved in cash crop production. But beyond the political argument or the dichotomies in banking operations between modern and pre-modern systems, it is important to consider why a pre-modern credit system involving an unusual species of lending called crop loans persisted in the National Bank throughout the 1920s.

In this connection, some data on the agricultural loans of the National Bank during the 1920s are worth examining in detail. Table 15 shows that, as of the end of 1925, the total amount of loans and discounts of the Bank reached 92.4 million pesos, 15 percent of which was in the form of agricultural loans with real estate as collateral and 7 percent of which consisted of crop loans. Table 16 indicates the amount of agricultural loans made available by the Bank by crop and by branch or agency as of the end of 1928.[61] It is noteworthy that nearly 70 percent of mid- and long-term agricultural loans and crop loans were provided for sugarcane agriculture, particularly by the branches of Bacolod and Iloilo. Comparing these two tables, one also sees that the amount of crop loans declined from 6.25 million pesos to 4.36 million pesos in the three years from 1925 to 1928. It is no idle speculation to read this decline as one consequence of the Bank's preference for agricultural loans over crop loans in the progress of land registration.[62]

This declining trend in the Bank's crop loan business is also borne out in the statistics compiled by the Bacolod and Iloilo branches. The amount of crop loans provided by the Bacolod agency declined as follows: 3.88 million

Table 15. Outstanding Loans and Discounts of the Philippine
National Bank by Sector, as of 31 December 1925

(1000 pesos, %)

| | | |
|---|---|---|
| Agricultural | 13,486 | (14.6) |
| Sugar Centrals | 48,549 | (52.6) |
| Crop loans | | |
|    Sugar | 6,041 | (6.5) |
|    Others | 208 | (0.2) |
| Commercial | 13,750 | (14.9) |
| Coconut Oil & Others | 10,340 | (11.2) |
| Total | 92,374 | (100.0) |

Source: Draft of Annual Report of the Philippine National Bank for the Year 1925 with a letter from Rafael Corpus to Manuel Quezon (24 Feb. 1926), Philippine National Library, Manuel L. Quezon, Papers, Series IV, Subject File, Box 448.

Table 16. Outstanding Agricultural Loans of the Philippine National
Bank by Crop and Branch, as of 31 December 1928

(1000 pesos)

| | Sugar | Rice | Coconut | Manila Hemp | Others | Total |
|---|---|---|---|---|---|---|
| **1. Agricultural Loan** | | | | | | |
| Bacolod[1] | 4,324 | 0 | 0 | 0 | 0 | 4,324 |
| Cabanatuan | 0 | 1,042 | 0 | 0 | 0 | 1,042 |
| Cebu | 112 | 0 | 74 | 0 | 186 | 372 |
| Dagupan | 0 | 512 | 0 | 0 | 0 | 512 |
| Davao | 0 | 0 | 188 | 438 | 0 | 626 |
| Iloilo | 4,426 | 0 | 0 | 0 | 0 | 4,426 |
| Legaspi | 0 | 90 | 180 | 180 | 0 | 450 |
| Lucena | 0 | 0 | 1,172 | 0 | 0 | 1,172 |
| Total | 8,862 | 1,644 | 1,614 | 618 | 186 | 12,924 |
| **2. Crop Loan** | | | | | | |
| Bacolod[1] | 4,144 | 0 | 0 | 0 | 0 | 4,144 |
| Cabanatuan | 0 | 56 | 0 | 0 | 0 | 56 |
| Iloilo | 217 | 0 | 0 | 0 | 0 | 217 |
| Total | 4,361 | 56 | 0 | 0 | 0 | 4,417 |

Source: "Philippine National Bank, Manila, Examiner's Report of Condition at Close of Business, Sept. 30, 1929," BIA 6769-with 187.

Note: (1) Sub-agency till the mid-1920s.

pesos (as of 5 September 1927), 3.07 million pesos (as of 16 October 1929), 1.69 million pesos (as of 5 September 1930) and 0.84 million pesos (as of 30 April 1931). For the Iloilo branch, these figures are: approximately 250,000 pesos (as of 10 October 1929), 50,000 pesos (as of 27 April 1931) and 110,000 pesos (as of 16 October 1933).[63] Crop loans as the predominant form of credit thus practically ceased by the end of the 1920s, indicating the National Bank's ultimate departure from the dual structure of its lending business in export agriculture, that is, the offering of mid- and long-term agricultural loans based on real estate as collateral, and the facility of short-term loans premised on standing crops as security.

Why did the National Bank sustain this dual structure of its lending business in agriculture throughout its first fifteen years? The slow decline of crop loans in the practices and policies of the Philippine National Bank during the American period underscores certain characteristics of the contradictory modern banking system in colonial Philippines, especially when regarded from the wider perspective of economic history in the Southeast Asian region. At the end of the nineteenth century, when private landownership in the Philippines had not yet been legally established under Spanish rule, commercial agency houses provided cash advances to growers using future crops as collateral instead of the customary real estate security introduced by modern banking.[64] This "traditional" system was widely adopted particularly in frontier regions of the emerging export economy, such as Negros Island. Sugar haciendas in Negros tended to be of large hectarage, owned and managed by landowners who needed agricultural funds. The likely prototype of the crop loan system lies in the practice of overseas Chinese moneylenders of offering cash advances to farmers in return for their anticipated or future crops, a practice that probably goes back to the eighteenth century.[65] In Southeast Asia, modern banking and moneylending on a smaller scale grew in tandem, as various efforts to sustain cash crop production grew in importance from the late nineteenth century to the mid-twentieth century. However, the process by which, in the early twentieth century, the crop loan business was enlarged, first by private banks and then by the Agricultural Bank and finally the National Bank capitalized by Philippine government funds is unique to the Philippines, especially when seen in comparison to its regional neighbors.

Indeed, the National Bank's continuation of the crop loan system appeared to be a kind of deviation from the norms of modern banking. But the evolving characteristics of the Philippine export economy could only lead inevitably to the survival of the crop loan system at exactly the same time that the modern banking system was being put in place under the Americans. As agricultural exports under the so-called "free trade" policy arrangements expanded between the United States and the Philippines during the early 1910s, banks were forced to develop a lending facility for cash-strapped planters invested in production for export to the U.S. market. However, certain problems then began to arise; for example, the inadequacy of legal land titles forced the National Bank to continue its crop loan business for an extended period. It was these conditions that gave rise to the contradiction of a supposedly modern banking system, represented by the National Bank, to function, in point of fact, as a pre-modern (even hybrid) banking institution, forced to adapt its structures and operations to such contextual contingencies. And indeed the forays of the National Bank into the crop loan business led to the decline in financial market share of larger British banks that had been unchallenged even at the onset of U.S. rule. In the 1920s the National Bank became the largest and leading bank in the Philippines literally laying, in a systematic fashion, the foundations for local financial markets under the American dispensation and with the sanction of its colonial state. In this context, the conclusion is inescapable that the dual structure of agricultural loans in the Philippine National Bank itself embodied and reflected the very characteristics of the export economy of the Philippines in its evolving financial structure from the mid-1910s to the late 1920s.

# PART III
# DEBACLE

CHAPTER 5

# THE WOOD-FORBES MISSION AND THE FINANCIAL CRISIS

WITH THE PHENOMENAL rise and expansion of postcolonial theory that followed the publication of Edward Said's *Orientalism* and later *Culture and Imperialism*,[1] colonial discourse analysis has become a common methodology in Southeast Asian studies. This approach has proven crucial to our understanding of the nature of colonialism, particularly in the critique it offers of the process of knowledge production that has been deployed on the colonized or "Others" by their colonial masters.

In the field of Philippine studies, a significant number of important studies using colonial discourse analysis have appeared. Notable among these are Reynaldo Ileto's *Knowing America's Colony*,[2] Vicente Rafael's *White Love*,[3] Floro Quibuyen's *A Nation Aborted*,[4] and Michael Salman's *The Embarrassment of Slavery*.[5] The intention of this book is to contribute to this new wave in Philippine historical research. Conceived as a study of Philippine banking history during the period of the American colonial state, and extending from the sphere of economic history to that of political history, the use of colonial discourse analysis is inevitable. It is only in the context of the American colonization of the Philippines that the 1919–1922 corruption scandal that befell the Philippine National Bank can be fully understood. This chapter endeavors to show that the Philippine financial crisis that followed World War I was the ground on which the American colonial state in the Philippines was built.

In order to present the conventional view on the scandal of the Philippine National Bank—a view that was widely disseminated in the early 1920s and subsequently became the standard accepted "narrative" in Philippine discourse—this chapter first analyzes the Wood-Forbes Mission, an investigation commissioned by U.S. President Warren G. Harding in March 1921. This mission's report was submitted to U.S. Secretary of War John W. Weeks in October 1921. An analysis of the conventional view using postcolonial theory follows, revealing the means by which the report aligned the "facts" of the scandal with U.S. colonial ambitions. Finally, this chapter argues that the Wood-Forbes Mission functioned as a crucial factor in the development of the political rivalries that characterized the solidification of the American colonial state in the 1920s.

**THE WOOD-FORBES MISSION REPORT**

The discussion begins with a brief summary of the Philippine financial crisis of 1919–1922. The Philippine National Bank was established in 1916 as a multi-purpose semi-governmental bank to provide loans for the agricultural export industry; it was also permitted by law to issue bank notes while depositing government funds. In 1917 the National Bank opened an agency in New York in which it deposited a considerable amount of Philippine currency reserves, which were government funds that the National Bank was forbidden to use for commercial purposes. Initially these funds were twofold: the Gold Standard Fund and the Silver Certificate Reserve. As will be shown, the two were combined as the Currency Reserve Fund in 1918. By the end of 1918, most of these reserves had been transferred back to the Manila office in order to augment loans for export businesses. Before long, the Philippine economy had exhausted its currency reserves and spiraled into hyperinflation. This rapid sequence of events generated the most scandalous and sensational fiscal issue the Philippine government experienced under U.S. colonial rule.

The crisis of the Philippine National Bank and the exhaustion of currency reserves were disclosed at the end of Governor-General Francis Burton Harrison's term. Harrison took responsibility and resigned in March 1921,[6] at which point Vice Governor-General Charles E. Yeater briefly became acting governor-general. However, the governor-generalship had been vacant for six months when Leonard Wood assumed the role in October 1921 at the time the Wood-Forbes Report appeared.

Some background on U.S. policy towards the Philippines at this time is in order here. In December 1920, before leaving his presidency, Woodrow Wilson made a speech to the U.S. Congress in which he stated that the Philippines had accomplished various requirements and should be granted independence. However, incoming President Warren G. Harding did not agree. Harding had served on the Senate Committee on Territories and Insular Possessions and had his own ideas about the Philippines. In March 1921, shortly after becoming president, Harding made a decision to send a special mission to the Philippines to investigate the Philippine situation.[7] The mission was quickly put together, led by former Philippine Governor-General William Cameron Forbes and Major-General Leonard Wood—with the latter designated Chairman and already nominated as the next governor-general[8]—and thus was called the Wood-Forbes Mission.

The official purpose of this mission was to judge whether the Philippines was ready for independence. However, as will become clear, the real intention was—under the guise of finding a way to reconstruct the country's financial and currency system—to reverse the accelerated "Filipinization" of political and administrative institutions that had been under way during Harrison's governor-generalship. U.S. Secretary of War John W. Weeks explicitly requested the mission to look for the effects of Filipinization on the country's finances. In his instructions to Wood, Weeks wrote as follows:

> In passing now on the question of the stability of the existing government in the Philippines Islands if American support should be withdrawn therefrom and of the probability of the permanence of such a government thereafter and the likelihood that such a government would protect the people in their essential rights and privileges, the standard should not be one of perfection from our point of view, but the standard outlined in the instruction of Mr. McKinley.[9]
>
> We cannot neglect in considering the question of the maintenance of a government in the Philippine Islands the financial condition of the people. A study of the situation must embrace, therefore, a first-hand examination of the financial condition of the Philippine government and of the Filipino people— the present and prospective revenues of the government and the extent to which these revenues are dependent on the present relation of the islands to the United States. . . .

It is unnecessary to review the steps in the development of the existing government. It is sufficient to say that it is most liberal in its concession of powers to the Filipino people. . . .[10]

Carrying these instructions, the Wood-Forbes Mission departed the United States in April 1921 and arrived in Manila in May. During a four-month-stay in the Philippines, the mission traveled through various provinces to examine political, economic, and social conditions. Their *Report of the Special Mission on Investigation to the Philippine Islands* was submitted to Weeks in October.

The Wood-Forbes Mission Report was published both in Manila and Washington in 1921 and 1922.[11] Its twenty-seven pages first described briefly the schedule of the mission in the Philippines and then discussed various issues. The report's headings are: Historical Sketch; The Philippine People; Present Conditions; Constabulary and Public Order; Administration of Justice; Land Titles; Prisons; Public Instruction; The Bureau of Science, Health and Sanitation; Economic Condition; Finances; The Philippine National Bank; Public Works; Government in Business; Elections; Legislation; General Conclusions; and Recommendations.

As to the Filipinization of the legal, administrative, and legislative system in the Philippine government, the report commented: "There has been a progressive transfer of government to the people of the Islands, and at the present time it is very largely in their hands. So extensive has been the transfer that many fail to realize that there still continues in the Islands a decisive American control that assures the maintenance of an orderly government, secure against disturbing influences from within and without."[12]

This comment was reflected in the report's recommendations: first, that the present status of the Philippine government should continue until the people absorb thoroughly the powers already in their hands; second, the governor-general, as the representative of the United States, should have the authority commensurate with the responsibility of his position; third, in case of a deadlock between the governor-general and the Philippine Senate in confirmation of appointments, the U.S. president should make the final decision; and fourth, the American government should not allow any situation in the Philippines to develop that would leave the United States "in a position of responsibility without authority."[13]

The report did not spare the economic policy of the Harrison administration, targeting, in particular, the Philippine National Bank. The report's section on the bank begins: "The story of the Philippine National Bank is one of the most unfortunate and darkest pages in Philippine history,"[14] and proceeds as follows:

> This bank was started in 1916 and a law passed compelling all provincial and municipal governments to deposit all their funds in it; and at the same time arrangements were made to transfer from other banks all government funds there deposited, except trust funds which were held on deposit in the United States; later the bank was put into a position to get control of these moneys and reserve funds. The sum of $41,500,000, held for the conversion of currency, was transferred to the Philippine Islands, the bank making a large profit in exchange in doing so. Much of it was then loaned out to speculative concerns under circumstances which have led to grave doubt as to the good faith of the transactions.
>
> A man presumed to be experienced in banking was brought from the United States and took the first presidency which he held a short time. An American inexperienced in banking was then put in charge, and upon his death a Filipino also without banking experience became president.[15] The result of all this has been a series of banking losses estimated by the Insular Auditor to reach the severe total of $22,500,000....
>
> As a result of these findings, charges have been filed against General Concepción,[16] a former president of the bank.... The bank also established branches and agencies throughout the Philippine Islands, in charge of which they placed untrained Filipinos, and without exception these branches have been mismanaged. Of the four branches in which the examinations have been completed crime charges have been preferred against the managers of each one....[17]
>
> The currency resources have been depleted, the silver on deposit to redeem the currency has been pledged and used for other purposes. The fund for the maintenance of the parity of gold and silver is involved in these losses, with the result that instead of a metallic and cash basis for the currency, its principal support now is the pledge of the Philippine government and the confidence on the part of the public that the United States will not permit these things to happen again. The currency is now practically a fiat currency....
>
> The Philippine Islands, contrary to general belief, have maintained all of the expenses of civil administration since the beginning of American occupation from Insular revenues and without assistance from the Treasury of the United States, which has, however, defrayed all the costs of the military and naval

establishments and fortifications. The only aid received by the Philippine government from the United States has been a $3,000,000 appropriation for famine relief made in 1903.[18]

Based on the above remarks, three inferences may be made as to the Wood-Forbes Mission's view on the crisis of the Philippine National Bank and the Philippine currency system. First, the Philippine National Bank, established under the Harrison administration and falling into crisis within a few years of its start due to mismanagement, exhausted the currency reserves. Second, the losses in currency reserves undermined the fiscal competence of the Philippine government, though all had been well until the start of the Harrison administration.[19] Third, American colonial policy would not tolerate a fiscal system that could not be self-sufficient. The Wood-Forbes Mission claimed that the financial and fiscal policies of the Harrison administration led to total failure, and the responsibility for this failure must be shouldered by politicians in the U.S. Democratic Party and in the Philippines who had jointly promoted these policies.

What is important to note here is that the Wood-Forbes Mission's view, by emphasizing the inexperience of the Filipino bank officials and staff, was well situated to criticize the ill effects of the Filipinization promoted under Governor-General Harrison. Indeed, several Filipino officials appointed by Harrison were arrested and convicted. Thus, it was widely accepted in the Philippines that the crisis of the National Bank resulted from the bank's uncontrolled loans provided to export sectors with the strong support of politicians who protected the economic interests of Filipino landowners and manufacturing sectors of primary commodities. This view regarding the Philippine National Bank crisis had far-reaching influence in the Philippine political arena, as will be discussed later.

However, the graft and corruption in the Philippine National Bank, though widely recognized in the Philippines, was only one cause of the crisis and of the exhaustion of currency reserves. Another investigation, under the auspices of the U.S. Bureau of Insular Affairs (BIA), had been under way since 1919. In several reports—as well as in a 1921 memorandum by an independent bank examiner—it became clear that the crisis of the Philippine National Bank was due not only to graft and corruption in the bank itself, but also to serious shortcomings in the monetary policy of the Philippine government. The next section shows how the Philippine monetary policy of the time related to the uncontrolled loans extended to the export sectors of the Philippine economy.

## REVEALING THE TRUTH OF THE CURRENCY AND EXCHANGE CRISIS

It was George F. Luthringer who, in his 1934 study *The Gold-Exchange Standard in the Philippines*, provided the first well-researched discussion of the exhaustion of the Philippine currency reserves after World War I.[20] Luthringer tells us that it was the Bureau of the Treasury in the Philippine Department of Finance and Justice that took responsibility for the control of currency reserves. The Philippine National Bank had no legal competence as the central bank, despite its status as a depository of government funds in its quasi-governmental role. In this situation—given that the currency reserves deposited in the New York agency of the Philippine National Bank were illegally transferred to its Manila office and were utilized for massive loans to export sectors—what role did the Bureau of the Treasury actually play in the course of these transactions?

In order to answer this question, Luthringer stated "that the currency reserves deposited with the Philippine National Bank were dissipated in such a manner is indicative of inefficiency and crass ignorance of the principles of the currency system on the part of both the officials of the Bank and the responsible officials of the Insular Government."[21] He provides evidence that, in September 1918 the Insular Treasurer and the Philippine National Bank formally agreed that the Bank was to handle all the exchange for the Bureau of the Treasury, although the Bureau was legally responsible for the sale of exchange. He concludes that "if such an agreement was made, the Insular Government should have seen that the Bank conducted its operations in connection with the currency system in strict observance of the currency laws."[22]

Though not as clearly expressed as Luthringer's arguments, similar observations were available in 1919 and 1921. Francis Coates, Jr., who was sent to Manila by the BIA in late 1919,[23] wrote in one of his three unpublished reports:

> The fact the bank was allowed to continue under inefficient management, and to drift to the edge of insolvency before the condition became known to the Government Officials is due to the inefficiency of the Examiners in the Treasury Bureau and the Bureau of Audits, by whom it was examined and reported upon. . . .

The Executive Bureau indicates its inefficiency in the appointment of incompetent men in positions of importance—the President of the Bank, the Insular Treasurer, the Insular Auditor, the Attorney General, all of whom are so closely identified with the administration and safeguarding of the funds of the Government.[24]

Later, Ben F. Wright, a special bank examiner for the Philippine National Bank, stated outright in his memorandum of 1921 that the banking inexperience and fiscal ignorance of the Insular Treasurer had brought on the exhaustion of the currency reserves:

> The Insular Treasurer[25] at this time held some very peculiar views on the question of the relation of the sale of exchange to the settlement of the balance of trade, and the turning over of the government sale of exchange to the Philippine National Bank fitted in with these views. Had the Treasurer, at the same time, insisted that bank retire from circulation the money received from the sale of exchange little harm would have been done save in the loss of the premium to the government, which by law accrued to the currency reserve fund. However, the Treasurer apparently did not understand the fundamental principles of the currency system, and the result was that the proceeds of the sale of exchange, which should have been withdrawn from circulation either by the bank or the Treasurer, were instead invested by the bank in loans. The net result of this procedure was, on the one hand, that the government was deprived of the larger part of its gold reserve in New York with no means of replacing it, and, on the other hand, the circulation was not reduced as required by law. In fact the circulation was made more redundant with no possibility of a material reduction because of the depleted gold reserve in New York.[26]

Such comments by Luthringer, Coates, and Wright show that the currency and exchange crisis was caused not only by graft and corruption among the Philippine National Bank staff but also by serious loopholes in the monetary system of the Philippine government. Wright even singles out Insular Treasurer Fitzsimmons as the government official most responsible for the exhaustion of the currency reserves.

However, the BIA was aware as early as May 1919 that the lack of knowledge of the insular treasurer was a major cause of the currency crisis. Among a number of telegrams exchanged between the governor-general's office in Manila and the BIA in Washington that are presently housed at the U.S. National Archives, the author found the following telegram sent by Acting

BIA Chief Charles C. Walcutt, Jr. to Vice Governor-General Charles E. Yeater on 24 May 1919:

> Confidential. Does the Treasurer of the Philippine Islands understand the law governing the Currency Reserve Fund and does he appreciate his responsibilities for illegal circulation of Philippine National Bank notes? Failure to reply to inquiries from the Bureau is very disquieting. You should direct auditor to examine forthwith condition of Philippine treasury and report promptly location and condition of certificate reserve fund. The Bureau understands vaguely from cablegram that practically the entire currency reserve fund is now illegally held by Philippine National Bank and that the President of the Bank in effect refuses to return any part of this to the Treasury. Is this fact?[27]

This telegram indicates that, with information scarce on the causes of the massive losses in currency reserves, the BIA was very much concerned that the responsibility of handling the reserves had been transferred from the Insular Treasurer to the Philippine National Bank. Two days after Walcutt's telegram, Acting Governor-General Yeater sent the following reply:

> Treasurer Fitzsimmons will shortly be transferred to the office of Director of the Mint, and he will also be examined for clearance by government committee of three. In my judgment, his official conduct has been correct, and our troubles come from other sources. It is a fact that the National Bank sold exchange against the currency reserve funds deposited in the New York Branch, which automatically transferred such to the Bank here, which has loaned such funds to its customers.
>
> It is not a fact that the National Bank has refused to return any part of this to the Treasury. On the contrary, the Bank is turning over securities apparently as fast as possible.[28]

Here, Acting Governor-General Yeater insisted that the Insular Treasurer was not responsible for the exhaustion in currency reserves. Instead, he stated his opinion that the depletion occurred for other reasons, something relating to the operation of the Philippine National Bank. In this connection we should note that the Wood-Forbes Mission, over two years later, reiterated the view that the Philippine National Bank should take responsibility for the massive losses in currency reserves. Meanwhile, Coates's report of 1919 and Wright's memorandum of 1921, which emphasized loopholes in the Philippine government's monetary system as well as the incompetence of government officials as major causes of the crisis, apparently fell on deaf ears. Why were the findings of these special investigations almost totally ignored in the Wood-Forbes Mission report in October 1921?

It may be assumed that the reason the BIA took the initiative to investigate the causes of the exhaustion of Philippine currency reserves was that it was part of the BIA's duty to monitor the monetary policy of the Philippine government and set it on an improving course wherever possible. As a result of its investigations, the BIA observed that a major cause of the currency crisis, including the mismanagement of the Philippine National Bank, stemmed from the slipshod monetary policy of the Philippine Treasury, of which an American had taken charge. In political terms, however, disclosure of the incompetence of an American official would have cleared the ground for the Philippine legislature to attack him, and this would have shaken the legitimacy of American colonial rule.[29] Fortunately for the BIA, the political situation in the Philippines at the time made it easy to avoid such a risk. Because the financial crisis happened under the rapid Filipinization of the political and administrative system, the way was clear to shift almost all responsibility on to Filipino banking officials and staff and Filipino politicians.

The "official narrative" of the post-World War I Philippine financial crisis thus emerged in 1921. In the public statement, as shown in the Wood-Forbes Mission Report, the financial crisis was described as "the corruption scandal of the Philippine National Bank," unrelated to any deficiency in the government's monetary system. The view expressed in the Wood-Forbes Mission Report was widely dispersed and accepted, and in time became the standard "history" of the crisis. Responsibility for the financial crisis was fully shouldered by Filipino banking officials and politicians. The country's American administrators and banking officials had found a way to evade any such responsibility.

## BIA'S INVOLVEMENT IN THE 1918 REVISION OF THE PHILIPPINE CURRENCY LAW

In order to fully explore the BIA's concern with the Philippine financial crisis of 1919–1922, it is important to note that the BIA had been urging the revision of the Philippine currency law from at least as early as 1912. This was inevitable because, as Romero V. Cruz correctly argues, the BIA, formally instituted as a division of the U.S. Department of War in July 1902, was "virtually a colonial office, minus all but a modicum of statutory power;

and perhaps on that account, actually quite powerful."[30] "In the chain of the American imperial system, the BIA was the organizational link between Washington and Manila."[31] The first BIA chief was Clarence R. Edwards, who served until August 1912. Edwards was followed by Frank McIntyre, who had served as assistant chief since 1905. McIntyre—the most capable of the chiefs who served the bureau—was promoted to the rank of major-general in the U.S. Army in 1917, the only BIA chief to attain such distinction. Between July 1918 and December 1919, while McIntyre served in World War I as an assistant chief of staff, Charles C. Walcutt, Jr. served as acting BIA chief. McIntyre resumed his duties as BIA chief in December 1919, serving until his retirement in January 1929. He was knowledgeable about the Philippines, including matters of administration, law, currency, and finance, and exercised significant influence on U.S. policy in the Philippines.[32]

To the author's knowledge, the earliest BIA document which addressed the necessity to revise the Philippine currency law was a memorandum written by BIA Chief Clarence R. Edwards in 1912. In this memorandum Edwards stated that under the Philippine currency system there were two currency reserve funds, the Gold Standard Fund and the Silver Certificate Reserve. The Gold Standard Fund was established by Act No. 938 of the Philippine Commission in 1903 (known as the Gold Standard Act), and the Silver Certificate Reserve was set up by the Philippine Coinage Act of 1903 passed by the U.S. Congress. Act No. 938 was amended by the Philippine legislature in 1911 to fix the Gold Standard Fund at 35 percent of the face value of the government money in circulation. One half of this fund was to be maintained in cash and one half was to be available for investment loans to the municipalities and provinces of the Philippine Islands for public works. The U.S. Philippine Coinage Act provided for the issue of silver certificates and for a reserve to be maintained in the Philippine Treasury to secure such certificates. By a 1906 amendment to the Coinage Act, 60 percent of such silver might be replaced by U.S. gold of the same value.[33]

Thus, Edwards continued in his 1912 memorandum, under the current provisions the Gold Standard Fund could lend for investment in public utilities, but the Silver Certificate Reserve could not be used for that purpose. The Gold Standard Fund for the fiscal year 1911, he wrote, averaged approximately 10 million dollars, and the net income from the use of this fund for the year was 458,386 dollars. The Silver Certificate Reserve amounted to about 15 million dollars, but did not produce any revenue for the government; rather, it incurred expenses for coinage, storage, and shipment. Edwards proposed a plan to increase the Gold Standard Fund by authorizing two-thirds of the inactive Silver Certificate Reserve held in coined silver in the Philippine Treasury to be replaced by an equal amount in face value of gold or securities readily interchangeable for gold. In this plan, Edwards saw two advantages. First, it should provide for a distribution of the reserve between the United States and the Philippines. This was found to be very desirable and urgently recommended by Philippine officials including the acting insular treasurer, the governor-general, and the secretary of finance and justice. Second, it would enable the Philippine government to make profitable use of a part of the Silver Certificate Reserve while simultaneously increasing its value.[34]

As is clear from the above, during the early 1910s the BIA was endeavoring to increase the revenue of the Philippine government through an efficient management of both currency reserves. This thrust to amend the Philippine currency law for the purpose of utilizing currency reserves in search of financial resources continued after Edwards's resignation in 1912. In October 1914, the BIA commissioned Charles A. Conant to draft a bill amending the Philippine currency law. His draft bill, submitted to the BIA in October 1914 and entitled "An Act to Establish a Currency Reserve Fund for the Maintenance of the Parity of the Philippine Currency," proposed the abolition of the Gold Standard Fund, making the Silver Certificate Fund the sole currency reserve in order to maintain the parity of Philippine currency against the U.S. dollar.[35]

In a separate memorandum, Conant explained in detail the rationale of this revision. He strongly addressed the necessity to readjust "the reserve funds in the custody of the Philippine government, which have accumulated to an unnecessary amount under the operation of the currency system established in 1903,"[36] as long as this readjustment would not go beyond the authority of the original U.S. Philippine Coinage Act of 1903 and its amendments. He argued:

> The measure taken by the Philippine government in 1903 to insure a uniform and safe currency in the Philippine Islands were [sic] based upon a policy of abundant caution and larger reserves. . . . The currency of the Islands had been for many years in a chaotic condition, which was intensified by the violent price of silver bullion which had occurred during several years before the American occupation of the Islands. These fluctuations, reacting upon the foreign exchanges,

had seriously hampered the commerce of the Islands with gold standard countries, which had come to include not merely the chief European countries and the United States, but also British India and Japan, after the adoption of the exchange standard in the former country in 1893 and in the latter country in 1897.[37]

The gold exchange standard had been in operation on a restricted scale in the Dutch East Indies for a long time, and after 1898 it became an admitted success in British India. In the Philippines it was introduced in 1903, and the strong and consistent policy of the government in meeting demands for exchange at par assured the stability of this new currency system.[38]

Based on his understanding of the stability of the gold exchange standard in the Philippines, Conant gave the following three reasons for proposing revision of the currency law. First, it was no longer necessary for the Philippine Treasury to withhold the full amount of its currency reserves as a means of maintaining the parity of silver and paper circulation with gold. Second, extension of the use of paper certificates had diminished practical necessity for a larger use of silver pesos. Third, aside from the experience in the Philippines, the gold exchange standard had been widely supported in British India, Mexico, Panama, and the Straits Settlements. In this situation, it had become possible for the Philippines to modify the strict measures to defend the gold standard that had been introduced at the initial stage of its currency valuation and to appropriate some amounts for the development of the Philippine Islands and the benefit of the Filipino people.[39]

Conant's specific recommendations were as follows. First, the full amount of the present Gold Standard Fund should be transferred to the Philippine Treasury for general fiscal purposes. Second, the title of the Silver Certificate Reserve (Conant preferred the term "Certificate Redemption Fund") should be changed to the Currency Reserve Fund and its function should be recharacterized as the maintenance of parity of the silver and paper currency performed by the Gold Standard Fund. Third, a sufficient amount of gold should be transferred to the new Currency Reserve Fund to afford an adequate reserve against the entire amount of certificates and coin in circulation. Fourth, provision should be made for future increases in the currency supply by issuing paper money based upon gold.[40]

Needless to say, Conant's proposal fully reflected the BIA's intention. This assertion can be verified by an examination of various communications that passed among the BIA chief, the U.S. secretary of war, and the Philippine governor-general. For example, in April 1914 BIA Chief Frank McIntyre exchanged information with Conant regarding the currency reserves in the Philippines.[41] In May 1915, in a letter to Governor-General Harrison, McIntyre mentioned that for several years the BIA had been urging the U.S. Congress to modify relevant laws to make the efficient usage of the Silver Certificate Reserve possible.[42] In July 1915, Conant himself sent a letter directly to Governor-General Harrison suggesting that, as the Philippine Coinage Act of 1903 had been enacted by the U.S. Congress, in order to revise the currency reserve regulations it included it was necessary to propose and pass a bill in Washington. In the same letter, Conant further revealed that McIntyre had informally requested Secretary of War Lindley M. Garrison for an opinion on this matter, and that Garrison had replied that at this point proposing a revision of a law relating to currency reserves was not an appropriate initiative for the Department of War to undertake.[43]

In a letter addressed to Governor-General Harrison in July 1914, Garrison expressed his opinion on this matter more directly:

> Mr. Conant has been in consultation with the officers of the Bureau of Insular Affairs at intervals with the reference to the Philippine currency system. Mr. Conant's interest in theoretical finance is rather general and the correspondence indicates that his attention had not been called to the difference in the legal status of the gold standard fund created by the Philippine government and subject to legislation by that government and the reserve behind the silver certificates which was provided by Congress and with reference to which the Philippine government may not legislate.[44]

Secretary Garrison went on with some legislative history. When the 1906 amendment to the Philippine Coinage Act of 1903 was secured, he wrote, the Philippine government was directed to obtain authority to place a part of the Silver Certificate Reserve in the U.S. depositories of the Philippine government in order to profit by its possession. However, this had proven to be in vain, and successive efforts had also failed. Subsequently, the Philippine government amended the Gold Standard Act of 1903 to enable it to lend a part of the Gold Standard Fund to provinces, municipalities, and the Manila Railroad Company.

In this way, Garrison added support to Conant's idea of combining the two currency funds and granting the Philippine government the authority to use the combined fund for increasing its revenues. He found it timely to move on this issue because the matter had already received careful attention in the BIA for several years, and because there was a provision in a bill pending before the U.S. Congress (the Jones bill) that the Philippine government would be authorized to legislate on this matter if it was approved by the U.S. president.[45]

Garrison's letter to Harrison shows that, as early as the middle of 1914, the BIA had already begun a campaign to amend the Philippine currency law to combine the two currency reserves, on the premise that the Jones bill would be passed soon and would provide more autonomy to the Philippines. This could also be inferred from a telegram of BIA Chief McIntyre to Harrison in October 1914. In this telegram, McIntyre informed Harrison about Conant's report on the reform of currency reserves and also mentioned that it would be advisable to defer currency legislation given the likelihood that the Jones bill would pass in February of the following year.[46] McIntyre suggested to Harrison that the Philippine legislature should then pass an act embodying the following provisions: (1) authorizing the governor-general to designate such depositories in the United States as he deems advisable to be branches of the Philippine Treasury; and (2) authorizing the governor-general to transfer from the Gold Standard Fund to the General Funds of the Philippine Treasury such amount, not to exceed 5 million pesos, as may be necessary to meet fiscal requirements, such transfers to be regarded as a loan from the Gold Standard Fund.[47]

In August 1914, the judge advocate general of the U.S. Department of War had disclosed his view that the depositories of the Philippine government in the United States should be deemed branches of the Philippine Treasury, and this view was supported by the secretary of war.[48] Thus, when the Jones bill was passed by the U.S. Congress in February 1916, the Philippine legislature enacted Act No. 2603, providing that the governor-general might in his discretion designate such depositories of the Philippine government in the United States as he might deem advisable to be branches of the Philippine Treasury.[49] By the end of 1916 nearly 80 percent of the Gold Standard Fund was invested and over 50 percent of the Silver Certificate Reserve was held in the form of bank deposits in the United States.[50] This indicates that by the mid-1910s the Gold Standard Fund alone could not have maintained the parity of the Philippine silver peso with the theoretical gold peso, and the Silver Certificate Reserve began to be used to supplement the former, as has been discussed in chapter 1. In this context, the combination of the two currency reserves was the order of the day.

However, after Conant died in July 1915, it took some years for the BIA to finalize Conant's draft of 1914. In December 1916, the Philippine insular auditor drafted a bill based on Conant's proposal, but BIA Chief McIntyre found it improper and asked Bernard Herstein, a member of the Board of Public Utility Commissioners in the Philippines,[51] to draft a new bill. In April 1917, Herstein's bill was submitted by McIntyre to Governor-General Harrison, and in October Insular Treasurer Fitzsimmons made some revisions.[52]

In November 1917, Sergio Osmeña, the Speaker of the Philippine House of Representatives, sent a telegram to Jaime C. de Veyra, Philippine Resident Commissioner in Washington, asking him to seek advice from renowned economist Edwin W. Kemmerer, who taught at Princeton University at that time. Osmeña's and de Veyra's crucial concerns were, first, the recoinage of the old Philippine pesos and second, whether the parity and suitability of the currency system could be insured if a currency redemption fund was created to take the place of the present Gold Standard fund and Silver Certificate Reserve.[53]

De Veyra sought Kemmerer's opinion, and immediately relayed the economist's reply to Osmeña as follows:

> [H]e is somewhat reluctant to render an opinion regarding monetary question in the Philippines as he has not kept himself in touch with the financial developments since 1913. However, his experience in the Philippines brought him to the conclusion that monetary problems of this type are nothing like as simple as they appear at first glance; that the recoinage plan proposed seems at first glance to be a doubtful one, and that the proposal for combining the Gold Standard Fund and the Silver Certificate Reserve seems to envolve [sic] a complete change of fundamental policy that is of very doubtful advisability. Neither plan should be adopted without very careful study.[54]

Kemmerer, a prominent financial expert known for his strong support of the gold exchange standard in a strict sense, thus showed his suspicion of the Conant-Herstein proposal from the beginning.

In January 1918, after some consideration, Kemmerer submitted to Osmeña through de Veyra his plan for the Philippine currency reform in a sixty-nine-page report entitled "Memorandum Concerning Certain Proposals for Currency Legislation in the Philippine Islands Submitted to the Speaker of the Philippine Assembly by E. W. Kemmerer." It first explained briefly the necessity to maintain two currency reserves under the fundamental principles of the gold exchange standard. Then it described the transformation and deviation process of the Gold Standard Fund and the Silver Certificate Reserve from their original purposes and functions between 1903 and the mid-1910s. Then, concluding that neither the combination of the two currency reserves nor the recoinage of Philippine pesos was advisable, Kemmerer proposed the reorganization of the Gold Standard Fund and the changing of silver certificates into currency notes.[55]

Why did Kemmerer consider the combination of the two currency reserves inadvisable? The principal reason, he stated, was that the Gold Standard Fund and the Silver Certificate Reserve had fundamentally distinct functions. While the former was a currency reserve intended to maintain the parity of pesos by regulating foreign exchange, the latter was structured for the redemption of silver certificates.[56] How then should the Philippine government meet the situation by which the recent deposits of the Silver Certificate Reserve in U.S. banks had changed the character of the silver certificate from "coin certificate" to a kind of currency note? Kemmerer suggested the following three possible plans: (1) substitute for the present silver certificates bank notes of the Philippine National Bank; (2) return to the certificate form of silver certificates that had been departed from; or (3) accept as permanent a form of government currency notes. Among the three, the safest plan in Kemmerer's opinion was the introduction of government currency notes. For this purpose, the notes should be supported by currency reserve equivalent to at least 100 percent of their face value. This currency note fund should consist of a coin part and an invested part. The coin part of the fund should not be below 40 percent of the total, which was the legal minimum gold reserve required for Federal Reserve notes in the United States.[57]

As for the Gold Standard Fund, Kemmerer continued, if it were to be an entirely liquid fund consisting only of Philippine currency in the Philippines and U.S. currency deposits in the United States, the gold standard fund at 25 percent of the amount of currency in circulation would be adequate. Kemmerer further opposed a plan to reduce silver content in the coinage, and proposed instead to recoin a substantial number of pesos into half-peso pieces and also issue new peso currency notes. At the end of his report, he also advised that U.S. government funds provided to the Philippines for army and navy purposes should be transferred directly through the banks and not through the Gold Standard Fund.[58]

Even before Kemmerer submitted his proposal, the BIA had contested Kemmerer's involvement in the campaign to reform the Philippine currency system. Rather, the BIA affirmed the standpoint of the Conant-Herstein bill. Referring to the telegram sent by de Veyra to Osmeña in November 1917, the BIA immediately informed Governor-General Harrison that a Philippine currency reform plan had been carefully studied by Conant and Herstein under the auspices of the BIA, and that Kemmerer could add nothing new to the information available. The Gold Standard Fund and the Silver Certificate Reserve had been created by the Philippine Commission and the U.S. Congress respectively, and they would have been combined long ago if the Philippine Commission or legislature had had the authority to do so. The legislation combining them was not radical as long as the new fund was safeguarded.[59] Thus, Kemmerer's proposal was rejected by BIA Chief McIntyre.[60] As has been discussed in chapter 1, the Philippine Currency Act was revised in May 1918 (Act No. 2776), the major revisions being the combination of the two currency reserves into the Currency Reserve Fund and the creation of Treasury certificates in place of silver certificates, following the Conant-Herstein plan.

A memorandum exists (May 1918) that briefly explains the contents of the revision of the Philippine currency act by directly contrasting the opinions of Kemmerer and McIntyre. It shows that the revision of the act to provide for one reserve fund to be designated the Currency Reserve Fund followed McIntyre's recommendation instead of Kemmerer's recommendation that the separate reserve funds be retained. The new law, also following McIntyre's preference, provided for the issue of a Treasury certificate whose lowest denomination was one peso. Kemmerer had advised that a larger quantity of the pesos should be recoined into half-pesos, but there should not be a general recoinage unless silver advanced to a much higher level, whereas McIntyre opposed the fixing of a new weight and fineness for the silver coinage and rather recommended recoinage when necessary. The revised act further followed McIntyre's recommendations by giving the governor-general, with the concurrence of the presiding officers of both houses of the Philippine legislature, the authority to order a reduction in the weight and fineness of Philippine pesos. The other main difference in the views of Kemmerer and McIntyre was that the former recommended that transfers of funds between the U.S. and Philippine governments for army and navy purposes should be effected directly through banks instead of through the Gold Standard Fund or similar reserve fund of the Philippine government, whereas the latter considered that this profitable business should not be handed over to private banks. According to the memorandum, this question was not taken up in the revised act, but some administrative action was taken by Philippine officials so that transfers of funds were made through the Philippine National Bank and its New York agency.[61]

Thus, after years of machinations, the BIA's plan was adopted in the revision of the Philippine Currency Act in 1918. The two currency reserves were combined in order to compensate for the depletion of the Gold Standard Fund. This kept sufficient funds available to maintain the profitability of the Philippine colony. However, as it ignored and deviated from the fundamental principle of the gold exchange standard system, this policy eventually brought confusion to currency and exchange in the Philippines, and evolved into the grave financial crisis of 1919–1922. This outcome showed that, absent the maintenance of two currency reserves to ensure the parity of pesos and the redemption of silver certificates, the gold exchange standard system could easily subvert its fundamental basis. Thus, the consolidation of the Gold Standard Fund and the Silver Certificate Reserve into the Currency Reserve Fund in 1918 was a *causa remota* of the financial crisis of 1919–1922. Its history reveals how the BIA dealt with the theoretical interpretation of the gold exchange standard system. This is the long-neglected historical background of the post-World War I Philippine financial crisis.

## PHILIPPINE POLITICS AT THE CROSSROADS UNDER THE FINANCIAL CRISIS

It would be useful to conclude this chapter by showing how the viewpoint of the Wood-Forbes Mission in 1921 on the Philippine financial crisis revealed the nature of U.S. colonial policy and how the characterization of the financial crisis as the "corruption scandal of the Philippine National Bank in 1919–1922" subsequently functioned in Philippine politics. An unpublished 1963 dissertation by Frederick G. Hoyt provides valuable insight on this matter.[62] Hoyt shows how, from the very beginning of their mission, Wood and Forbes, while noting the critical fiscal condition of the Philippine government, paid their keenest attention to the insolvency of the Philippine National Bank. Returning from their first provincial inspection visit, they jointly sent the following telegram to Secretary of War John W. Weeks on 10 June 1921:

After examination and conference with [Acting] Governor-General, auditor, and manager National Bank, we find that the bank is practically insolvent. The government cannot purchase exchange, even to meet current running expenses payable in United States, and has had to ask other local banks not to present its circulating notes for redemption. Cash reserves are now about ten percent of legal requirements. If bank should fail, it would mean practical bankruptcy of insular government . . . besides bankrupting many provinces and municipalities which have been required by law to deposit all funds with the bank. We feel the faith of United States is pledged in support of solvency of this government, and situation is so critical that we concur in urging immediate relief measures on general lines recommended by Governor-General in extending debt-making power of government. Unnecessary publicity might precipitate crisis here.[63]

Secretary Weeks released this cable to the press on 17 June 1921, except for the first and last sentences, ignoring the advice on avoiding unnecessary publicity. His purpose in doing so was presumably to urge the U.S. Congress to take immediate emergency measures for the fiscal relief of the Philippine government. The news was widely publicized in newspapers in the United States. In the Philippines, Venancio Concepcion, former president of the Philippine National Bank, was arrested for violation of the National Bank Law on 24 June. The arrest of Concepcion immediately after the public disclosure of the critical financial condition may be understood as a purposeful response by the Philippine government with the object of obtaining emergency relief from the United States.[64] On 21 July, the U.S. Congress passed a bill authorizing an increase in the limit of legal indebtedness of the Philippine government from 15 million dollars to 30 million dollars, to save the Philippine government from bankruptcy.[65]

Concepcion's arrest plunged Philippine politics into the issue of how Filipinos should cope with the chaotic situation which had been brought about under the Harrison administration. The arrest of the former president of the Philippine National Bank provided the Democratic Party (Democratas) with a pretext for attacking the two leaders of the majority party of Nacionalistas, Manuel L. Quezon and Sergio Osmeña. The Democratas urged in their newspaper *La Nacion* that former Governor-General Harrison should be arrested and be returned to Manila to stand trial with Quezon and Osmeña for illegal bank management.[66] Harrison, along with Quezon and Osmeña as senate president and speaker of the House of Representatives respectively, had composed the Board of Control that had kept the power of influence in the management of the Philippine National Bank and other governmental corporations since 1918.[67]

As criticism of Quezon and Osmeña intensified, the former responded quickly to protect his political career. Quezon admitted freely to Wood that the Philippine fiscal conditions were "a great blow to the hopes of the people," but that the responsibility "must be shared between themselves and Governor Harrison, who neglected to use his prerogative as Governor."[68] In early July 1921, shortly after the arrest of Concepcion, Quezon had a long private interview with Frank R. McCoy, Chief of Staff of the U.S. Department of War, who had come to the Philippines as one of the attached members of the Wood-Forbes Mission. Quezon told McCoy that there were honest and capable Filipinos in the cabinet and the judiciary; finance was the exception. He also agreed that the Philippine government had to retain American financial experts until Filipinos could become more experienced. However, he refused to assign much blame to himself, saying "our terrible position [is] now largely due to Osmeña, thinking that Concepcion could run the bank and he [Concepcion] made an awful mess of it."[69] Concepcion was from the Visayas region, as Osmeña was, and for this reason Osmeña had strongly recommended Concepcion as the third president of the Philippine National Bank.[70] In the extremely critical situation spawned by the arrest of Concepcion, Quezon initiated his tactic to emphasize the responsibility of Osmeña for the chaotic condition of the Philippine National Bank.

With this keen intuition, Quezon wildly and drastically changed the direction of Philippine politics. This appeared in the abrupt dissolution of the friendly relations between Quezon and Osmeña. Their long-lasting relations further deteriorated after Leonard Wood became governor-general in October 1921, and culminated at the national convention of the Nacionalista Party in December the same year. At this convention, all the leaders were called upon to help in drafting a broad platform that would include an adequate answer to the Wood-Forbes Mission Report.[71] Although Quezon and Osmeña cooperated closely on this issue, when the question of leadership came up the differences in opinion between them became apparent. While Quezon with his Senate members declared the principle of collective leadership, Osmeña with his House members insisted on his unipersonal leadership in the party as before. From then on, Quezon with the Colectivistas and Osmeña with the Unipersonalistas antagonized each other.[72]

In February 1922, Quezon's newly created Nacionalista Colectivista Party denounced Osmeña for having conducted an "inefficient, corrupt autocratic administration indifferent to the welfare of the people." In the election of 1922, Quezon's new party won, campaigning on the issue of collective leadership. As a result, Quezon was re-elected Senate president, and in the lower house Claro M. Recto from the Democratic Party was elected speaker. Osmeña was relegated to Senate president pro tempore. Thus, Quezon became the top Filipino leader, with Osmeña playing second fiddle. When the two wings of the Nacionalista Party merged into a new party called the Nacionalista Consolidado Party in 1924, Quezon was elected president, with Osmeña as vice-president.[73]

The split and reunification of the Nacionalista Party in 1922–1924 can be understood as the political consequence of the financial crisis of 1919–1922. Quezon, as an influential member of the Board of Control, was as responsible for the insolvency as Harrison and Osmeña. However, taking advantage of the fact that it was Osmeña who had taken leadership in Philippine politics during the Harrison administration, Quezon intentionally aimed his attack at Osmeña, denouncing his "unipersonal" leadership. In this way, the post-World War I Philippine financial crisis was a fundamental catalyst in changing the course of Philippine politics.

Thus in the early 1920s the leadership in Philippine politics shifted from Sergio Osmeña to Manuel L. Quezon in the context of the mystification of the Philippine financial crisis. Quezon, without pointing out the shortcomings of the monetary system or the incompetence of American administrators, told the "official" story of the financial crisis as "the corruption scandal of the Philippine National Bank," using the occasion as a political maneuver by which Osmeña was held responsible for the chaotic financial situation. Quezon remained the top Philippine politician throughout the American colonial period. Thus, the struggle between Quezon and Osmeña over Philippine leadership under the financial crisis could be understood as a political scenario manipulated by American colonial discourse. In other words, it was within the framework of the colonial discourse of "the corruption scandal of the Philippine National Bank in 1919–1922" that colonial democracy strengthened its foundation in Philippine politics after World War I.[74]

CHAPTER 6

# THE PHILIPPINE NATIONAL BANK AND CREDIT INFLATION

THIS CHAPTER DISCUSSES the mismanagement of the Philippine National Bank during the financial crisis, with special reference to its extravagant commercial and industrial loans. It also reviews the contemporary debates on the remedies for the Bank's slipshod business practices. The crisis of the Philippine National Bank and the drain of the currency reserve were two sides of the same coin of the Philippine financial crisis in 1919–1922. During World War I, a large part of the currency reserve of the Philippine government was deposited at the New York agency of the National Bank, but was soon transferred to Manila in order to provide massive loans for Philippine businesses. The bank extended these loans to companies, landowners, and entrepreneurs engaged in the export business of primary commodities that had swollen enormously during and since the war years.

First, this chapter examines the financial condition of the Philippine National Bank from about 1913 through the early 1920s against the background of the expansion of loan business and the export boom. Second, the Bank's role in the development of three major export sectors—Manila hemp (*abaca*) trading, coconut processing, and sugar processing—is brought to light. Third, the chapter details the blatant illegitimacy of the Bank's lending, given the virtual across-the-board direct involvement of the Bank's board members in the ownership and management of the companies active in these businesses.

## THE FINANCIAL CONDITION OF THE PHILIPPINE NATIONAL BANK

As has been discussed in chapter 2, the "free trade" relationship between the Philippines and the United States was established by two acts of the U.S. Congress, the Payne-Aldrich Tariff Act of 1909 and the Underwood-Simmons Tariff Act of 1913. This trade relationship tied the Philippine economy to the U.S. trade sphere, based on the export of Manila hemp, sugar, and coconut products (copra and coconut oil) to the United States as well as the import of industrial products from the latter. After the outbreak of World War I, Philippine foreign trade expanded rapidly. During the war years, the Philippines' export revenue increased tremendously, due not only to the increase in volume but also to skyrocketing prices.

Table 17 shows the average volume and revenue of exports of Manila hemp, sugar, and coconut oil during the 1911-1918 eight-year period. During 1915–1918, the average revenue from the export of Manila hemp and sugar was double that of the prior four-year average. In a phenomenal growth, the average revenue from coconut oil exports during 1915–1918 jumped to eleven times, and the volume ballooned to thirteen times, what they had been during the prior four years, due to rapid development in the coconut process industry at this period to meet a growing demand in the United States. This huge expansion in the export of primary commodities inevitably augmented domestic commercial activities. The value of merchandise sold in the Philippines increased from approximately 488 million pesos in 1915 to 1,327 million pesos in 1918. In 1915 alone, 114 new domestic corporations were registered in the Philippines, with a total authorized capital of nearly 13 million pesos. In 1918, 299 corporations were registered, nominally capitalized with over 72 million pesos. The resources of commercial banks, 63.7 million pesos in 1913, had increased to nearly 400 million pesos by the end of 1918.[1]

What role did the Philippine National Bank play during the export boom of primary commodities after the outbreak of World War I? Table 18 shows the annual change in the financial statements of the Philippine National Bank during the 1916-1925 ten-year period. Assets increased from approximately 50 million pesos in 1916 to 223 million pesos in 1919 and then to a high of 288 million pesos in 1920. However, after the reform of the National Bank in 1921, a drastic decline in bank assets set in, reaching a low of 129 million pesos in 1925. Throughout the period loans and discounts maintained the largest share of assets, from 26 percent in 1916 swelling to 56 percent in 1918

Table 17. Export of Manila Hemp, Sugar, and Coconut Oil, 1911–1918

|  | 1911–14 (average) | | 1915–18 (average) | |
| --- | --- | --- | --- | --- |
|  | Volume (tons) | Revenue (1000 pesos) | Volume (tons) | Revenue (1000 pesos) |
| Manila Hemp | 139,887 | 38,438 | 154,508 | 76,515 |
| Sugar | 199,988 | 19,484 | 256,917 | 28,990 |
| Coconut Oil | 4,239 | 1,883 | 47,509 | 24,910 |

Sources: Peter W. Stanley, *A Nation in the Making: The Philippines and the United States, 1899-1921*, Cambridge, MA: Harvard University Press, 1974, p. 238; Philippines (Commonwealth), Bureau of Customs, *Annual Report of the Insular Collector of Customs for the Fiscal Period Ending June 30, 1940*, Manila: Bureau of Printing, 1941, pp. 101–105.

Table 18. Financial Statements of the Philippine National Bank, 1916–1925

(1000 pesos)

| Year (as of 31 Dec.) | Assets (or Liabilities (%) | Assets | | Liabilities | | |
| --- | --- | --- | --- | --- | --- | --- |
|  |  | Loans and Discounts[1] (%) | Paid-up Capital (%) | Deposits (%) | | Bank Note Circulation (%) |
| 1916 | 50,786.5 (100.0) | 13,012.6 (25.6) | 4,364.4 (8.6) | 42,341.1 (83.4) | | 520.0 (1.0) |
| 1917 | 138,276.1 (100.0) | 40,766.9 (29.5) | 7,395.3 (5.3) | 102,037.3 (73.8) | | 4,560.0 (3.3) |
| 1918 | 248,798.1 (100.0) | 139,193.4 (55.9) | 9,210.3 (3.7) | 186,182.3 (74.8) | | 4,407.4 (1.8) |
| 1919 | 223,141.7 (100.0) | 130,344.8 (58.4) | 10,977.4 (4.9) | 134,726.4 (60.4) | | 14,082.5 (6.3) |
| 1920 | 288,441.4 (100.0) | 151,506.8 (52.5) | 12,216.2 (4.2) | 134,728.9 (46.7) | | 24,370.9 (8.4) |
| 1921 | 185,631.1 (100.0) | 122,031.8 (65.7) | 35,300.0 (19.0) | 84,390.1 (45.5) | | 32,704.5 (17.6) |
| 1922 | 149,429.6 (100.0) | 130,671.9 (87.4) | 35,300.0 (23.6) | 76,670.8 (51.3) | | 31,885.7 (21.3) |
| 1923 | 146,905.8 (100.0) | 122,505.1 (83.4) | 35,300.0 (24.0) | 72,700.4 (49.5) | | 31,639.0 (21.5) |
| 1924 | 132,573.3 (100.0) | 80,156.9 (60.5) | 10,000.0 (7.5) | 46,386.9 (35.9) | | 31,773.9 (24.0) |
| 1925 | 129,340.5 (100.0) | 80,577.4 (62.3) | 10,000.0 (7.7) | 51,139.2 (39.5) | | 30,540.1 (23.6) |

Source: United States National Archives, Record Group 350, Records of the Bureau of Insular Affairs (hereafter cited as BIA), 6769-187A, 6769 with 187, 6769-190A.
Note: (1) For some years, overdrafts were included.

and to 58 percent in 1919. The amount of loans and discounts then declined under the bank reform of the early 1920s, but to a lesser degree than that of the assets overall; in fact, the percentage of assets represented by loans and discounts increased sharply, settling at around 60 percent by 1925. On the liability side, the larger percentage of deposits before 1920 is notable.

For example, in 1919 paid-up capital represented only 5 percent of liabilities as against 60 percent for deposits. After that, due to the increase in bank note circulation, the percentage of deposits decreased, but without losing a strong liability presence. It is also noteworthy that the amount of loans and discounts exceeded that of deposits in 1920, clearly revealing the National Bank's practice of allowing its lending to exceed its capacity.

It was during the term of the Bank's third president, Venancio Concepcion, who served from March 1918 to November 1920, that massive loans were extended to companies engaged in the production and export of primary commodities. The demand for loans came as a result of the collapse of primary commodity prices after the war. As the Bank approached the brink of insolvency, Concepcion was forced to resign in recognition of his responsibility for the Bank's mismanagement.[2] The near-bankruptcy of the National Bank had caught the attention of Newton D. Baker, the U.S. Secretary of War. In October 1919 Baker sent Francis Coates, Jr. to Manila to investigate the Philippine National Bank (as partially discussed in chapter 5). One of three reports that Coates submitted to the Bureau of Insular Affairs (BIA) in Washington was the "Report of an Examination of the Philippine National Bank Manila, P. I. as of at Close of Business Nov. 30, 1919" (hereafter cited as the Coates Report of 1920). This report presented the results of Coates's investigation from 30 November 1919 to 11 April 1920, exposing the reckless loan business of the Bank.[3] Later, the prestigious accounting firm of Haskins & Sells also examined the management of the Bank and submitted its report to the BIA in 1922 ("Haskins & Sells Report of Examination of P. N. B. as of May 19, 1921," hereafter cited as the Haskins & Sells Report of 1922).[4] Both reports revealed that massive loans were provided to subsidize Manila hemp trading, the coconut oil industry, and sugar processing. In the loan business of the Bank, Filipino firms largely benefited; however, in the Manila hemp trade and the coconut industry American firms also enjoyed privileges through their special connection with Filipino and American bank officials.

**EXTRAVAGANT LOAN BUSINESS**

**Manila hemp trading.** The Manila hemp industry was the most detrimentally affected by the end of World War I. As has been mentioned earlier, among major export commodities Manila hemp had the largest share, comprising 30–40 percent of the total exports of the Philippines during World War I (see Table 5 and Table 17). The crash of export prices of Manila hemp as well as the sharp decline in its export brought the Manila hemp trading firms to ruin. In spite of this rapid change in circumstances during 1918–1919, the Philippine National Bank continued to finance hemp trading firms with irrecoverable loans. The Coates Report of 1920 provided precise information on the Bank's loans to trading firms for Manila hemp like the Philippine Fiber and Produce Co., G. Martini Ltd., U. de Poli, Babcock & Templeton, and the Compañía Mercantil de Filipinas. Among them, the Philippine Fiber and Produce Co., G. Martini Ltd., and U. de Poli incurred huge indebtedness to the Bank as a result of irrecoverable loans provided to them.[5]

For example, between December 1917 and July 1918 the National Bank approved loans or credits of 1.65 million pesos to the Philippine Fiber and Produce Co., with *quedans* (warehouse receipts) and other assets as collateral. However, by March 1919 the credit actually provided to the firm had reached 4.6 million pesos, or 2.8 times the original plan. A certain Kaufman, president of the company during 1917, disclosed that the company had obtained a credit of one million pesos from the bank in July 1917, with *quedans* as collateral. Soon after that a certain Wicks, who had taken over the company's management during 1918, negotiated with an American vice-president of the Philippine National Bank, J. Elmer Delaney, who approved a credit of four million pesos for the company. As of 30 November 1919, 2.3 million pesos of the company's indebtedness remained unpaid—a figure much larger than the value of the collateral specified in the loan agreement.[6]

For U. de Poli, the National Bank approved credits of 300,000 pesos with *quedans* as collateral during 1918. This firm also received from the Bank demand drafts of 250,000 pesos, time loans of 150,000 pesos, an overdraft of 596,200 pesos, and other credits, adding up to 179,300 pesos—a total of 1,175,500 pesos in credit. The collaterals the firm offered for these credits were tobacco (16,449 quintals [one quintal = 46kg]), maguey fiber (2,095 bales), and Manila hemp (3,455 bales, 1,200 piculs [one picul = 63.25 kg], and 3,982 kilos).[7]

G. Martini Ltd. presents an even more egregious case. This firm first applied for credit of 200,000 pesos, but the Bank declined the loan. However, in March 1917 the company obtained the more modest credit service of 100,000 pesos from the Bank. Then, as the price of Manila hemp rose after the United States entered World War I in April 1917, the Bank approved a loan of 3.5 to 4 million pesos to Martini as an advance for purchasing Manila hemp from local producers, on the condition that it should be paid back within six months. Although Bank President Samuel Ferguson, recognizing the riskiness of such a large loan, recommended to the Bank's board of directors that the amount be reduced to a mere 390,000 pesos, the Bank approved six credit lines totaling 2.69 million pesos during the first half of 1918. From October to November of the same year, the firm separately applied for a further credit of 3 million pesos in order to expand its export business to the United States, but this was rejected. Nonetheless, at the end of November, the Bank's board approved yet another credit line for the firm, this time for 2 million pesos. The board accepted the opinion of Vice-President J. Elmer Delaney and President Concepcion that, by supporting the business expansion of G. Martini Ltd., skyrocketing prices could be contained.[8]

When World War I ended in mid-November 1918, and the export prices of Manila hemp collapsed, G. Martini Ltd., its business threatened, requested additional loans from the Bank in January 1919. This time the Bank refused. By that time, the firm owed the Bank 2.5 million pesos and nearly 700,000 pesos to five other banks. The firm also held unsold stock of Manila hemp valued at 1.32 million pesos. Seeing no chance of improvement, the Bank took over the properties of G. Martini Ltd. in July 1919. The credits that the Bank had extended to the firm as of November 1919 amounted to 8.5 million pesos, including overdrafts of 2 million pesos and unmatured foreign bills of 4 million pesos.[9] The Coates Report of 1920 also disclosed a further complication: that the National Bank itself became directly involved in Manila hemp transactions in order to keep its losses to a minimum. To disguise its direct involvement, in February and March 1919 the Bank provided loans to two trading firms, V. Madrigal & Co. and Fernandez Hermanos, amounting to 2.63 million pesos. These two firms were managed by two directors of the Bank. The two "firms" purchased Manila hemp to sustain prices that had already sharply declined. The market value of the collateralized hemp of the two firms was 1.36 million pesos, only half of the amount of the loans, incurring great losses to the Bank.[10]

The Coates Report of 1920 noted: "[T]he names of Madrigal and Fernandez were used to disguise the transactions so that the public would not know that the bank or government were behind the deal—that the notes were 'dummy notes' and while both makers are amply responsible, and might be so held—that the loss would be borne by either the government or the bank, as to be later decided."[11] Table 19 shows the amount of outstanding

Table 19. Estimated Losses of Loans and Discounts of Manila Hemp Trading Firms to the Philippine National Bank, as of 19 May 1921

(1000 pesos)

| Name of Corporation | Estimated Recoverable | Estimated Loss |
|---|---|---|
| 1. G. Martini Ltd. | 4,923.8 | 4,923.8 |
| 2. Philippine Fiber & Produce Co. | 2,161.9 | 2,106.9 |
| 3. U. de Poli | 1,362.0 | 1,317.0 |
| 4. Sundry hemp purchases | | |
|     Fernandez Hermanos | 1,186.9 | |
|     Madrigal & Co. | 1,031.2 | |
|     G. Martini Ltd. | 21.2 | |
|     Estimated accrued interest | 330.0 | |
| Sub-total | 2,569.3 | 1,694.3 |
| Total | 11,017.0 | 10,042.0 |

Source: "Haskins & Sells Report of Examination of P.N.B. as of May 19, 1921, with 16 Exhibits," BIA 6769-708A, Exhibit: General Sheets, May 19, 1921, and Consolidation.

loans and losses of the trading firms for Manila hemp as of May 1921. The Bank's losses reached 10 million pesos, indicating the gravity of its irresponsible management.

**Coconut processing.** The first coconut processing mill in the Philippines had been established in 1906 and the industry grew rapidly during World War I. In the beginning, coconut oil was produced mainly for the domestic market. However, at the outbreak of World War I more than thirty coconut processing mills, large and small, were established in the vicinity of Manila by American or Filipino entrepreneurs. After the war, exports declined sharply and many mills were closed. It was not until 1921, when the United States imposed an import tax on coconut oil from other countries, that the Philippine export of coconut oil was revitalized.[12]

Most of the coconut mills established in the Philippines during World War I obtained large and often questionable financial support from the National Bank. Due to the crash of the export market after the war, these coconut mills suddenly faced financial difficulties as they fell behind in their loan repayment schedules. For example, as of June 1919, the Philippine Vegetable Oil Co., the largest coconut mill in the Philippines,[13] had credits of 26 million pesos from the Bank, with collaterals in *quedans*, as well as overdrafts and time papers. Of this 26 million pesos, only 3.6 million had been authorized by the Bank's board. Moreover, 11 million pesos had been provided as a "blanket mortgage"; that is, the real estate and chattel mortgage or vessels that the company held both in the Philippines and the United States should have been recorded as mortgages for 11 million pesos. However, with the exception of the company's two steamers, the mortgages were not properly recorded at the Bank and the Bank did not acquire definite title to the property as collateral for its loans.[14]

The Cristobal Oil Co. also benefited initially from the rampant loan business of the National Bank. Through its stockholders and management, this company was closely associated with two other companies, the Compañía Mercantil de Filipinas and the Compañía Naviera de Filipinas. The stockholders of all three companies included Filipino and American board members of the National Bank. In early 1918 Cristobal had a capital of about 910,000 pesos with fixed assets of 340,000 pesos. Then, under a "reorganization," the fixed assets were inflated ten times in the book, showing nearly 3.3 million pesos. Thus, together with 1.53 million pesos of the "good-will account" of the directors of the corporation (which was created by another tactic to inflate the assets), the company's capital ballooned to 4 million pesos by the end of July 1918. In 1919 it had acquired loans from the National Bank totaling 1.5 million pesos with collaterals of mortgage on plant (600,000 pesos), the Philippine Guarantee Co. (200,000 pesos), copra (41,600 piculs), and coconut oil (300 tons); however, only 1 million pesos was evidently authorized by the Bank's board in July 1919.[15]

Based on data from the Haskins & Sells Report of 1922, Tables 20 and 21 illustrate the overall picture of loans of the Philippine National Bank provided to coconut oil companies in 1921 and 1922. Table 20 shows that, as of February 1922, twelve mills owed a total of 23.7 million pesos to the Bank. Of twelve mills, the Philippine Vegetable Oil Co., the Philippine Manufacturing Co., and the Cristobal Oil Co. were the most indebted. The Philippine Vegetable Oil Co., a Filipino firm, accumulated debts of 17.2 million pesos to the Bank, while the Philippine Manufacturing Co. (American)[16] and the Cristobal Oil Co. (Filipino) owed the Bank 2.7 million pesos and 1.7 million pesos respectively. The total liabilities of the above twelve mills, which included debts to the National Bank as well as other loans and unpaid accounts, amounted to 51.8 million pesos, as against total assets of 21 million pesos.[17] These figures

Table 20. Liabilities of Coconut Oil Companies to the
Philippine National Bank, as of February 1922
(1000 pesos)

| Name of Corporation | Liabilities |
| --- | --- |
| 1. Philippine Vegetable Oil Co. | 17,251.0 |
| 2. Philippine Manufacturing Co. | 2,736.0 |
| 3. Cristobal Oil Co. | 1,690.0 |
| 4. Copra Products | 612.0 |
| 5. Philippine Oil Products Co. | 385.0 |
| 6. Philippine American Oil Co. | 320.0 |
| 7. Manila Cocoanut Oil Co. | 208.0 |
| 8. Manila Oil Refining & By-Products Co. | 187.0 |
| 9. Central Oil Corporation | 143.0 |
| 10. Laguna Cocoanut Oil Co. | 90.0 |
| 11. Insular Philippine Cocoanut Oil Co. | 47.0 |
| 12. National Cocoanut Oil Co. | 41.0 |
| Total | 23,710.0 |

*Source*: Same as Table 19, p. 7.

Table 21. Estimated Losses of Loans and Discounts of Coconut Oil
Companies to the Philippine National Bank, as of 19 May 1921
(1000 pesos)

| Name of Corporation | Estimated Loss |
| --- | --- |
| 1. Philippine Vegetable Oil Co. | 12,297.2 |
| 2. Philippine Manufacturing Co. | 664.2 |
| 3. Cristobal Oil. Co. | 559.0 |
| 4. Philippine American Oil Co. | 270.4 |
| 5. Philippine Oil Products Co. | 172.4 |
| 6. Manila Oil Refining & By-Products Co. | 137.0 |
| 7. Central Oil Corporation | 99.6 |
| 8. Laguna Cocoanut Oil Co. | 90.0 |
| 9. Insular Philippine Cocoanut Oil Co. | 26.4 |
| 10. Manila Cocoanut Oil Co. | 30.0 |
| 11. Copra Products | 20.0 |
| Total | 14,366.2 |

*Source*: Same as Table 19, Exhibit: General Balance Sheets, May 19, 1921, Consolidation.

clearly show that the twelve mills received massive loans far beyond their ability to repay.

Table 21 specifically shows the amounts of loans of eleven coconut oil companies in the National Bank as of May 1921. The Philippine Vegetable Oil Co. obtained the largest loan, over 12 million pesos, followed by the Philippine Manufacturing Co. and the Cristobal Oil Co. at 664,200 and 569,000 pesos, respectively. In May 1921, the Philippine Vegetable Oil Co. was already in the hands of a receiver, and the Bank's board was considering whether some other coconut oil companies should be sold either to the Bank itself or to other creditors.[18] According to the Bank's annual report of 1922, the Bank was holding assets of fourteen coconut oil companies in pledge as of the end of the year. Among them, only five still maintained efficient production capacity. When the remaining nine companies declared no possibility of further profitability, the Bank shut them down and dismantled their machinery for sale.[19]

In March 1925 Rafael Corpus, at that time president of the National Bank, sent a report to Manuel L. Quezon, president of the Senate, on the operation and condition of the Bank. Corpus wrote that, of fifteen coconut oil companies indebted to the Bank for a total of over 24 million pesos at the beginning of 1922, all had been taken over by the Bank except two companies against which foreclosure proceedings were pending in court. Corpus continued:

> A number of these mills has[sic] been dismantled and the salvaged materials and machinery are being sold from time to time; two of these mills are leased and another one was sold. At this writing, the sale of one other mill is being consummated with the present lessee. The old storage plant in San Francisco, California, has been sold for forty thousand dollars ($40,000): Every effort is being made to dispose of these oil properties in the most advantageous way at an early date. Loans to these companies have substantially been decreased from ₱17,761,267.00 on December 31, 1923, to ₱5,566,733 on December 31, 1924.[20]

Furthermore, the annual report of the National Bank in 1925 showed that the indebtedness of the coconut mills to the Bank had decreased to 2.32 million pesos by the end of 1925: the Philippine Manufacturing Co. owed 1.12 million pesos, while the Philippine Vegetable Oil Co. and the Cristobal Oil Co. were indebted for about 730,000 pesos and 480,000 pesos, respectively.[21] As a new export boom began in the late 1920s, it was American, British, and German corporations that entered into the Philippine coconut industry, while the Philippine National Bank gradually retreated from financial involvement with this industry.[22]

**Sugar processing.** The first "sugar central" (i.e., large sugar processing mill with modern equipment) was established by the Mindoro Development Co., an American firm that bought the San Jose Estate of 22,500 hectares in Mindoro, one of the former Spanish friar lands. Its operation began in crop year 1912–1913.[23] Subsequently, many sugar centrals were established in rapid succession by American, Filipino, and Spanish entrepreneurs in the islands of Luzon and Negros. The number of operating sugar mills increased from three to sixteen during the 1910s and from twenty-two to forty-two during the 1920s, reaching 45 by the early 1930s. During the modernization of sugar processing, there were two periods of the boom for the establishment of sugar centrals. The first was toward the end of the 1910s, when sugar prices increased rapidly after the U.S. entry into World War I, and the second was the late 1920s, when the United States became almost the sole export market for Philippine sugar. Of thirty-nine sugar centrals operated in crop year 1924–1925, eighteen mills were Filipino, ten were American, ten were Spanish, and one was Spanish-Filipino. The massive loans provided by the National Bank during the first boom made it possible to establish a larger number of Filipino sugar centrals by the early 1920s.[24]

It is noteworthy that the National Bank extended loans to the sugar processing industry from the very beginning. Immediately after the opening of the National Bank in 1916, even before its first president H. Parker Willis arrived in Manila, a loan of 1.5 million pesos to the Mindoro Development Co. was approved under the recommendation of Governor-General Francis Burton Harrison. This loan was initially provided by the International Banking Corporation, an American bank. Just before Willis assumed the presidency of the National Bank, Samuel Ferguson, vice president of the Bank, informed the International Banking Corporation that, out of 1.5 million pesos of the loan to the Mindoro Development Co., the Philippine National Bank was prepared to shoulder 1 million pesos, composed of an ordinary loan of 600,000 pesos with an advance of 400,000 pesos. Section 37 of Act No. 2621 (National Bank Act of 1916) provided that the Bank could approve a loan of up to 1.5 million pesos under special circumstances. However, Willis expressed apprehension about this particular transaction.[25]

The Coates Report of 1920 provided detailed data regarding the Bank's loans to the Mindoro Development Co. The first agricultural loan made by the Bank to this company, as has been mentioned above —Loan No. 1, for one million pesos—was paid up on April 30, 1919. However, the company had obtained an additional loan of 800,000 pesos in July 1918, and between October 1918 and July 1919 it received six further advances amounting to 395,000 pesos. These advances (evidently capital loans) were provided without formal authorization of the board of directors of the Bank. They were given under personal judgments of President Concepcion and Vice-President Delaney. The company ostensibly needed these advances for running expenses, but they were not properly secured. Demands for payment were made repeatedly but without result. The president of the company stated that "the loan was to be paid as soon as certain shipments of sugar arrived in Manila for the Japan markets, which shipments it was stated were due to arrive in the fall of 1919."[26]

Among the American-owned sugar centrals, the Calamba Sugar Estate also received credits from the National Bank. It obtained a demand bill of 500,000 pesos from the Bank in November 1919. This line of credit was authorized on the basis of *quedans* as collateral, but Coates's investigation showed that in reality the loan was provided without proper security; only the note of discount from the president and the secretary of the Bank was provided.[27]

It was the Filipino-owned sugar mills that enjoyed the largest lending services from the National Bank. Taken from the Coates Report of 1920, Table 22 shows the lending services of the Bank to eleven sugar mills as of November 1919. Ten of the mills were Filipino and one (Palma Central) was Spanish. The total amount of their borrowing reached approximately 13 million pesos, 15 percent of which represented agricultural loans, 74 percent other loans and overdrafts, and 11 percent letters of credit. All eleven sugar mills received loans from the Bank between May 1918 and March 1919, during the term of Bank President Concepcion. The Bacolod-Murcia Milling Co., the Isabela Sugar Co., the Talisay-Silay Milling Co., and the Ma-ao Sugar Central Co. enjoyed the biggest loans or overdrafts, all without secured collateral. The Coates Report of 1920 pointed out that 10 million pesos in loans to six sugar mills—the Bacolod-Murcia Milling Co., the Central Azucarera de Bais, the Talisay-Silay Milling Co., the Ma-ao Sugar Central Co., the Binalbagan Estate Co. and the Pampanga Sugar Development Co.—were unlisted in the Bank's books or financial statements.[28]

The following details describe the outstanding loans of nine sugar mills at the Bank as reported in the Coates Report of 1920:

Table 22. Outstanding Loans and Credits to Sugar Centrals Provided by the Philippine National Bank Outstanding, as of 29 November 1919
(1000 pesos, %)

| Name of Corporation | Amount Authorized | | Date Authorized |
|---|---|---|---|
| 1. Agricultural Loans | | | |
| Hinigaran Sugar Plantation | 710.0 | (5.5) | Nov. 29, 1918 |
| Gomez Hermanos | 281.8 | (2.2) | May 31, 1918 |
| Kabankalan Sugar Co. | 1,000.0 | (7.7) | Feb. 22, 1918 |
| Sub-total | 1,991.8 | (15.4) | |
| 2. Other Loans and Overdrafts | | | |
| Bacolod-Murcia Milling Co. | 1,127.6 | (8.7) | Mar. 5, 1919 |
| Central Azucarera de Bais | 490.6 | (3.8) | Nov. 23, 1918 |
| Isabela Sugar Co. | 1,599.9 | (12.3) | unknown |
| Palma Central | 606.5 | (4.7) | Dec. 19, 1918 |
| Talisay-Silay Milling Co. | 1,076.7 | (8.3) | Mar. 5, 1919 |
| Ma-ao Sugar Central Co. | 4,662.0 | (35.9) | Mar. 24, 1919 |
| Sub-total | 9,563.3 | (73.7) | |
| 3. Letters of Credit | | | |
| Binalbagan Estate, Inc. | 862.0 | (6.6) | Mar. 24, 1919 |
| Pampanga Sugar Development Co. | 553.6 | (4.3) | Mar. 5, 1919 |
| Subtotal | 1,415.6 | (10.9) | |
| Total | 2,970.7 | (100.0) | |

Source: Francis Coates, Jr., "Report of an Examination of the Philippine National Bank Manila, P. I. as of at Close of Business Nov. 30, 1919," BIA 6769-565A, p. 85.

**Hinigaran Sugar Plantation.** A loan of 710,000 pesos was provided by the Bank with a term of twenty years. Capitalized at 140,000 pesos, Senator Esperidion Guanco and his father-in-law (named Victoriano Siguenza; see chapter 4 on crop loans in Negros Occidental) were its principal owners. Since the lands of the company were subject to inundation. A large amount of sugarcane had been destroyed in the last flood and the company faced financial difficulties. A loan of 73,179 pesos and its interest, due 30 November 1919, had not been paid.[29]

**Kabankalan Sugar Co.** Incorporated in January 1919, this company owed 1 million pesos to the Bank. Its term was twenty years.[30]

**Bacolod-Murcia Milling Co.** In March 1919, a loan of 2,169,000 pesos was approved by the Bank to this company capitalized at only 1,039.50 pesos. The security offered was 10,779 hectares of land owned by sugar planters and company stockholders. The loan was approved without proper assessment of the land's value. As of November 1919, 1,127,600 pesos of the loan had been advanced, 450,000 pesos of which was issued as a demand note with 21,400 pesos of interest due April 1919. The central was not yet completed; machinery was on order, on advances made by the Bank, but undelivered.[31]

**Central Azucarera de Bais.** This firm applied for an industrial loan of 500,000 pesos in December 1918, to be used in the purchase of machinery, with security of 1,275,000 pesos in assets. The loan was approved by the Bank for a period of one year. However, no appraisal of the pledged property was filed and the loan was past due. At the time of investigation, the firm had an overdraft of 490,563.67 pesos, but its paid-up capital was only 37,500 pesos.[32]

**Isabela Sugar Co.** A loan was authorized in April 1918, on the condition that the Bank should purchase 1.5 million pesos in company bonds and the proceeds would be used by the company for the purchase of 6,000 hectares of agricultural land and to finance the importation of sugar machinery. However, in November 1919, thirteen months after the loan was negotiated, certain irregularities in connection with a mortgage were discovered. The mortgage did not cover any property belonging to the company, but, instead, certain haciendas attached to the company's sugar mill. The Bank made a resolution to authorize the loan, provided that the mortgage should cover land, buildings, machinery, and improvements belonging to the company. Meanwhile, due to serious discord between the stockholders and the management of the central, its operation was to be taken over and managed by the Bank. The subscribed capital and paid-up capital of this company were 9,000 pesos and 6,000 pesos, respectively.[33]

**Ma-ao Sugar Central Co.** As shown in Table 22, the Bank's loan offered to this company reached 4,662,000 pesos, the largest among the eleven listed sugar mills. The company's paid-up capital was only 25,000 pesos. The security for the loan was 20,478 hectares of land valued at 9 million pesos and machinery valued at 3 million pesos. Based on this security, the maximum loan could be calculated at 7,229,030 pesos. No re-appraisal on the land actually covered by mortgage was made by the Bank. However, the correct calculation by the investigation showed that the value of the mortgages was 5,183,030 pesos.[34]

**Palma Central.** A loan of 600,000 pesos was authorized by the Bank in January 1919. However, as of November 1919, this appeared as an overdraft of 606,548.45 pesos (see Table 22). No report was made of this irregularity.[35]

**Talisay-Silay Milling Company.** The Bank offered credit of 1,076,600 pesos to this company, including a demand note of 400,000 pesos and an overdraft of 676,600 pesos. The paid-up capital of the company was only 1,450 pesos. The stated mortgage value was 1,450,000 pesos on land appraised at 2,430,000 pesos.[36]

**Binalbagan Estate, Inc.** The Bank advanced 862,000 pesos to this company. This advance was made in the form of "customer's liability" under a letter of credit. However, the Bank had taken no mortgage or other security at the time this advance was made, and late in January 1920 the Bank made a further advance in the form of a demand loan of 1,120,500.50 pesos without security.[37]

The loans to the sugar centrals ballooned further after 1919. The Bank continued to support these sugar centrals by additional lending to complete the construction of the mills and to start their operation, but to no avail. In May 1921, the board of directors of the Bank passed a resolution to organize the Philippine Sugar Centrals Agency to bring six sugar centrals under its direct control. These six sugar centrals were the Bacolod-Murcia Milling Co., the Isabela Sugar Co., the Ma-ao Sugar Central Co., the Pampanga Sugar Development Co., the Talisay-Silay Milling Co., and the Binalbagan Estate, Inc. The supervising contract between the six sugar centrals and the Bank was concluded in August 1921. Later, these sugar centrals were called "Bank Centrals." The power given to the Sugar Centrals Agency was stated as effective for five years or until loans secured by the centrals were fully paid.[38]

Table 23 shows the liabilities of seven sugar centrals and the Sugar Centrals Agency to the National Bank as of February 1922, based on data from the Report of Haskins & Sells of 1922. This report stated that the total debts reached over 40 million pesos, and that it was doubtful if even 25 million pesos could be recovered. These sugar mills were constructed mostly during 1918, 1919, and 1920, when materials, freight, and labor costs were considerably higher than normal. The administration and control of the construction program were neither efficient nor economical. The Report of Haskins & Sells of 1922 confirmed:

Table 23. Liabilities of Sugar Centrals and the Philippine Sugar Centrals Agency, as of February 1922
(1000 pesos)

| Name of Corporation | Liabilities |
| --- | --- |
| Binalbagan Estate, Inc. | 9,300 |
| Ma-ao Sugar Central | 9,400 |
| Talisay-Silay Milling Co. | 5,610 |
| Pampanga Sugar Development Co. | 5,360 |
| Bacolod-Murcia Milling Co. | 5,310 |
| Isabela Sugar Co. | 3,160 |
| Palma Central | 1,090 |
| Philippine Sugar Centrals Agency | 1,700 |
| Total | 40,930 |

Source: Same as Table 19, p. 5.

The book value of the plants is about ₱34,000,000.00 but it is doubtful whether ₱15,000,000.00 could be obtained by their sale. In addition to mortgages held upon the plants and equipment the bank holds real estate mortgages upon cane lands supplying the mills aggregating 37,847 hectares in Occidental Negros and 14,240 hectares in San Fernando [Pampanga], equal to about 128,700 acres in all. . . . The planters who own these cane lands as well as the majority of the shares of the sugar companies owe the bank well over ₱10,000,000.00 individually, secured by sugar shipments, lands and personal properties.[39]

Under the management of the Sugar Centrals Agency, the Pampanga Sugar Development Co. and the Talisay-Silay Milling Co. decreased their debts rapidly and paid their debts fully by the end of the 1920s. However, the debts of the other four mills actually increased during the 1920s and it was not until the late 1930s that they finished paying their debts to the Bank.[40]

## ON THE ILLEGITIMACY OF THE DIRECTORS' RELATED LIABILITIES TO THE NATIONAL BANK

As pointed out by the Coates Report of 1920, Act No. 2747 (the revised Philippine National Bank Act of 1918) included two provisions: (1) "The National Bank shall not, directly or indirectly, grant loans to any of the members of the board of directors of the bank nor to agents of the branch banks" (Sec. 35); (2) "Any persons who shall violate any of the provisions of this Act shall be punished by a fine not to exceed ten thousand pesos, or by imprisonment not to exceed five years, or by both such fine and imprisonment" (Sec. 49).[41] This shows that, as a modern banking system, the Philippine National Bank was prohibited from offering its loan business to corporations with which the Bank's directors or other Bank agents were affiliated. However, in defiance of these regulations, massive loans were in fact provided by the Bank to its board members' affiliated corporations. The Coates Report described fourteen of these violations in detail. It is important to bear in mind that the Coates Report was merely preliminary, the result of only four and a half months' investigation. Moreover, due to various obstacles, Coates's survey was confined to an examination of the records in Manila, and information on the operations of various branches and agencies of the Bank was obtained only by correspondence. Coates made it clear that his report was not complete, and that further investigation would be necessary.[42]

Presumably in response to Coates's determination, a separate report was prepared in November 1923 by the Philippine government regarding the irregularities of loans provided to corporations with which board members of the Bank were affiliated. This report, written by F. C. Fisher and Michael Camus, was entitled "Report Concerning Liability, Civil or Criminal of Former Directors of the Philippine National Bank Arising from Commissions Connected with the Management of its Affairs." Over three hundred pages long, the report was in two parts. The first part discussed the illegitimacy of the loan to the Bank's board member-affiliated corporations, and the second part described various cases of violation of the Bank's regulations on loan service to the above corporations.[43] The following are two cases among them.

**Compañía Naviera de Filipinas.** This company was founded in May 1918. Its president was Senator Vicente Singson Encarnacion (a National Bank board member) and the treasurer was Carlos Cuyugan. The company had paid-up capital of one million pesos that was fully deposited with the Bank. Upon its organization, it sought 175,000 pesos from the Bank for the purchase of a steamer. The requested loan, representing 70 percent of the purchase value of the steamer, was approved by the Bank's board. Senator Singson was present at the board meeting, but did not vote on the matter of the loan to his company. In June of the same year, the company applied to the Bank for another loan of 50 to 75 percent of the purchase price of two wooden ships. This loan, of 1 million pesos, was also approved by the board. For these two loans, the three ships were mortgaged at a total value of 1,054,000 pesos in wartime prices. After the war, in July 1919, this security was devalued to 395,000 pesos. As the company fell into financial difficulties, two of the Bank's mortgages were foreclosed and both ships were bought in 1921 by the National Exchange Company, a subsidiary corporation controlled by the Bank, for 150,000 pesos in total. The books of the Bank showed that, as of November 1923, the total advances to the company by the Bank amounted to 1,349,455 pesos.[44]

The report of Fisher and Camus stated that directors J. Elmer Delaney, R. J. Fernandez, Vicente Madrigal, Fred N. Berry, and Archibald Harrison, all of whom had approved the first loan of 175,000 pesos in violation of the Bank's charter, should be jointly and severally liable with Senator Singson for the balance due on the loan. With regard to the second loan of 1 million pesos, because Director Fernandez was absent at the board meeting when it was approved, he could not be liable unless independent evidence could be found to show that he was a stockholder in this company and directly participated in granting the illegal loan.[45]

**Compañía Mercantil de Filipinas.** As has been mentioned above, this company was one of the Manila hemp traders that maintained credits at the National Bank. Incorporated on 14 March 1917, it had authorized capital of 40,000 pesos and subscribed capital of 8,000 pesos. Two weeks after the company's incorporation, the authorized capital was increased to 250,000 pesos with a paid-up capital of 35,500 pesos. In May 1918 the capital stock of the company was increased to 1 million pesos, of which 600,000 pesos were paid up. Vicente Singson Encarnacion and Vicente Madrigal, board members of the Bank, were the subscribers of the increased capital stock, the former for 22,000 pesos and the latter for 5,000 pesos. Both were also members of the board of directors of this company. It is not clear when Senator Singson first became a stockholder in the company. His connection with the company first appeared in the public record as a stockholder at its meeting in May 1918; however, he was almost certainly a stockholder prior to that time. The minutes of the board meeting of the National Bank in May 1918 showed that Singson personally requested the board to make a loan of 1 million pesos to the company, but refrained from voting on the proposition upon the ground that he was an "officer" of the borrowing company. On the other hand, there was no evidence that Madrigal was a stockholder of the company prior to the increase of the capital stock authorized at the meeting of the stockholders in May 1918.[46]

The National Bank offered loans and financial support to this company from May 1918 to January 1920. The first loan was approved on 18 May 1918. Bank President Concepcion submitted a report to the Bank's board that stated:

> Senator Singson Encarnacion solicits the financial help of the Bank for Compañía Mercantil de Filipinas to absorb the assets and business of Froehlich & Kuttner and increase its capital and surplus to ₱570,000 fully paid. For this purpose, a loan of ₱1,000,000 is requested at an annual interest of 7%, guaranteed by the two combined concerns mentioned above, which amount to approximately ₱2,000,000. Senator Singson anticipates the liquidation of the loan within 18 months, more or less. Approved.[47]

According to the minutes of a Bank board meeting, a second loan was approved on 30 October 1918 as an overdraft line of ₱750,000, and a third credit of ₱500,000 was approved in the form of rediscounts and commercial letters of credit.[48] On 6 August 1919, in a re-arrangement of financial support, the Bank approved the company's proposal to set its merchandise in stock (Manila hemp) as security for its outstanding indebtedness to the Bank.[49]

On 9 January 1920, at the Bank's board meeting, President Concepcion submitted a report regarding the financial condition of the company. It stated that on 20 August 1919, an overdraft of 2.4 million pesos had been allowed for this company against pledge of its stock of merchandise, on the condition that it would pay 700,000 pesos on or before 30 November 1919. The company would then continue making payments at the rate of 100,000 pesos monthly so that the amount due should be reduced to 1 million pesos payable on demand on 30 June 1920. However, in view of the fact that the said conditions were not duly complied with, the company was required to pay the difference of 329,496.65 pesos. In order to cope with this situation, the company requested that its overdraft line be fixed at 2,082,500 pesos and that from January 1920 it would gradually reduce its obligation to the Bank.[50]

As of 31 March 1919, the net worth of the company was 792,289.02 pesos, of which 650,000 pesos was capital and 63,138.99 pesos surplus, with 97,150.25 pesos in reserve. The total outstanding indebtedness of the company to the Bank was 2,757,565.72 pesos, of which 2,093,860.19 pesos was overdraft. Furthermore, the company owed three local branches of the

Bank; in Cebu 125,000 pesos (overdraft) and 50,000 pesos (rediscounting), in Iloilo 157,500 pesos (overdraft), and in Aparri 35,000 pesos (overdraft).[51]

Later documents obtained by the Bank showed that the company adopted a resolution at its board meeting of 16 December 1922 which stated that as of 16 October 1922, the company was indebted to the Bank in the amount of 1,252,884.95 pesos. The Bank had demanded the liquidation of this long overdue obligation, but the company had no funds to pay it. In this situation, the company agreed to liquidate all its properties and pay the Bank. On the same day, upon this resolution, a contract was signed by Senator Singson for the company and E. W. Wilson, general manager of the Bank, that the company should transfer all its property to the Bank as full payment of its debts.[52]

What opinion then did Fisher and Camus disclose on the illegitimacy of the loan business of the Bank to the Compañía Mercantil de Filipinas? The report argued that the case of the Compañía Mercantil was practically identical with that of the Compañía Naviera and the same conclusion could be reached regarding the criminal liability of the directors by whom the loans were authorized. As for civil liability, in the case of Senator Singson, who was a director of the Compañía Mercantil as well as of the Bank, the repayment of the indirect loan to himself should be examined. On the other hand, the case of other directors of the Bank must be investigated on the ground that they authorized the loans knowing the relationship of Senator Singson with the Compañía Mercantil. The report concluded that all of the directors of the Bank should be jointly and severally liable for the payment of the unpaid balance, unless that liability had been affected by the above contract of 16 December 1922.[53]

Fisher and Camus went on to express their opinion: "There is no doubt, we believe, that if the contract of December 16th, 1922, constitutes a valid discharge of the debt of the Compañía Mercantil to the Philippine National Bank, it likewise constituted a discharge of the liability of Mr. Singson as the indirect borrower of the money, and of the other Directors of the Bank jointly and severally bound with him."[54] However, careful examination of the minutes of the meeting of the board of directors showed that no record remained to disclose any prior authority to E. W. Wilson, the Bank's general manager, to discharge the debt of the Compañía Mercantil. Therefore, the question was whether Wilson was legally authorized to bind the Bank by contract with the Compañía Mercantil or not.[55]

The report further argued that General Manager Wilson understood that the debtor corporation was absolutely insolvent, yet never considered the possible effect of a complete discharge of the Compañía Mercantil from all liability to the Bank upon the personal responsibility of directors, either of the Compañía Mercantil or of the Bank. Wilson also did not recognize that his authority as general manager should be bound by the decision at the meeting of the board of directors of the Bank. Citing court cases in the United States, Fisher and Camus disclosed their view that the charter of the Philippine National Bank provided that, when its president or general manager concluded a contract with its creditors, he was required to secure the "advice and consent" of its board of directors. In the light of this interpretation, the validity of the contract between the Bank and the Compañía Mercantil of 16 December 1922, which Wilson undertook, should be in very grave doubt.[56] The report concluded: "In the absence of a direct ruling by our Supreme Court, we hesitate to give a definite opinion as to what the outcome of the litigation would be, but we are strongly inclined to the belief that the attempted discharge would be regarded by the courts as invalid."[57] If such litigation were undertaken, as the report suggested, then not only Senator Singson, director of both the Bank and the Compañía Mercantil, but also the other directors of the Bank who consented to the making of loans to this company, should take unqualified responsibility for the unpaid balance of the company's debt.[58]

In examining the report by Fisher and Camus, it is important to consider the reasons why there were so many cases of violation of the National Bank's regulations prohibiting loans to companies in which board members of the Bank were stockholders or managers. What was the socioeconomic background to these irregularities of the National Bank in the light of modern banking practice in the Philippines?

By way of answer to this question clues abound in the moneylending practices of the Chinese banking business in the Philippines. In Wong Kwok-Chu's *The Chinese in the Philippine Economy: 1898–1941,* chapter 5, "Credit and Banking," illustrates the distinctive features of the Chinese banking business in the Philippines. According to Wong, commercial business was conducted based on *xinyong* (trustworthiness) and personal relationships among the Chinese community in the Philippines. With the commercial expansion of the U.S. colony, money transactions that had previously been conducted through verbal promises took the form of "promissory notes" (*jie ju*)—written promises made by a debtor to pay a creditor some amount of money, specifying the principal and interest and due dates. The use of promissory notes became the basis of Chinese money transactions and remittances to China. While in British Malaya or Thailand Chinese merchants were able to obtain ample credits from Western banks, commercial banks in the Philippines were not active in providing credit services to the Chinese. This was the situation when the China Banking Corporation (CBC) was founded in the Philippines in 1920.[59]

Most stockholders of the CBC were Chinese living in the Philippines. In 1921 the CBC was owned collectively by 500 Chinese resident merchants. In 1937, 91 percent of the stocks were owned by Chinese and the remaining 9 percent by Filipinos, Americans, and others. Its paid-up capital had increased from 2.9 million pesos in 1920 to 5.7 million pesos in 1924, and the latter figure remained the same until 1941. From 1924 to 1935, the percentage of the combined shareholding among eleven board members increased from 26 percent to 47 percent. The single biggest stockholder held 1 million pesos throughout this period.[60] It is noteworthy that the CBC granted large loans, discounts, and overdrafts to its directors. Wong calculates that "[t]he percentage of directors' related loans relative to total loans and total deposit between 1923 and 1940 was on average 47.3 percent and 47.6 percent, respectively."[61]

Another Philippine Chinese bank, the Mercantile Bank of China (MBC), as Wong shows, was incorporated in Manila in 1924, with authorized capital of 2 million pesos, half of which was paid up. During the period 1924–1931, eleven Chinese directors of the board shared 20–25 percent of its total paid-up capital. Unlike CBC, MBC had no single major shareholder among its directors. In 1926 this bank had about 300 shareholders, mostly Chinese. However, MBC also granted a high percentage of loans to its directors. The total direct and indirect liabilities of its directors made up 44 percent of the total deposits in 1926; this figure had grown to around 80 percent by 1931.[62]

Both the CBC and the MBC continued to grant a large proportion of loans to their directors, despite official bank examiners' frequent criticism of such a lending policy in their reports. In Wong's view, this lending policy can be justified because these banks were founded primarily to meet the needs of Chinese businessmen. For these banks, "*xinyong* and close personal relations were deemed more important than rational credit analysis and sufficient collateral."[63] Thus, despite repeated official criticism and warnings on violation of banking regulations, the CBC and the MBC maintained the large proportion of loans to directors throughout the 1920s.

We might discover here some common points between the findings from these case studies of Chinese banks and the report by Fisher and Camus regarding the irregularities of the loan business of the Philippine National Bank to its directors. The National Bank was founded as a modern banking system, that is, in accordance with strictly professional managerial principles. Yet in actual practice, various loan transactions were conducted under the sole decision of the Bank's president or general manager, even with inadequate collateral. In previous studies of Philippine banking history, these practices have been characterized as deviations—"corruption" or "violation of regulations"—from the proper governance principles of modern banking management. The slipshod management of the National Bank could thus be regarded as an exceptional phenomenon at the time of a rising market in export-oriented primary commodities during World War I. However, if we place the irregularities of the loan business of the National Bank alongside Chinese banking practices based on *xinyong* and close personal relations, this might make it possible for us to understand them in the context of historical and traditional moneylending practices in the Philippines.

As has been discussed in chapter 2, the Philippine economy was incorporated into the British-led world economy in the late nineteenth century. With the expansion of the country's export economy, a domestic commercial and financial network was established by 1900 with British and Spanish banks at its center. Under this financial umbrella, British or American agency houses and Spanish or Chinese traders conducted business through various local networks composed of numerous middle-sized or smaller Chinese merchants or usurers who lent funds for agricultural production and bought the products. Within these networks, lending services were provided with standing crops as collateral, without accurate information or papers on the price or size of land as security. Personal ties and connections were also efficiently used by Chinese merchants or usurers for the expansion of their financial network. This kind of commercial and financial business practice continued in the Philippines into the early twentieth century. In this context, such peculiar lending practices of the Philippine National Bank as director-related liabilities may be understood rather as the "rational" banking service of the Philippines, following traditional business practice based on *xinyong* and close personal relations that had been well-rooted since the nineteenth century. Although not the whole story, this insight may help us to understand why the National Bank continued to protect the economic interests of Filipino elites through director-interlocking relationships even after its rehabilitation in the 1920s.[64]

CHAPTER 7

# RECONSTRUCTING THE PHILIPPINE NATIONAL BANK AND THE CURRENCY SYSTEM

AS WAS DISCUSSED in chapter 1, the Philippine government revised the currency law in 1918. This revision consolidated the two currency reserves, the Gold Standard Fund and the Silver Certificate Reserve, into the Currency Reserve Fund which then came to embody two functions: that of stabilizing the foreign exchange rate of the peso against the U.S. dollar, and that of guaranteeing the credibility of the Philippines' Treasury certificate. However, because the Philippine currency system was based on the gold exchange standard, the operation of the new reserve fund exposed an inherent contradiction in monetary policy. Under this currency system, the Philippines had required two different currency reserves, one to guarantee the stability of the exchange rate (pesos to dollars) and the other to fund government paper like the silver certificate or Treasury certificate. The strict separation of the two funds had been deemed essential for fiscal security under the American colonial regime.

In order to correctly maintain the gold exchange standard under the single currency reserve, it was necessary to strictly limit moneys used for lending and investment to ensure that the remaining larger proportion of available currency was not appropriated for purposes other than exchange. In other words, if the amount of the former Silver Certificate Reserve was not set aside, the gold exchange standard in the Philippines would not be able to function smoothly after the consolidation of the two reserves. What actually happened in the Philippines after World War I was that most of the consolidated currency reserve was deposited at the New York agency of the Philippine National Bank and subsequently appropriated by its Manila office for massive loan business, thus precipitating credit and paper money inflation.

Reviewing briefly the Philippine financial crisis of 1919–1922 in this way, we might point out the following four reasons as its major causes. First, the revision of the currency law in 1918 conflated the gold and silver standards. Second, there is evidence that the Philippine Treasury did not fulfill its responsibility to manage the currency reserve properly. Third, the Philippine National Bank intentionally appropriated the currency reserve for large investment loans. And fourth, the political and administrative system in the Philippines was more than willing to tolerate the appropriation of the currency reserves to extend large loans to the private sector. The second of these causes has been discussed in chapter 5. In this chapter, the remaining three points are discussed; the chapter also shows how the Philippine government dealt with (or failed to deal with) the near bankruptcy of the Philippine National Bank, as well as with the exhaustion of its currency reserves.

## THE ARREST OF VENANCIO CONCEPCION, FORMER PRESIDENT OF THE NATIONAL BANK

As early as May 1919 the Bureau of Insular Affairs (BIA) at the U.S. War Department in Washington suspected links between the depletion of the Philippine currency reserves and the mismanagement of the Philippine National Bank. The BIA sent an investigating team headed by Francis Coates, Jr. to Manila late in the same year. During 1920–1921 Coates submitted three reports exposing the slipshod management of the National bank as well as the irregular administration of the currency reserves.[1] In 1921 the accounting firm Haskins & Sells conducted an independent investigation of the questionable large loan business of the National Bank.[2] In addition, Ben F. Wright, special examiner of the National Bank, issued a memorandum on the chaotic condition of the Philippine currency system in August 1921.[3] Wright submitted another report to Governor-General Leonard Wood in November 1922 that included a summary of the reports by Coates and Haskins & Sells.[4] The official view of the financial crisis, delivered by Wood to the Philippine legislature in February 1923, was based on this second Wright report.[5]

While the BIA had quickly taken an initiative in 1919 to grasp the actual situation and true causes of the financial crisis, a full year passed before any actual responsibility on the part of the Philippine government and bank officials for this grave matter was publicly expressed. Almost immediately after receiving the news of the exhaustion in currency reserves at the New York agency of the Philippine National Bank in May 1919, the BIA had understood that a serious problem might exist in the management of their currency system by the Philippine authorities. During 1919–1920 numerous telegrams were exchanged between the BIA in Washington and the governor-general's office in Manila. In the Philippines, however, the issue was not discussed openly until late 1920. The financial crisis was so grave, and its true causes were so complicatedly interwoven with the conduct of the Philippine administration, that candid public disclosure held the potential to endanger the very foundation of the U.S. colonial system in the Philippines.

Yet various rumors were circulated among government and financial circles in Manila regarding the mismanagement of the National Bank as well as the currency crisis. In November 1920, assuming responsibility for various irregularities connected with National Bank loans, Venancio Concepcion resigned from the Bank's presidency. In March of the next year, Francis Burton Harrison resigned the governor-generalship of the Philippines. In May 1921, the Wood-Forbes Mission was sent to Manila to investigate political and economic conditions in the Philippines, as well as the autonomous role of the Philippine government. As a result of the mission's investigation, the fundamental cause of the Philippine financial crisis came to be understood solely as "the mismanagement of the Philippine National Bank," with no consideration of the grave defects in the currency system, which was administered by the Philippine Treasury under the indirect supervision of the BIA. Thus, all responsibility for the Philippine financial crisis came to be shouldered by the officials and staff of the National Bank, as well as by some leading Filipino politicians. It was in this milieu that Venancio Concepcion was arrested in Manila for violation of the National Bank Law on 23 June 1921. It is important to note here that the arrest coincided with the emerging discourse of "the corruption scandal of the Philippine National Bank," masking the full truth of the currency-based crisis from the public.

Among the documents relating the arrest of Concepcion in the holdings of the U.S. National Archives, there are three articles originally written in Spanish and translated by the BIA that comment on his arrest, and provide some overview of the facts presented in the indictment. Official gazette clippings also describe three judicial trials and their judgments. In addition, Concepcion himself later wrote a memoir in which he analyzed the scandal and justified his position.[6]

There was some critical reaction in Manila to the official apportionment of blame. Three days after Concepcion's arrest, the daily newspaper *El Ideal* carried an article with the headline "The Conduct of General Concepcion as President of the National Bank." Under the sub-heading "To whom losses suffered were due," the author of this article comments:

> The gold reserve was totally exhausted when he [Concepcion] assumed the management. The National Bank of the Philippines is one of the institutions that have been most furiously attacked. The most distressing thing is that the attacks were made thoughtlessly and unadvisedly, and censorious pens have not thought as to whether they were fully acquainted with the condition of the Bank. Those attacks came with renewed force when a Filipino was seen at the head of the institution, and all the more so when they considered that this Filipino was a Nationalist. . . .
>
> The Filipino president of the Bank, the Philippine administration attracted all the censures, and he [Concepcion] was the center thereof. . . .[7]

In spite of this criticism, Concepcion was arrested on 23 June. On the following day, *La Vanguardia* described this incident in detail:

> VENANCIO CONCEPCION, EX-PRESIDENT OF THE NATIONAL BANK, INDICTED.
>
> He was arrested at 9:30 p.m., and was in jail until two in the morning. Concepción is accused of having drawn from the bank 750,000 pesos by illegal means. . . .
>
> The rumor that because of the late hour yesterday [when he was arrested] it was arranged that the accused should pay only 5,000 pesos of the 20,000 pesos fixed as bail, is entirely unfounded. . . . The bond given by Concepción is personal. . . .
>
> In connection with this notorious affair of Mr. Concepción, it is known that there are other matters besides that Auditor Nolting has under investigation, which will be taken to the city fiscal also.[8]

Moreover, *El Comercio* of 25 June 1921 reported the arrest of Concepcion sensationally with the headline "The First Arrest in the Bank Case." Like *El Ideal*, *El Comercio* stood on the side of Concepcion. It claimed that the crucial responsibility for the loss of money at the National Bank should be taken not by the president of the Bank but rather by the governor-general: "Whoever it be that has lost this money, and wherever it has gone, the truth is [that] it has disappeared because of the acts of commission or omission of the man whose voice exercised or which, under the law, should have exercised the greatest influence—Francis Burton Harrison."[9] Thus, from the beginning, the arrest of Concepcion was an incident with a strong political flavor.[10]

Concepcion was indicted on three charges, for which the Supreme Court issued three separate decisions. The first judicial trial was on the illegal loan of 750,000 pesos that *La Vanguardia* had reported. Concepcion was charged for making a loan of 750,000 pesos to the Binalbagan Estate, Inc.,[11] a company in which he himself was an owner controlling 40 percent of its capital stock upon the unsecured promissory note of the corporation. This was a violation of Section 35 of Act No. 2747.[12] Concepcion was convicted of this charge by the Supreme Court on 15 August 1922, with a minimum fine of 10,000 pesos or imprisonment not to exceed five years or both fine and imprisonment.[13]

Grounds for the second trial were as follows. By overstepping his powers and without authorization from the board of directors of the National Bank, Concepcion extended the Philippine Vegetable Oil Co.[14] a loan in the amount of 725,000 pesos, and this loan had not been repaid. He was accused of violating Section 17 of Act No. 2747.[15] However, on 11 September 1922, the Supreme Court acquitted Concepcion of this charge for lack of sufficient evidence.[16] At the third trial, Concepcion was charged with violation of Section 35 of Act No. 2747: as president of the National Bank he had authorized an extension of credit of 300,000 pesos in favor of the firm named "Puno y Concepcion, S. en C." without proper securities. On 29 November 1922, he was found guilty of this charge.[17]

Two and a half years later, on 25 June 1925, the *Manila Bulletin* carried the news that Concepcion had been released from Bilibid prison the previous day, having served the term imposed by the court following his conviction for two violations of the charter of the National Bank. Upon release he made a statement of his intention to write a memoir offering his own account of the Bank's role in the financial crisis, as well as the causes of the depletion of the currency reserves.[18]

Concepcion's memoir was published in 1927 under the title "*La Tragedia" del Banco Nacional Filipino*. In this small book, Concepcion covered a host of topics: the purpose of the establishment of the National Bank, the "Filipinization" of the important positions in the Bank, the management of the Bank before Concepcion took its presidency, the state of the Bank's business under Concepcion as its president, the criticism of his administration, his resignation, the subsequent management of the Bank under E. W. Wilson as general manager, responsibility for the near-bankruptcy of the Bank, the exhaustion in currency reserves, the loss in the Shanghai branch, large loans to sugar centrals, and his trials.[19] Although all of these points are important, it is particularly significant to look into the matter relating to responsibility for the mismanagement of the Bank and Concepcion's remarks on his trials.

In chapter VI of the memoir, Concepcion presented his view of the mismanagement of the Bank. He strongly opposed the contention that only Filipino bank officials and staff were responsible. Instead, he especially aimed his attack at J. Elmer Delaney, American vice-president of the Bank. Delaney, a New York banking expert, had the foreign department of the Philippine National Bank under his absolute control and was the sole functionary of the Bank who handled letters of exchange covering the export of Manila hemp to New York and London, mainly of the firms G. Martini, Ltd., the Philippine Fiber & Produce Co., and the U. de Poli.[20] He handled his business in the context of the high market prices prevailing during World War I. When the market collapsed after the war, he himself went to New York to attend the liquidation of export products that had stagnated in the market. However, the situation proved too serious to find a way to safeguard the interests of the Bank. The abovementioned firms went into bankruptcy and the Bank suffered great losses. Here Concepcion emphasized the fact that Delaney, while he was still in New York, resigned his position at the Philippine National Bank and accepted a vice-presidency at another bank, the Bank of the Philippine Islands. By doing so, according to Concepcion, Delaney succeeded in relieving himself of responsibility for his direct actions in financing the export of Manila hemp (*abaca*) and other foreign deals. After Delaney's resignation, two other Americans took over export management at the Bank. Concepcion claimed that, when he assumed the general management of the Bank in March 1919, the business of the Bank was severely distressed.[21]

In chapter X of his book Concepcion presented his own justification of the accusations proffered against him. According to him, he had been arraigned in four cases. Two of them, citing violation of the law chartering the Bank that prohibited board members from obtaining loans from the National Bank directly or indirectly, were the cases discussed above as the first and third trials, and one of the others was the second trial mentioned earlier. The fourth, according to Concepcion's memoir, was for alleged embezzlement, in which trial he was found not guilty.[22]

At the end of the memoir, Concepcion expressed his view that the matter of the National Bank was so complex and intricate that it could not have been the work of one man. He concluded:

> Authorities on banking, such as Dr. H. Parker Willis, Mr. Chas. C. Robinson, Mr. J. Elmer Delaney, Mr. Adolph Kopp, Mr. Henry J. Belden and Mr. Reilly, have succeeded each other in the Bank and have contributed to [the] said institution their wealth of technical knowledge and experience in all branches of banking. And, nevertheless, according to a statement of the banker, Mr. Francis Coates, Jr., the errors which he discovered in the operation of the National Bank were not only those of origin but those accumulated during four years of operation, and this explains the fact that I found the Bank's affairs very badly involved when I undertook the management thereof.[23]

It is possible to understand the arrest of Venancio Concepcion not as a result of structural issues of the Bank's management but rather of Concepcion's lack of talent as a banker. Interestingly enough, Concepcion was not the only Filipino convicted. Among the officers and employees of the bank who were prosecuted and convicted of embezzlement and other criminal charges were the vice-president-cum-assistant general manager, the manager and assistant manager of the Foreign Department, the assistant chief note teller, the managers of the Iloilo branch and of the Aparri branch, and various subordinate employees. It was reported that the manager of the Aparri branch committed suicide.[24]

**DEBATES ON THE REVISION OF THE CURRENCY LAW**

While the arrest of Venancio Concepcion and other officials and staff of the National Bank stirred an awareness in Philippine society of the gravity of the banking scandal, preparation was under way for reforming the currency law that was now acknowledged as one of the fundamental causes of the exhaustion in currency reserves. The initiative for this currency reform came not from the Philippine government but from the BIA in Washington. As has been discussed above, the BIA had sent investigators to determine the causal correlation between the depletion of the currency reserve and the scandal of the National Bank during 1919–1922. Six reports in all were submitted to the BIA, all vital and instrumental in disclosing the true picture of the Philippine financial crisis. However, they have remained unpublished. These reports are now housed in the U.S. National Archives, the Library of Congress, and the Seeley G. Mudd Manuscript Library of Princeton University. To the author's knowledge no previous research has examined all six of these unpublished reports to build an overarching study of the Philippine financial crisis of 1919–1922.[25] By examining these six reports carefully, the author has found that the Coates Report of 1921 and the Wright Report of 1921 were the ones that most critically and analytically focused on the exhaustion in currency reserves. It was primarily these two reports that led the BIA to perceive the problem of the Philippine financial crisis in two aspects: the legal basis of the National Bank as depository of the Philippine government in the United States, and the transformation of the nature of the gold exchange standard necessitated by the merger of the Gold Standard Fund and the Silver Certificate Reserve.

As suggested by its long title—"Report to the Honorable, The Secretary of War–United States of America, Washington, D.C., Covering an Investigation of the Operation in the Gold Standard Fund and the Certificate Reserve Fund of the Treasurer of the Philippine Islands in Connection with the Operations of the Philippine National Bank of the Philippine Islands"—the Coates Report of 1921 grappled squarely with the question of the legal basis of the National Bank as depository of the Philippine government in the United States.

In this 1921 report—his third and last—Coates said that the purpose of his inquiry was

> to investigate the entire transaction to determine how diversion of the funds [the Gold Standard Fund and the Certificate Reserve Fund] had been made possible—how they had been invested, and to place, if possible, the responsibility for their diversion and misapplication—meaning by misapplication their conversion by the bank into loans, investments and advances instead of having them retained as collateralized deposits [of Philippine currency], subject to the order and control of the Treasurer of the Philippine Islands.[26]

In order to fulfill his task, Coates paid particular attention to the question of the legal basis of the National Bank as depository of the Philippine government in the United States. In pursuit of this issue, he examined the Administration Code of the Philippines of 1917 (Act No. 2711), the Philippine currency law of 1918 (Act No. 2776),[27] the Philippine National Bank Act of 1916 (Act No. 2612), and its revision of 1918 (Act No. 2747).

Indeed, in Section 625 of Article VII, at Chapter 26 of the "Bureau of Audits" in the Administration Code of the Philippines of 1917, the following regulation was stated regarding the depositories and depositary accounts:

> Sec. 625. Appointment of depositaries by Governor-General or Secretary of War. The Governor-General may appoint any bank or banking institution in the Philippine Islands, and the Secretary of War any similar institution in the United States, as depositary of the Government of the Philippine Islands, after such institution has filed sufficient evidence of its sound financial condition and has deposited, as security, either in the Insular Treasury or in the Bureau of Insular Affairs, at Washington, bonds of the United States or of the Government of the Philippine Islands or other bonds or securities satisfactory to and approved by the officer making the appointment and in such amount as shall be required by him.[28]

Under this regulation, a bank in the United States was required to obtain permission from the Secretary of War before it could accept a deposit of any currency reserves of the Philippine government. At the same time, Act No. 2603 provided for the governor-general of the Philippines to designate the depositories of the Philippine government in the United States as "branches of the Philippine Treasury."[29] Thus, to deposit any currency reserves of the Philippine government, banks in the United States were required to obtain permission both from the U.S. secretary of war and the governor-general of the Philippines. However, Coates also pointed out in his report of 1921 that, subsequent to the establishment of the Federal Reserve System in the United States in 1913, depositories of the Philippine government in the United States were limited to the banks in the Federal Reserve System.[30] The Federal Reserve Act of 1913 provided as follows:

> Sec. 15. . . . No public funds of the Philippine Islands, or of the postal savings, or any Government funds, shall be deposited in the continental United States in any bank not belonging to the system established by this Act. . . .[31]

Coates further explained how the Philippine National Bank Act of 1916 (Act No. 2612) provided for the regulation of the depositories of government funds:[32]

> Sec. 19. The Philippine National Bank is hereby authorized to receive deposits of funds of the Insular Government, the provinces, municipalities, Postal

Savings Bank, associations, corporations, and private persons, and it is hereby made obligatory for the aforesaid Insular, provincial, and municipal governments to make their deposits in the National Bank. The interest paid by said Bank on deposits so made shall not exceed four per centum per annum: *Provided, however*, That whenever in the judgment of the Governor-General it is in the public interest to make deposits from public funds in other banks he is hereby authorized to cause the same to be done under such terms and conditions as he may deem proper.[33]

By the revision of Philippine currency law of 1918 (Act No. 2776), Chapter 41 of the Administration Code relative to the currency system was largely amended. Among its revised sections, Coates paid particular attention to the regulations relating to the National Bank as the depository of the Philippine government in the United States:[34]

> Sec. 1624. . . . The currency reserve fund shall be held in the Treasury at Manila or may in part, at the discretion of the Governor-General and upon the recommendation of the Secretary of Finance, on terms accepted by the former, be kept on deposit with branches of the Philippine Treasury in the United States; and the Governor-General is hereby authorized, upon recommendation of the Secretary of Finance, to designate such depositaries of the Philippine government in the United States among the federal reserve banks as he may deem advisable to be branches of the Philippine Treasury: *Provided, however*, That not more than twenty-five per cent of the currency reserve fund shall be deposited with any single branch depositary in the United States, except branches of the Philippine National Bank in the United States.[35]

If we follow the above regulation of Act No. 2776, we might understand that the New York agency of the National Bank duly fulfilled the function of depository of the Philippine government in the United States as the "branch of Philippine Treasury" under the discretion of the governor-general and the secretary of finance. However, as we have seen from Section 625 of the Administration Code of 1917, a bank was required to obtain permission from both the U.S. secretary of war and the governor-general of the Philippines to become a depository of the Philippine government in the United States. Moreover, depositing any funds of the Philippine government at any bank which was not part of the Federal Reserve System in the United States clearly violated the U.S. Federal Reserve Act of 1913. And, in addition, Coates claimed that the business activities of the New York agency of the Philippine

National Bank as the depository of the Philippine government conflicted with a New York banking law which prevented branches of foreign banks from carrying deposits.[36]

Thus, Coates discovered four legal discrepancies regarding deposits of the Philippine government in the United States: the Philippine National Bank law, the revised Philippine currency law, the Federal Reserve Act of the United States, and a New York banking law. He pursued an in-depth investigation of how currency reserve transfers to the New York agency of the National Bank were conducted. It was particularly after the revision of the Philippine currency law in 1918—which endowed the New York agency of the National Bank with special status among the depositories of the Philippine government in the United States—that currency reserves of the Philippine government which had formerly been deposited at the Federal Reserve Banks were transferred to the New York agency of the National Bank. In his 1921 report Coates cites numerous letters and cablegrams exchanged between the Manila office of the National Bank and its New York agency, as well as correspondence between the insular treasurer of the Philippine Islands and the governor-general securing permission for the transfer of such reserves from private banks in the United States to the New York agency of the National Bank.[37]

Then, Coates showed, the currency reserves were transferred to Manila and largely appropriated for loan business to the export sector (Manila hemp, sugar, and coconut industries) by the Manila office of the National Bank.[38] As a result, Coates came to the conclusion that the depletion of the currency reserves at the New York agency of the National Bank was not due solely to the irresponsibility of a few officials at the National Bank or the Philippine Treasury; rather, it should be understood as an outcome of corporate graft in which many high officials at pivotal positions in both the Philippine and the U.S. governments were deeply involved.[39]

The second issue arising from debates on the revision of the currency law was the transformation of the nature of the gold exchange standard as the background of the merger of the Gold Standard Fund and the Silver Certificate Reserve. In this connection, the Wright Report of 1921 is most informative. The formal title of this report is "Memorandum Concerning the Development of the Currency System of the Philippine Islands with Special Reference to Existing Conditions and to the Philippine National Bank." Written by Ben F. Wright as special bank examiner, this report was composed of thirteen chapters (sixty-one pages) with seven exhibits. It discussed generally the fundamental principles of the gold exchange standard, delineated the characteristics and functions of the two Philippine currency reserves, and explained the background of their combination. Then, examining the currency reform of 1918 critically, Wright described the chaos prevailing in the currency system since 1918 and proposed some solutions. He also discussed the mismanagement of the National Bank and made some recommendations for its remediation.[40]

As Wright explained, the gold exchange standard was based on the fundamental principle that a country whose currency was circulated under the silver standard could maintain the parity of its currency for foreign exchange based on the gold standard. There was no gold in circulation in the Philippines under the gold exchange standard. ". . . [T]o settle foreign balance it was provided that such balances could be settled by purchasing from the Treasurer a bill of exchange upon New York payable in gold at a rate representing the actual cost of shipping gold to New York, and similar provision was made for the sale of exchange in New York payable in Manila in pesos at the same rate."[41] Therefore, the Gold Standard Fund was necessary to maintain the gold parity of the silver peso, while the Silver Certificate Reserve functioned to keep the convertibility of the silver certificate into silver domestically.[42]

However, as time went by the Gold Standard Fund was gradually appropriated as the lending or investment funds of the Philippine government, and the government required an enlargement of the Gold Standard Fund as prices rose before the outbreak of World War I. As for the Silver Certificate Reserve, the government had originally been required to deposit it in its Treasury in Manila in the form of silver. However, the rising prices of silver made it difficult for the government to do so. The change in regulations made it possible for the Philippine government to deposit those Silver Certificate reserves not required domestically in the form of U.S. dollars at Federal Reserve Banks in the United States. More and more of the Silver Certificate Reserve was transferred to U.S. banks, to a point at which 76 percent of the reserve was held in the United States.[43] Wright expressed his opinion that "the officials responsible did not realize at the time that their action changed the fundamental nature of the currency system."[44] At this juncture, when the Philippine currency system was at a crossroads with its nature transformed, the currency law was revised, the two currency reserves were combined into one, and an enormous confusion of the currency system ensued in the Philippines, with almost total depletion of the currency reserve in the United States.

A consistent claim in the Wright Report of 1921 was that the fundamental cause of the Philippine financial crisis after World War I was the deviation of its currency system from the original gold exchange standard. He stated that the crisis deepened because government and bank officials did not recognize their responsibility for currency control. To bolster his argument, Wright traced the passage of the changing role of the two currency reserves through the following four processes: (1) the depositing of a part of the Gold Standard Fund in private banks in Manila in 1908–1911; (2) the investment of half of the Gold Standard Fund provided for in an Act of 1911; (3) the investment of 80 percent of the Gold Standard Fund provided for in an Act of 1915; and (4) the opinion of the Judge Advocate General of the United States that the Silver Certificate Reserve could be deposited in Federal Reserve Banks in the United States—this last changing the nature of the silver certificate.[45] As Wright correctly pointed out, "[t]he original silver certificate was changed into a form of a government currency note (the present [T]reasury certificate), I believe it safe to say, without any realization that a fundamental change had been made in the currency system."[46] Wright explained how the revision of the Philippine currency law in May 1918 by Act No. 2776 provided that gold coin could be substituted for any portion of the Currency Reserve Fund by removing the former limit of 60 percent. The law also enacted that the combined fund should not be less in amount than the nominal value of the Treasury certificates in circulation, plus 15 percent of the money of the Philippine government in circulation.[47]

In his critique of the revision of the currency law in 1918 Wright focuses on two main points. First, the Gold Standard Fund and the Silver Certificate Reserve performed two distinct functions. To combine these two into one introduced ambiguity into the fundamental principle of the gold exchange standard. Second, the combined currency reserve was required to be merely no less than the nominal value of the [T]reasury certificates in circulation plus 15 percent of other Philippine government money. This latter provision represented a drastic reduction from the previous regulation of 1911 that the Gold Standard Fund should be equivalent to 35 percent of government money in circulation. In fact, by simple calculation, the revision of the currency law in 1918 cut the amount of the currency reserve by at least 20 percent, seriously undermining the foundation of the currency reserve.[48]

Needless to say, Wright's argument endorsed his own theory of an ideal currency system for the Philippines. For Wright, the Philippine currency system should never have deviated from the Gold Standard Act of 1903—a point of view espoused by Edwin W. Kemmerer as financial advisor to the Philippine Commission (see chapter 3). From the standpoint of Wright, the revision of the Philippine currency law of 1918 was nothing but a justification by fiat of the gradual deviation from the gold exchange standard that had been going on since before the outbreak of World War I.

Wright went on to consider the most recent revision of the Philippine currency law, Act No. 2939 of January 1921. In view of the "unfortunate experience through which the government in the meantime lost control of the larger part of the currency reserve fund in New York,"[49] the new act prohibited the deposit of any currency reserves in any branch of the Philippine National Bank in the United States.[50] Among other aspects of this act, the further revision of the minimum currency reserve concerned Wright. The new act reduced the minimum of the Currency Reserve Fund to 60 percent of the Treasury certificates in circulation, up to 120 million pesos (this amount should have been reached by 1921, due to the large actual circulation of Philippine National Bank notes; see Figure 1 in chapter 1). This further reduction of the minimum of the Currency Reserve Fund was understood by Wright as "a clear abandoning of the [T]reasury certificate as a certificate of deposit." Wright believed that, while the nominal designation of silver certificate had been changed to Treasury certificate by the revisions of currency laws in 1918 and 1921, the Philippine government lacked knowledge of the difference in character between the two currency instruments.[51]

Wright then summarized a memorandum that Edwin W. Kemmerer submitted to the Speaker of the House of Representatives in the Philippines in January 1918. Kemmerer, concerned with the deviation of the Philippine currency system from the original gold exchange standard and the combination of the two currency reserves, had recommended that the silver certificate should be replaced by a currency note supported by 100 percent reserve, and a gold standard fund of 25 percent should be maintained separately from the currency note fund.[52] However, Kemmerer's recommendations were totally ignored in the Philippine Legislature and Act No. 2776 was passed there to revise the currency law in May 1918, as has been discussed above. Wright, in support of Kemmerer's recommendations and as proposed remedies for the financial crisis, offered two suggestions: first, the introduction of a government currency note backed up by a reserve equivalent to 100 percent, and second, the restoration of the gold standard fund.[53]

The Francis Burton Harrison Papers at the U.S. Library of Congress contain numerous telegrams between Governor-General Harrison and the BIA during his term (1913–1921). These telegrams reveal the intensity of exchanges of information between the governor-general's office in Manila and the BIA in Washington regarding Philippine financial policy. They clearly betray that most of the decision-making initiative came from the BIA.[54] This is particularly true in matters concerning the two currency reserves; as discussed in chapter 5, from as early as 1914 the BIA had been considering measures to revise the currency law and to appropriate the Silver Certificate Reserve efficiently for the colonial administration.

Indeed, the consolidation of the two currency reserves in 1918 was the architecture that the BIA had aimed to construct for many years. Its principal advocate was Frank McIntyre, chief of the BIA since 1912. When the exhaustion of currency reserves in the New York agency of the Philippine National Bank was detected in Washington in 1919, McIntyre was temporarily absent from the BIA as U.S. Army assistant chief of staff, to which capacity he had been appointed in July 1918. However, due to the gravity of the Philippine crisis, he was re-engaged at the BIA in January 1920. Upon resuming his position as BIA chief, he thoroughly examined the various investigative reports and sent opinions to the U.S. secretary of war and to the governor-general of the Philippines. McIntyre's view was different from that of the Coates and Wright Reports of 1921. McIntyre argued that the legal basis of the Philippine National Bank as the depository of the Philippine government in the United States was adequate, and that the combination of the Gold Standard Fund and the Silver Certificate Reserve was an appropriate measure toward the transformation of the Philippine currency system.[55]

While Wright supported Kemmerer's recommendation to maintain the gold exchange standard, McIntyre was the adherent of another theorist, Charles A. Conant, who proposed a plan to manage the gold exchange standard under the single currency fund.[56] In this context—aside from the irregular exchange operations of currency reserves, as well as the mismanagement of the National Bank—there arose conflicting theoretical understandings of the role of the gold exchange standard system in the Philippine financial crisis in 1919–1922. Boasting that "the Bureau of Insular Affairs of this Department, whose experience with the Gold Exchange Standard is greater than that of any office in the United States,"[57] McIntyre candidly admitted the erroneous appropriation of currency reserves, but never considered how the unification of two reserves had compromised the currency system of the Philippines.

Ultimately, however, the BIA's longtime policy toward the Philippine currency system, as manifested in McIntyre's intransigence, was forced to change drastically under the grave financial crisis. When Leonard Wood assumed the governor-generalship in October 1921, he at once began a discussion by letter with U.S. Secretary of War John W. Weeks on measures to restore the Philippine currency system.[58] It was partly as a result of these discussions that the Philippine legislature in June 1922 passed Act No. 3058, again amending the currency law. This act had three major new provisions. First, the Currency Reserve Fund was abolished, and the Gold Standard Fund and the Treasury Certificate Fund were separately established. Second, the Treasury Certificate Fund was to be held only in the vaults of the Insular Treasury in Manila. Third, the Gold Standard Fund was deposited either in the vaults of the Insular Treasury in Manila or held by the member banks of the Federal Reserve System in the United States that were designated as the branches of the Philippine Treasury.[59] Here it should be noted that this 1922 revision of the currency law followed fairly closely the guidelines that the Coates and Wright Reports of 1921 had suggested. Two currency reserve funds were separately established, and depositing currency reserves at the New York agency of the Philippine National Bank was prohibited. The Philippine Treasury at last gained strength in its monetary control, under which the currency system was based on the gold exchange standard, as Edwin W. Kemmerer had recommended.

**THE ABOLITION OF THE BOARD OF CONTROL**

The Philippine government policy to reconstruct the currency system and the Philippine National Bank under Governor-General Wood did not stop at the amendment of the currency law and the arrest of the bank officials. As argued by the Coates Report of 1921, the financial crisis of 1919–1922 was one of the gravest debacles of the American colonial state in the Philippines—one in which numerous government and bank officials were directly or indirectly involved, both in the United States and in the Philippines. The BIA's involvement, which was never openly discussed in public in either the United States or the Philippines, should particularly be noted here. However, Governor-General Wood concentrated on reconstructing the National Bank in order to free it from graft and corruption among banking officials and Filipino politicians. For this purpose, Wood considered it imperative to abolish the Board of Control, a Philippine institution by which the leading Filipino politicians influenced the officials of the National Bank.

During the Harrison administration, a series of government-owned corporations were established. Besides the Philippine National Bank (a semi-governmental institution), these included the National Development Company, the National Coal Company, and the National Cement Company. The Manila Railroad Company, originally a private corporation, was also purchased by the Philippine government. In 1918, the Philippine legislature passed an act to create a committee with authority to control the voting stock of these corporations. This committee of three (later known as the Board of Control) was composed of the governor-general and the presiding officers of the Senate and the House. Under Harrison's Filipinization policy, Sergio Osmeña as House speaker and Manuel L. Quezon as Senate president strengthened their influence on these government corporations by their powers at the Board of Control.[60]

As discussed in chapter 4, the formal nomination of the committee of three as the "Board of Control" first appeared in the revised charter of the Philippine National Bank of 1921 (Act No. 2938).[61] As for the Manila Railroad Company, Act No. 2923 of March 1920 granted its voting power to the committee of the governor-general, the president of the Senate, and the speaker of the House. In March 1923, by Act No. 3066, the powers of the Bureau of Audits were reduced with reference to jurisdiction over the accounts of government corporations. Under this act, the insular auditor, with the approval of the Board of Control, was authorized to appoint a representative in a corporation in which the government owned the majority of stock.[62]

Thus, even under the Wood regime, the power of the Board of Control over the government corporations continuously expanded, despite Governor-General Wood's intentions. Before assuming the governor-generalship, as chairman of the Wood-Forbes Mission he had recommended the withdrawal of the Philippine government from the business corporations established under the Harrison administration.[63] In his inaugural address and message to the Philippine legislature in December 1921, Wood stated: "... the government should, as soon as possible and as far as possible, get out of business and keep out. This is, of course, easy to say, but hard to do under the commitments already made and it can only be successfully accomplished with your earnest cooperation."[64]

The road toward reform and reconstruction of the government corporations, like that of the Philippine National Bank, was not easy. As quickly became evident, the Wood policy toward the Philippines was characterized by draconian measures against the Filipinization that had been promoted by Governor-General Harrison, antagonizing the Filipino elites who had expanded their vested interests in political and business circles. Predictably, Wood and the Philippine legislature engaged in several confrontations, culminating in a joint resolution by the two houses of the Philippine legislature in October 1923 demanding Wood's recall.[65] Despite resistance from Filipino leaders, however, Wood tried hard to secure the government's withdrawal from business activities. Towards this end, Wood aimed primarily at the abolition of the Board of Control, which continued to exercise enormous power over the government corporations as well as over the National Bank. To realize this challenging reform, Wood recognized the importance of blocking the intervention of Filipino political leaders. The following letter from Wood to U.S. Secretary of War John W. Weeks candidly expressed his difficult position:

> The Board of Control, consisting of the Governor-General, the President of the Senate, and the Speaker of the House, knew too little of the condition of the [National] Bank. This condition had existed for a long time. The Board of Directors, so far as I could judge, had tolerated and even encouraged by their own example unsound business methods, and conditions which the Coates report had long before predicted had developed. In a word, the situation was chaotic, the policy unsound, and adequate government supervision lacking. . . .
>
> Neither Manager or [sic] Directors are heavy stockholders and they have little at stake other than their personal reputations; and as you can see, it has been necessary to exercise strong control, not only to secure a thoroughly conservative conduct of affairs but to avoid getting the Government deeper and deeper into business. . . .
>
> Between you and me, the Board of Control constituted as above indicated— the Governor-General, President of the Senate and Speaker of the House—is not fair to the Governor-General, for after all whatever goes rightly or wrongly in the Philippines is charged in large measure either to his credit or discredit, and to place the Governor-General responsible to the home government and public opinion where he is one in a board of three, the other two members being the political heads of the two houses of the Legislature with little responsibility to public opinion here and absolutely none to public opinion in the United States, is to place him in a position greatly to his disadvantage. . . .[66]

The reply from Secretary Weeks was unequivocal:

> I agree with you that the Board of Control, constituted as at present, is unfair to the Governor-General. I agree fully that all of the other Acts which require the approval of the presiding officers of the two houses before an executive act can be performed are unwise and are probably in violation of the organic act. I would suggest that you attempt to have provisions of this nature omitted from future appropriation and other acts....[67]

During the period 1922–1926, Governor-General Wood tried in vain to negotiate with Quezon and Osmeña, his partners on the Board of Control, for the reform of the government corporations and the National Bank in various ways.[68] Finally, on 9 November 1926, Wood issued Executive Order No. 37, abolishing the Board of Control mandatorily:

> Office of the Governor General
> of the Philippine Islands,
> Manila, November 9, 1926.
>
> Whereas it is held in an opinion of the Judge Advocate General of the United States Army, confirmed by an opinion of the Attorney General of the United States, received at the office of the executive November 7, 1926, that the provisions of the statutes passed by the Philippine Legislature creating a "board of control" or "committee" and enumerating the duties and powers thereof, with respect to certain corporations in which the insular government is the owner of stock, are nullities; that the remaining portions of said statutes are valid; that the duties imposed by said statutes upon said board or committee are executive in their nature and subject to the provisions of the organic act relating to the executive functions that said executive duties and powers may be performed as in other cases not specifically provided for by law.
>
> Now, therefore, acting under authority of said opinion, the duties and powers heretofore exercised by said "board of control" or "committee" shall, from and after this date, be exercised solely by the Governor General pursuant to the executive power vested in him by the organic act.
>
> Leonard Wood,
> Governor General.

This mandatory order of Governor-General Wood stirred resentment and confrontation among members of the Philippine legislature as well as among top officials of the government corporations and the National Bank. The Filipino political and business elites simply could not accept the abolition of the Board of Control. On 29 November 1926, acting as members of the Board of Control as if it still existed, the Senate president and the House speaker asked the governor-general to convene the Board to decide upon the manner in which the stock held by the government in the National Coal Company should be voted. A special meeting of the stockholders of the National Coal Company was called on 6 December 1926 for the purpose of electing directors. Both presiding officers of the two houses at the legislature attended, but Wood merely sent a representative. In this situation, the chair of the meeting recognized the two presiding officers of the legislature in their capacity as majority members of the voting committee, and new directors of the corporation were elected accordingly. Governor-General Wood contested this decision and filed a suit against the new directors.[69]

Complications also arose at the board meeting of the Philippine National Bank. In December 1926, one of its directors submitted a petition signed by the governor-general that three of its nine board members should be removed. In January 1927, a special meeting of the stockholders was called. The meeting was attended by twenty-six private stockholders as the owners of 94 shares of the Bank and the governor-general representing the government, which owned 97,332 shares of stocks. The Senate president and the House speaker failed to attend the meeting, and contented themselves with sending a letter of protest against the meeting on the ground that the governor-general had no right to represent the Philippine government in relation to the exercise of the voting power of its stock in the Bank. The president of the Bank, as chairman of the meeting, ruled that he could not recognize the right of the governor-general to vote the government stock without the consent of the presiding officers of both houses of the legislature, and that a quorum was present. Thus, he declared the meeting adjourned. However, Wood and twenty stockholders remained and elected a chairman pro tempore and a secretary pro tempore. This group, declaring itself the bonafide board of directors of the Philippine National Bank, removed three directors and elected three new directors. A few days later, at a regular meeting of the board of directors, the president of the Bank refused to recognize the three new directors, and allowed the removed directors to exercise their votes. Wood protested this action and filed a suit against the three removed directors of the Bank.[70]

These two lawsuits—the "National Coal Company case" (The Government of the Philippine Islands vs. Milton E. Springer et al., No. 26979) and the "National Bank case" (The Government of the Philippine Islands vs. Gregorio Agoncillo et al., No. 27225)—were decided in favor of Governor-General Wood by the Philippine Supreme Court on 1 April 1927. In the National Coal Company case, the court stated: "[w]e have no hesitancy in concluding that so much of section 4 of Act 2705, as amended by section 2 of Act 2822, as purports to vest the voting power of the government-owned stock in the National Coal Company in the President of the Senate and the Speaker of the House of Representatives, is unconstitutional and void."[71] In the National Bank case, the court stated that "the original statute vested the voting power of the stock owned by the Government in the bank exclusively in the Governor-General, which was legal, while the amendments found invalid, without express repeal, attempted to transfer this power to an illegally constituted Board of Control."[72] Thus, the governor-general's office gained sweeping victories at the Philippine Supreme Court. These decisions were reaffirmed in May 1928, when appeals from Manuel Quezon and other Filipino elites were rejected.[73]

In previous literature, the Philippine financial crisis of 1919–1922 has focused on the consequences of the overacceleration or failure of the Filipinization of the political system and government corporations under the Harrison regime. This perspective can be understood as a result of the deliberate characterization of the crisis as "the corruption scandal of the Philippine National Bank." This view stresses the Bank's appropriation of large amounts of the currency reserve funds that were deposited at its New York agency; and indeed, given their corrupt relationships, the Filipino political and business elites saw to it that the loan business of the National Bank was fully committed to the major export sectors. In following this argument, it is convenient to find roots of the Philippine crises in the incompetency of the Filipino elites who autonomously controlled the political, administrative, and banking systems in the Philippines due to rapid "Filipinization." It could be claimed, therefore, that the Philippine political and administrative systems and other economic institutions were emboldened by the continuing effect of rapid Filipinization under the Harrison administration.

However, after examination of relevant documents in the National Archives, the Library of Congress, and various university libraries in the

United States, it becomes clear that this prevailing interpretation of the Philippine financial crisis of 1919–1922 reflects a bias that masks the true picture of this complicated issue. The Philippine financial crisis could not have been precipitated solely by the corrupt and privileged triangular relationships among the National Bank, the Philippine legislature, and the landowners and entrepreneurs in export business sectors. It can no longer be doubted that the appropriation of the currency reserves for the massive loan business of the National Bank was engineered by the interests active in this corrupted structure for their own advantage.

In this connection it is vitally important to emphasize that the crucial factor which made possible the unparalleled appropriation of currency funds for the extravagant loan business of the Bank was the revision of the currency law of 1918. This law was implemented with an inadequate understanding of the fundamental principle of the gold exchange standard. The merger of the Gold Standard Fund and the Silver Certificate Reserve into the Currency Reserve Fund undermined this principle, and the authorization of the New York agency of the Philippine National Bank as depository was in violation of the U.S. Federal Reserve Act. This consolidation plan, however, had been conceived and discussed at the BIA since the early 1910s. The BIA and the governor-general's office had prepared for its implementation through numerous telegrams and letters over many years. A bill for the revision of the currency law was drafted under the initiative of the BIA and it was submitted to and passed by the Philippine legislature in response to the BIA's explicit encouragement.

Thus, if we consider that one of the main causes of the financial crisis of 1919–1922 was corruption among Filipino elites in regard to National Bank business, we must recognize an equally serious cause in the interference with the currency policy by the BIA—a policy that took the strong initiative of combining the two currency reserves in flagrant disregard of the fundamental principle of the gold exchange standard. In this context, it is clear that the financial crisis of 1919–1922 was the most severe debacle that shook the bedrock of the American colonial state in the Philippines. Parties responsible for this debacle included the BIA, the governor-general's office, the Philippine Treasury, the Philippine legislature, the Philippine National Bank, and Filipino landowners and entrepreneurs in the major export sectors.

# CONCLUSION

THIS BOOK HAS SOUGHT to paint the overarching historical picture of the Philippine financial crisis of 1919–1922 that shook the foundations of the American colonial state. It has illustrated clearly that the series of events referred to as "the corruption scandal of the Philippine National Bank" in most previous literature should instead be understood as "the Philippine financial crisis." In other words, this book has argued that the focus on corruption at the National Bank is merely colonial discourse masking the true picture of the devastating financial crisis that overtook the Philippines after World War I. Furthermore, the analysis has exposed the mechanisms and means by which this colonial discourse was created and how this interpretation of the crisis was imposed on Philippine society. However, the discussion was not limited to economic history; indeed, it was necessary to engage with scholarship on the Philippine administration and politics of the time. Such an approach reveals the linkages among banking, the currency system, Philippine politics, and the U.S. colonial administration.

If we regard the mismanagement of the Philippine National Bank as one of two major causes of the financial crisis of 1919–1922, we must recognize that the failure of currency policy—manifested in the ill-advised consolidation of the two currency reserves, with its flagrant disregard for the fundamental principles of the gold exchange standard—is the other major cause.

While the mismanagement of the National Bank was largely brought about by corruption among banking officials, the failure of the currency arose from the policy largely promoted by the Bureau of Insular Affairs (BIA) in Washington, and which was supervised in a slipshod manner by the Philippine Treasury during 1918–1919. If the whole truth of the Philippine financial crisis had been exposed to public scrutiny at the time, government officials in both the Philippines and the United States would have had to admit responsibility along with the accused National Bank officials and politicians. Clearly, this would have given the Philippine legislature opportunity to seriously undermine the U.S. administration and would have gravely damaged the foundation of the U.S. colonial system.

There can be little doubt that, knowing the gravity of the situation, the U.S. government, and in particular the BIA, masked the fatal flaw in Philippine currency policy, thus permitting the American administrators to escape accountability. Governor-General Harrison resigned, ostensibly for overaccelerating his Filipinization policy, but neither he nor any other American administrator was openly accused of mishandling the currency reserves of the Philippine Treasury. From the American point of view it was expedient to characterize the crisis as merely a corruption "scandal," shifting all responsibility to Filipino banking officials who were accused of incompetence in modern banking business and of collusion with political and business leaders.

As in other colonial systems, the formation of the American colonial state in the Philippines generated various discourses that served as common or prevailing social notions intended to legitimize the mastery of the United States over Philippine society. In order to establish colonial rule, such discourses are designed to become widely accepted as justifications of colonial policies, thus facilitating many complicated tasks necessary for the formation and establishment of an advantageous power structure beyond the binary of ruler and ruled. Thus, "the corruption scandal of the Philippine National Bank" is best understood in terms of such a colonial discourse.

If we understand colonies as politico-economic entities built to serve colonial masters, it becomes clear that these kinds of colonial discourse function as ideological pillars supporting the colonial administration. Such discourse settles deep in the consciousness of a colonial society and exercises a powerful influence on what the colonized people think, feel, and do. Colonial discourse allows hegemonic power to change the form of a colonized society by imposing myth-like systems of thought that transform and dissolve the collective social identity of the subject people. These processes obstruct any momentum the colonized might achieve on their own to "deconstruct" the discourse. The ideological operations generated by colonial discourse lead to its entrenchment in the colonized society, playing a crucial role in establishing the political, administrative, and economic realities most advantageous for the colonizer.

It is important to emphasize here the impact of the financial crisis on the formation of the American colonial state in the Philippines. Previous studies on Philippine history during the colonial period have tended to see several distinct sub-periods, rather than seeking to describe one overarching "American colonial period." Usually, the period is divided in accordance with the changes in the political administration. However convenient this scheme may be, it has proven inadequate for historians interested in the socioeconomic aspects of Philippine society under the American colonial regime.

Some studies have been written on the assumption that from the onset of the U.S. occupation, American influences penetrated consistently and decisively into the military, political, economic, and cultural spheres of the Philippine Islands, with the collaboration of Filipino elites and despite the massive resistance of the Filipino populace. Based on a study of the banking and currency system, this study contests that view and argues that the American colonial foundation in the Philippines was fragile before World War I, and that it was during the 1920s, beginning with the financial crisis, that the colonial regime took firm root.

In fact, it was due to the weak foundation of the colonial state that the financial crisis occurred in the Philippines after World War I; and the full strength of the American colonial foundation in the Philippines grew directly from the process of reconstructing the administrative and financial pillars of the colony during the 1920s. In this context, we might argue that the American colonial period could be divided into two parts: the first from 1898 to World War I, and the second from 1918 to 1941. (Philippine independence, prepared for since 1935, was interrupted by the Japanese occupation of 1942–1945. Independence came in 1946.) A number of facts support the adequacy of this two-period division, exemplifying in particular the character of the second period.

First, in the development of trade relations, two tariff laws were enacted in 1909 and 1913 establishing a "free trade" partnership between the

Philippines and the United States—a relationship greatly enhanced by the opening of the Panama Canal in 1914, which drastically shortened the ocean route from the eastern ports of the United States to the Pacific. These developments weakened the power of the British economic sphere which had been predominant in Asia. After World War I, the United States gained the paramount position in trade relationship with the Philippines, and a corresponding change occurred in banking. For decades, the Philippine financial system had been closely tied to the British financial network in Asia, but with the establishment of the Philippine National Bank in 1916 the United States was able to construct a Philippine financial system directly linked with its own banking regime.

Second, it was from the early 1920s that the budget of the Philippine government became professionally supervised under a consolidated accounting system. We learn this by examining the fiscal revenues and expenditures of the Philippine government listed in the annual reports of the governor-general. The Philippines was the first American colony in Asia, so the United States as the colonial master had to establish a budgetary system suited for it. As is widely known, the U.S. Congress approved the colonial status of the Philippines on the condition that the United States would grant independence to the country in the future. As a result, although the United States continued to allocate U.S. army and navy expenditures to the Philippines, it offered hardly any economic assistance to the Philippine government. This condition inevitably led to fiscal constraint in the Philippine government.

After the military pacification of the Philippine Islands, United States policy set about reshaping Philippine society as a "home base" for the American sphere of influence in Asia. Improvement and construction of economic and social infrastructure in the Philippine islands was very much needed, yet the Philippine government was expected to carry the entire expense. Under these circumstances, the Philippine government faced chronic and serious financial problems and came to tide over difficulties by appropriating currency reserves. In this way the currency reserves were used as investment funds not only for public works but also for processing primary commodities for export. It was this latter activity, as we have seen, that led to the mismanagement of the Philippine National Bank in 1918–1919.

Third, the United States sought to pave the way for the autonomy of the Philippine government under its declared mission of benevolent assimilation.

From the start of the colonization, the U.S. Philippine Commission functioned as the political, administrative, and legislative body of the insular government, endeavoring to establish close relationships with the Filipino elites who had served among the leaders of the Philippine Revolution. American administrators patronized and nurtured these elites as possible pro-American leaders who might promote the autonomy of the Philippines under American tutelage. This was not an easy task, however.

The Philippine legislature was established as a bicameral legislative body in 1916. Rivalries among leading politicians, such as Sergio Osmeña and Manuel L. Quezon, emerged within the Nacionalista Party. It was in the early 1920s that Quezon finally assumed the sole leadership in Philippine politics under American rule. Quezon was a brilliant tactical politician. On the one hand he understood what the United States aimed for as the colonial master in the Philippines, and on the other he insidiously practiced "colonial democracy," accommodating various demands of Philippine nationalists. The leadership shift from Osmeña to Quezon in the early 1920s is perhaps the most significant event in Philippine political history. It inaugurated a new era in Philippine politics: colonial "nationalism" was officially endorsed under American tutelage, subtly transforming the true nationalism whose origin should have been traced back to the Philippine Revolution at the turn of the century.

Fourth, in relation to the financial turbulence of the American colonial state in the Philippines during World War I, the role of the BIA in Washington must be understood. The BIA functioned as the U.S. outpost for supervising the Philippines (and other dependent territories) by linking overseas territories with the U.S. War Department. The BIA had played an especially important role in Philippine currency management in the absence of a central bank vested with the authority to control and govern the financial and monetary system of the country. In fact, the BIA was in constant communication with the governor-general's office in Manila about the management of the currency reserves throughout the first decade of the century.

However, following the U.S. declaration of war against Germany in April 1917, the BIA's commitment in the Philippines was greatly reduced. Much of the BIA staff was transferred to other sections of the U.S. War Department, which posed a serious problem for the Philippines. It was particularly so when BIA Chief Frank McIntyre, who had always taken a personal interest in the Philippine economy, was appointed to the U.S. Army as assistant chief of staff and was subsequently out of the BIA office from July 1918 to December 1919. He knew more than anyone in Washington about Philippine legal questions and financial or currency matters. Perhaps it was not merely a coincidence that the large-scale mismanagement of currency reserves happened at the New York agency of the Philippine National Bank during McIntyre's absence.

Thus, U.S. participation in World War I had an indirect effect on American governance in the Philippines by weakening the function of the BIA as the supervising and administrative organ of the colony. Moreover, the American colonial system in the Philippines had not yet fully asserted itself when the United States joined the war. This global historical background cannot be denied. Yet, although various financial crises occurred in Southeast Asia in the wake of World War I, the Philippine crisis was of a particularly devastating order, shaking the entire political, administrative, and economic system of the colony. Should we then understand the crisis as a single and peculiar phenomenon in the Philippines?

James C. Ingram's study of Thai economic history and Yasuo Gonjo's book on the Banque de l'Indochine, as discussed in the introduction, suggest answers to this question. Ingram shows that under the gold exchange standard Thailand experienced a serious financial crisis in 1919–1922, while Gonjo shows that French Indochina experienced difficulty sustaining the silver standard during the same period. In both cases the financial policies could not cope with the violent fluctuations of export prices during and after World War I. Clearly, the same was true of the Philippine financial crisis after the war; as has been extensively argued, it was precipitated by a sharp drop in export prices, leading exporters and producers of primary commodities to fall into debt after borrowing recklessly from the Philippine National Bank. Considering the various financial situations in Southeast Asia before and after World War I in this way, we can generalize that the skyrocketing export prices of primary commodities during World War I and their crashes after the war had an enormous impact on currency systems in Southeast Asian countries. However, it is important to note that what exacerbated the ultimate financial crisis in the Philippines was the mishandling of currency reserves by the Philippine Treasury.

In addition, similarities between the development of an export economy and a modern banking system in the Philippines and those of other Southeast Asian countries may be noted. Gonjo describes how the

Banque de l'Indochine extended loans to Vietnamese landowners. Most of these loans were secured by crop yields ("crop loans") until the bank started offering loans with land properties as collateral. Similarly, in the agricultural loan business of the Philippine National Bank, priority was given to major landowners engaged in the production of export crops.

The origin of crop loans can be traced to the late nineteenth century, when export-oriented agriculture developed in Southeast Asia. Commercial agency houses played a crucial role by providing advances to producers in the absence of lending institutions. It was an appropriate form of credit at a time when private landownership was not legally established. Then, in the Philippines especially, interlocking relationships among company directors and bank officials (in this case the Philippine National Bank) introduced nepotism and "cronyism" into the agricultural and industrial loan business. Although such practices were (and are) criticized as improper in modern banking, they can be seen as merely continuing commercial practices that were widely accepted in indigenous or traditional lending practices. In any event, it was this "cronyism" or nepotism that the Philippine National Bank incorporated into its business practice. Perhaps it was because the Bank incorporated these pre-modern lending practices that it came to dominate the banking system of the Philippines. It is important to understand this seemingly contradictory phenomenon of the Bank's business practice as one of its distinctive features in the context of Philippine economic history.

After studying the Philippine financial crisis of 1919–1922, it is possible to open a new perspective on Southeast Asian economic history, recognizing a particular watershed in the Philippines during World War I. There is a tendency to treat the Philippines as an exception, a special case among Southeast Asian countries for its distinct historical experience; it sometimes seems that the Philippines is considered part of Southeast Asia merely by its geographical location. However, looking at Southeast Asian economic history from a Philippine perspective, does a new historical pattern come to light?

In considering the expansion of export economies for primary commodities in Southeast Asian economies from the 1870s to the outbreak of World War II, parallels among the Philippines and other Southeast Asian countries are immediately apparent. At the turn of the twentieth century, as colonial power in the Philippines went from Spain to the United States, the Philippine economy was still within the British-led Asian economic network, like other

Southeast Asian countries before World War I. After the war, however, the Philippine economy was rapidly incorporated into the U.S. economic sphere in Asia and cut its ties to the British-led trade network in Asia. As the Philippines' economic relationship with the United States grew more intimate, its ties with neighboring countries in Southeast Asia weakened. This is the major reason why the development of the Philippine economy took a different path from that of other Southeast Asian economies during the first half of the twentieth century.

Until World War II most Southeast Asian countries remained under the influence of the British economic sphere in Asia and were only loosely connected with the U.S. economy. However, it is noteworthy that beginning in the 1920s the United States became a major importer of tin and rubber from British Malaya and the Dutch East Indies, reinforcing the economic process that led to U.S. trade domination of the Asia-Pacific area by the onset of World War II. This process can also be understood as a gradual shift of the trade relationships among the Southeast Asian countries themselves from the British economic sphere to a distinct Asia-Pacific sphere. In this context, the Philippines appears as the forerunner: the first Southeast Asian country to be integrated into the American economic sphere. From this perspective the Philippines is perhaps not an exceptional case in Southeast Asia, but rather predicts the eventual experience of other Southeast Asian countries. By exploring the financial history of the Philippines under American rule, this book has endeavored to reposition the Philippines in Southeast Asian history.

# NOTES

## INTRODUCTION: UNDERSTANDING THE PHILIPPINE FINANCIAL CRISIS 1919–1922

1. Harrison & Quezon to Yeater (7 Apr. 1919), U.S. National Archives, Record Group 350, Records of Bureau of Insular Affairs (hereafter cited as BIA), 6769-after 207. A copy of the original document appears among the photos in this book.
2. Willis to Harrison (17 Apr. 1919), BIA 6769-245-A; Churchill 1983, 13–17; Golay 1997, 222–23; McCoy 2009, 271.
3. Forerunners of the BIA included the Division of Customs and Insular Affairs (DCIA), created in December 1898 and reorganized as the Division of Insular Affairs (DIA) in December 1900. Then, in July 1902, under the Philippine Autonomy Act, this agency was formally renamed the Bureau of Insular Affairs. For a detailed study, see Cruz 1974)
4. Often called the "New York branch." Its official name was the "New York agency."
5. What follows summarizes research based on an examination of numerous telegrams and letters exchanged among U.S. and Philippine government officials, mainly between the governor-general's office in Manila and the BIA in Washington, from March to October 1919. See BIA 6769-201 to 6769-336. See also Willis to Harrison (14 Aug. 1920), BIA 6769-584-A.
6. For further observations on this aspect of the crisis, see Golay 1997, 217–21.
7. Luthringer 1934, 116.
8. Ibid., 117.
9. Ibid.
10. For public disclosure of the financial crisis and the debacle of the Philippine National Bank, see: "The Truth about the Financial Situation in the Philippine Islands," *Manila Times* (6 Mar. 1921); "Bank's Millions Dissipated," *Manila Daily Bulletin* (17 Aug. 1923); "Philippine National Bank Conditions Bared by Wood Message: Losses of More Than 72 Million Pesos Incurred," *Manila Times* (19 Aug. 1923); "The Governor's Message on the Philippine National Bank," *Philippine Herald* (19 Aug. 1923); "No More Reports on Bank to Be Issued: The Less Said About It the Better, Says Wood," *Manila Times* (24 Aug. 1923);"Present is Favorable

Time for Starting New Currency Says Wright," *Manila Times* (23 Dec. 1923). See also "An Orgy of Mismanagement: The Story of the Philippine National Bank," *Far Eastern Review* (Sept. 1923), 584–85, 615–20, BIA 6769-A-80.

11  Kalaw 1965, chap. 16; Agoncillo and Guerrero 1973, 354–59.
12  Onorato 1968, chap. 4; for a revised version, see also Onorato 1988, chap. 3.
13  Stanley 1974, see particularly chaps. 8, 9, and 10.
14  Luthringer 1934, see particularly chaps. 6 and 7.
15  For studies of U.S. colonial expansion with particular reference to the Philippines, see Go and Foster (2003), and McCoy and Scarano (2009). For a special study of the Philippines as the first modern surveillance state, see McCoy (2009), which sheds light on the elusive role of scandals as a means of legitimizing the colonial regime. For an illuminating discussion of colonialism in the Philippines, tracing its origin to the Spanish occupation late in the eighteenth century, see Blanco (2009), Introduction and chap. 1.
16  Thailand preserved a quasi-independence on the strict requirement that it maintained a stable, readily convertible currency for trade. In this respect it was no different from the formal colonies.
17  For a discussion of British "colonial banks" in Asia, such as the Hongkong and Shanghai Banking Corporation, the Chartered Bank of India, Australia and China, and Oriental Banking, see Hamashita 1990, 157–60, 173, and Ishii 1979. For French Indochina's Banque de l'Indochine, see Gonjo 1985, 13–17.
18  Allen and Donnithorne 1968b, 23, 181–94.
19  Ibid., 200–209.
20  Brown 1988, chap. 4.
21  Legarda 1999, part 2.
22  "Agricultural Bank of the Philippine Government" was the name registered under the law, although the bank was often called the "Agricultural Bank of the Philippine Islands" or simply the "Agricultural Bank."
23  Legarda 1999, 288–89. See also Allen and Donnithorne 1968a, chaps. 6 and 12; Allen and Donnithorne 1968b, chaps. 10 and 11. For major works on the Philippine business history, see Yoshihara 1984.
24  Spalding 1918, 116–18, 209–10, 228, 239–40; Legarda 1999, 274–75.
25  For a brief study of the process by which the silver standard changed to the gold exchange standard in Asian countries, see Eng 1993. For relevant studies of the financial history of the Dutch East Indies, see: Laanen 1980; Laanen 1990, 244–66; Klein 1990, 419–53; Eng 1996, vii–xxvi.
26  Yanaihara 1963, 490. The classic study of the gold exchange standard in India is Keynes 1924.
27  For a contemporary study of the gold exchange standard in the early twentieth century, see Hanna et al. 1903 and Hanna et al. 1904.
28  Kemmerer 1916; Spalding 1918.
29  For a recent balanced historical overview of the Philippine currency system and

Notes to Introduction    197

the creation of the Central Bank after World War II, see Valdepeñas 2003, 14–91. Other recent studies of currencies in the Philippines in the nineteenth and early twentieth centuries include Diokno (2000), Wolters (2001) and Wolters (2007). For a contemporary Philippine study of the American period, see Hernandez 1937. Regarding the post-World War II Philippine currency board, see Treadgold 2003. For the political economy of Philippine banking after independence, particularly with regard to the private banks, see Hutchcroft 1998. For details on the establishment of the Philippine Central Bank after World War II, see Cullather 1992.

30  For a discussion of the changing structure of Southeast Asian economies after World War I, see Foster 2010, chap. 2.
31  Ingram 1971, 152–55. For a discussion on the gold exchange standard in Thailand, see also Brown 1979, 381–99.
32  Gonjo 1985, 256–66. For a study of banking and the currency system in Southeast Asia during the Japanese occupation, see Banyai 1974.
33  For a detailed discussion of the Philippine export economy, see Doeppers 1984, chaps. 1–2.
34  For a detailed discussion of intra-Asian trade, see Sugihara 1996.
35  For major studies of Southeast Asian economic history, see: Tate 1979; Dixon 1991; Elson 1992, 131–95; R. A. Brown 1994; Ian Brown 1997; Lindblad 1998. For a detailed discussion of the Philippine export economy, see Doeppers 1984, chaps. 1–2.
36  Adas 1974. See also R. A. Brown 1993, 254–87.
37  Suehiro 1989, chaps. 2–4; Cushman 1991; Butcher and Dick 1993. For the translation of earlier works on overseas Chinese, see Hicks 1993. This is a compilation of two studies; one was conducted by the Bank of Taiwan in 1910s and the other was published by the Taiwan Governor-General's Office in 1940s.
38  Huff 1989, 161–89.
39  Allen and Donnithorne 1968b, chaps. 10 and 11; Hamashita 1990, chap. 5. For a study of the overseas Chinese network in Southeast Asian economies from the end of the nineteenth century to the 1930s, see Sugihara 1996.
40  Gonjo 1985, chap. 6.
41  For a classic study of Western agency houses, see Greenberg 1951. On the activities of agency houses in nineteenth-century Philippines, see Legarda 1999, part 3. For the continuity between modern banking business and earlier small lending business or local commerce, see: Fukuda 1995, chap. 5; Hicks 1993, 65–106, 295–314. Major studies of the economic activities of overseas Chinese in the Philippines include Wickberg 1965b and Wong 1999.
42  Paredes 1989a.
43  For studies on "knowledge and power" and "orientalism," see Foucault 1990, Said 1979, 1993, and Cohen 1984. For discussions of the American empire and colonial discourse, see Ileto 1999, Quibuyen 1999, Rafael 2000, Salman 2001, Shaw

and Francia 2002, Kramer 2006, Go 2008, McCoy and Scarano 2009, part 4, and Tyrrell 2009. Rafael (2008) provides a useful review of recent directions in Philippine studies in the United States.

## PART I. OVERVIEW
## CHAPTER 1: THE PHILIPPINE CURRENCY SYSTEM UNDER U.S. RULE

[1] Rosenberg 2003, 12.
[2] Ibid., 5.
[3] Ibid., 11; see also 15, 24–25. In the Philippines, Charles A. Conant played an instrumental role in the adoption of the gold exchange standard, while Edwin W. Kemmerer directed the currency reform in the Philippines during 1903–1906. Kemmerer had been a student of Jeremiah Jenks at Cornell University. Both Conant and Jenks worked for the U.S. Commission on International Exchange; Conant was a leading proponent of the passage of the Gold Standard Act. Kemmerer began his career as financial adviser in the Philippines, later becoming a well-known financial adviser in more than a dozen countries.
[4] Elliot 1968, 96–126; Hayden 1945, 166–67; Stanley 1974, 54–55, 63.
[5] Kemmerer 1916, 249–51.
[6] Ibid., 252. For some details on the Philippine currency system from the end of the nineteenth century to the early twentieth century, see: Stanley 1974, 92–96; Diokno 2000; Wolters 2001, 511–38.
[7] Forbes 1928, vol. I, 241.
[8] Ibid., vol. I, 241–42; Golay 1997, 112. The official aid to the Philippines that the U.S. Congress approved from 1898 to 1935 (when the Commonwealth government was established) was only 3 million dollars for disaster relief assistance. For details of the Philippine government revenues from 1907 to 1920, see Golay 1984, 231–60.
[9] Reyes 1967, 174–75.
[10] Conant 1902, 45.
[11] Kemmerer 1916, 277–81; Conant 1902, 45–46.
[12] Kemmerer 1916, 281–98.
[13] This plan was repeatedly proposed during the U.S. military rule of the Philippines during 1898–1901. For details see: Harden 1898, 10; Edwards 1900, 50–63.
[14] Kemmerer 1916, 300; Conant 1902, 47; Reyes 1967, 176.
[15] Kemmerer 1916, 298–301.
[16] Kemmerer 1916, 301–6; Conant 1902, 48.
[17] United States, War Department 1901, pt. 1, 99–102; Kemmerer 1916, 307–8; Conant 1902, 49–92; Reyes 1969, 176.
[18] Rosenberg 1985, 176–83; "Charles Arthur Conant," *Dictionary of American Biography* (1930), vol. IV, 334–35; Rothbard 2002, 210–16.
[19] Conant 1901; Willis 1970, 301–2; Cruz 1974, 73; Parrini 1993, 52.
[20] Kemmerer 1916, 308–9; Reyes 1967, 177–78; Willis 1970, 303. For details of

the discussion on Philippine currency reform in the U.S. Senate Committee in February–March 1902, see United States, Senate 1902a, 1902b.
21 Regarding the currency system, the Philippine Organic Act gave the authority to the Philippine government to issue only subsidiary silver coins. Kemmerer 1916, 309; Reyes 1969, 178.
22 Kemmerer 1916, 309, 311–13; Reyes 1969, 178–79; Hanna, Conant, and Jenks 1904, 283–94; Kemmerer 1905a, 585–609.
23 Public Law No. 137 1903, 952–53.
24 Cruz 1974, 74; Shafer 1964, 88; Legarda 1976, 55; Licuanan 1985, chap. X; Rothbard 2002, 221–24.
25 Spalding 1918, 6–14; Matsuoka 1936, 95–102, 152–81; Kemmerer 1905b, 302–4; Giesecke 1987, 91–99; Rothbard 2002, 208–9.
26 Act No. 938 (1903), 797–99.
27 The Chief of the Division of the Currency was required to submit the annual report to the Treasurer of the Philippine Islands under the Gold Standard Act. The first annual report of the Philippine Treasurer was published in 1904 (Philippine Islands, Bureau of Treasury [1904]). Edwin W. Kemmerer served as the first chief of the Division of the Currency, retaining this position until February 1906. See Kemmerer 1916, 318.
28 No actual exchange between Philippine currency and U.S. gold coin or gold bars ever occurred. Kemmerer 1916, 322; Luthringer 1934, 6.
29 Luthringer 1934, 28–34.
30 Ibid., 16–17; Philippine Islands, Bureau of the Treasury 1910, 5, 25.
31 Act No. 2067 (1911), 1316.
32 Act No. 2083 (1911), 2177–79. For details of the Manila Railroad Company, see Corpuz 1999.
33 Public Law No. 274 (1906), 453–54.
34 Luthringer 1934, 42–44.
35 For a detailed discussion, see Chapter 5.
36 Luthringer 1934, 44.
37 Ibid., 45.
38 For a detailed discussion, see Chapter 5.
39 Act No. 2776 (1918), 877–81.
40 Until 1916 the Insular Treasurer was appointed by the U.S. president as the position of the Insular Auditor; however, under the Administrative Code of 1917 it became the governor-general of the Philippines who appointed the Insular Treasurer. Elliott 1968, 121–22, 520–21; Kalaw ([1921]), 13, 82–83; Malcolm and Kalaw 1923, 113, 189–91.
41 Luthringer 1934, 43–44.
42 Act No. 2612 (1916), 1097–1102; Willis 1917a, 425.
43 For details on the Federal Reserve System, see Beckhart 1972; Meltzer 2003.
44 Willis 1917a, 425–46; *The Federal Reserve Act (Approved 23 December 1913)*,

*as Amended 4 August 1914, 15 August 1914, 3 March 1915, 7 September 1916, 21 June 1917*, Washington: Government Printing Office 1917, 28–30, BIA 17128-57.
45  Luthringer 1934, 113–14.
46  Ibid., 116.
47  Ibid., 75–79, 114–15. For the post-World War financial crisis, see also Ybiernas 2007, 359–64.
48  Luthringer 1934, 115–17. As the original source of this estimate, see Philippine Islands, Governor General 1923, 80. For the figures related to the transferred currency reserves and the loans provided by the National Bank, cf. the Introduction.
49  Ibid., 75; Philippine Islands, Bureau of the Treasury 1920, 23–24.
50  Act No. 2939 (1921), 601–2.
51  Luthringer 1934, 82.
52  Act No. 3058 (1922), 1543–48.
53  Ibid., 1547–48. For details on the discussion in the U.S. Congress on the issuance of the government bonds, see United States, House of Representatives (1922a).
54  Luthringer 1934, 201–2; Philippine Islands, Bureau of the Treasury (1924), 39.
55  Luthringer 1934, 220–22.
56  Perkins 1947, 39–42; Nawa 1943, 16–18; Luthringer 1934, 249–50; Hernandez 1937, 61–62; Rothbard 2002, 467.
57  Act No. 4199 (1935), 737–38.
58  Philippines (Commonwealth), Bureau of the Treasury 1936–1941, various pages.

**CHAPTER 2: THE EMERGENCE OF MODERN BANKING IN THE PHILIPPINES**

1  For a useful study on U.S. tariff policy toward the Philippines, see Abelarde 1947.
2  For details see Nagano 1986, chap. 1.
3  Ibid., chap. 3. See also Larkin 1993, chap. 5.
4  Hawes 1987, 59–60.
5  For the formation of entrepreneurs and the development of haciendas in the Philippine sugar industry, see Nagano 1986, chaps. 3–6; Larkin 1993, chap. 3.
6  For the oligopolistic structure of Philippine sugar industry, see Nagano 1988, 170–81.
7  For the business activities of Tabacalera, see Raventos (1981), an excellent company history. Spanish capital, at this time, is hence classifiable into two categories, that is, "domestic investment" for those firms established in the Philippines and "foreign investment" for those whose headquarters were based in Spain. If Filipino and Philippine-based Spanish investments were lumped together as "domestic" in nature, both in combination would compose approximately 70 percent of the total investments in sugar mills.
8  In other parts of colonial Southeast Asia like British Malaya, by contrast, it was the overseas Chinese who played the pivotal role in capital formation in, for example,

the tin industry. For the formation of Chinese mestizos in the Philippines, see Wickberg 1965a.
9   United States, War Department 1901, pt. 1, 102–3; Nawata 1943, 104–5.
10  "Appendix C: Organic Act of the Philippine Islands, Public – No. 235," In Kalaw 1916, 273; Elliot 1968, 6, 8, 100–102; Kalaw 1926, 298; Barrows 1914, 14–16.
11  Philippine Islands, Governor General 1919, 131; Central Bank of the Philippines 1974, 143.
12  Philippine Islands, Bureau of Banking 1930, 5; Nawata 1943, 111.
13  Stine 1966, 108; Central Bank of the Philippines 1974, 142. For the regulations on banking in the Corporate Law of 1906, see Villalon 1926, 27–50.
14  Philippine Islands, Bureau of Banking 1935, 46–71.
15  Ibid., 33–37.
16  Ibid., 46–71.
17  Ibid., 43–45.
18  For details, see Doeppers 1983, 189–215.
19  Philippine Islands, Bureau of the Treasury 1925, 79–80; Philippine Islands, Bureau of Commerce and Industry 1918, 78–79. In the latter document, some insurance companies were listed as among the banks in operation. At present, this author only has data for the total assets of ten building and loan associations in the 1930s, the amount of which was approximately 10 percent of the combined assets of savings and mortgage banks, commercial banks, trust companies, and branches of foreign banks throughout the 1930s. Philippine Islands, Bureau of Banking 1933, 13; Philippines (Commonwealth), Bureau of Banking 1938, 34.
20  This author relies on comments from Dr. Benito J. Legarda, Jr. for the observation on the situation in the late 1930s. Email communication with Benito J. Legarda, Jr. (9 Apr. 1999).
21  Mauro Prieto established a short-lived bank with government approval in 1913 under Act No. 2215; see Espiritu and Magno-Mijares 1957, 5. One record states that the Central Luzon Agricultural Students' Bank was "reopened" in 1925. However, its year of establishment and business activity remain unknown; see Philippine Islands, Governor General (1927), 107.
22  Abreu, Newberry and Reyes Bank was the first bank established by Filipinos in 1902 and was dissolved in the same year; see Buencamino 1977, 21–22. Rodriguez Bank, although it was not a modern bank but a small lending institution, was established in 1830, but was dissolved later due to stiff competition; see Regidor and Mason 1950, vol. V: 104–6; Licuanan 1985, 64–66. Since the mid-nineteenth century, the Oriental Banking Corporation, which first established a branch in China as a British bank, assigned an agent in Manila for foreign exchange and loan business, but withdrew from business in 1884; see King 1988a, 103–4.
23  For details about the Manila branch of Banco Peninsular Ultramarino de Madrid, see Herrera 1883. For a general review on the development of the Philippine banking sector in the nineteenth century, see Balanon (n.d.).

24   For the Philippine Bank of Commerce, see Licuanan 1988, chap. 1; Reyes-McMurray 1998, 92–93.
25   The Postal Savings Bank, established in 1906, had not been supervised by the Bureau of Banking since 1930, while the Agricultural and Industrial Bank was newly opened in 1939 and data on its activities in 1940 are missing from the annual report. For the establishment of the Philippine Postal Savings Bank, see Kemmerer 1907. With Act No. 1493, the Postal Savings Bank was established under the supervision of the Bureau of Posts. Within a year it had a nationwide network of 233 offices and at its peak in 1930 had 983 branches. See Doeppers 1983, 191–95; Tirona 1987–1988, 60. The Agricultural and Industrial Bank was established by Commonwealth Act No. 459, stipulating for the bank a capital of 150 million pesos, with exclusive subscription by the Philippine government, with 25 million pesos payable upon subscription. Philippines (Commonwealth), Bureau of Banking 1940, 21–22.
26   United States, War Department 1901, pt. 2: 468–70; Conant 1901, 51–55; Ide 1907, 27–32; Colayco 1984, 63, 83, 96. The major stockholder of the Bank of the Philippine Islands (and of the Philippine Trust Company and the Monte de Piedad and Savings Bank) around 1940 was the Archbishop of Manila. Ibid., 116, 127.
27   Tirona 1987–1988, 61; Nawata 1943, 122–23; *Firipin ni okeru Ginko-hattatsushi* 1942, 12; *Senzen ni okeru Hito no Zaisei, Kinyu, Tsuka, Boeki-ippan* 1942, 16.
28   "China Banking Corporation: Golden Anniversary" (1970), 8, 10. For the China Banking Corporation, see Wong 1999, 132–42. Wong gives the date of the establishment of this bank as 1928. For the articles of this bank, see China Banking Corporation, Manila, P. I. 1920.
29   *Firipin ni okeru Ginko-hattatsushi* 1942, 122. For Peoples Bank and Trust Company, see Colayco 1984, 171–79.
30   *Eighty Years of Public Service* 1962; Vibal 1960, 52, 75; "Monte de Piedad's 106th Year" (1988), 17–20; Email communication with Benito J. Legarda, Jr. (9 Apr. 1999).
31   Mackenzie 1954, 132–41, 217: United States, War Department 1901, pt. 2, 471; Hamashita 1990, 157–59, 201–2; Philippines (Commonwealth), Bureau of Banking 1939, 15.
32   King 1988a, 103, 115; Hamashita 1990, 201; Legarda 1999, 208.
33   Bankers Association of the Philippines 1957, 74; Ji 2003, 152. Some other sources give the year of the merger of the International Banking Corporation with the National City Bank of New York as 1914. For example, see "In the Lives of These People, There Is a Bank. . . " (1971); Tirona 1987–1988, 60.
34   Philippine Islands, Bureau of Banking 1931, 5; Philippine Islands, Bureau of Banking 1932, 5; Philippine Islands, Bureau of Banking 1935, 8.
35   Espiritu and Magno-Mijares 1957, 11: Hamashita 1990, 202–3.
36   For the controls on the banking sector under Japanese rule, see "Rehabilitation of Philippine Banking Structure," in Romualdez 1962, 475–94.

37 For the financial network of the Chinese in the Philippines during the U.S. colonial period, see Wong 1999, part 2.
38 Ybañez 1983, 451; King 1988a, 118.
39 Ybañez 1983, 437–42; King 1988a, 111–14.
40 Ibid., 102–8.
41 Ybañez 1983, 453–54; King 1988a, 119–20.
42 Ybañez 1983, 454; King 1988a, 120–21.
43 Ybañez 1983, 456, 464–66; King 1988b, 535–39.
44 *Banco de las Islas Filipinas* 1928, 1–3; Colayco 1984, 18, 23–26; Legarda 1999, 208–211.
45 *Banco de las Islas Filipinas* 1928, 14–17, 23, 25, 43; Colayco 1984, 30, 36, 40, 57–58.
46 *Banco de las Islas Filipinas* 1928, 56–57, 62–63: Colayco 1984, 79–80, 83; "Charter of the Bank of the Philippine Islands" (n.d.), 13–45; "The Bank of the Philippine Islands" (1918), 372. Act No. 3330 of 1928 limited the maximum amount for the issuance of bank notes by the bank to nine million pesos and stipulated that all of its bank notes were to be retired within fifteen years. See Nawata 1943, 47–48.
47 Colayco 1984, 39–40, 48–49, 52–53.
48 *Banco de las Islas Filipinas*, 66–68; Colayco 1984, 84; Vergara 1954, 34–35.
49 Colayco 1984, 105.
50 Act No. 2612 (1916), 1097–1102; Willis 1917a, 415–16; Nagano 1993, 218–19.
51 However, the Philippine government showed some interest in establishing cooperative-type rural credit institutions among small farmers. In 1915, Act No. 2508, known as the Rural Credit Law, was enacted, and in 1924 Act No. 3154, known as the Guanco Act, was passed. These two laws promoted the establishment of small-scale financial institutions. In 1931 Act No. 3895 and Act No. 3896 were enacted. The former urged the Philippine National Bank to organize agricultural financial institutions in ten rural areas, while the latter encouraged the setting up of rural banks by smaller private capitalists. Yet only seven financial institutions were created under the former act, while only two rural banks were established as a result of the latter act. Espiritu and Magno-Mijares 1957, 10–11; Balmaceda 1924, 5–16; Galang 1938, 109–13.

## PART II. START-UP
## CHAPTER 3: THE AGRICULTURAL BANK
## OF THE PHILIPPINE GOVERNMENT

1 Owen 1971.
2 Stanley 1984.
3 Paredes 1989a.

4   Cullinane 2003.
5   Golay 1997.
6   Salamanca 1984, 22.
7   Pérez 1887, 3; Romero 1974, 242–43; McCoy 1982, 307–26; Owen 1984b, 42–71.
8   For contemporary essays on the Agricultural Bank of the Philippine Government, see Elliot 1968, 369–92; Jenks 1907, 38–44; Kemmerer 1908, 262–79.
9   William H. Taft's actual term of Civil Governor and then Governor-General of the Philippines was 1901–1904. For a recent study of Taft's career in the Philippines, see Escalante 2007, who discusses the continuity of military occupation and civil government during the early period of U.S. rule in the Philippines.
10  Stanley 1974, 232–48.
11  United States, War Department 1900, vol. 1, 149.
12  United States, War Department 1904, 102–10.
13  Kemmerer 1916, 308; Rosenberg 1985, 176–86; Rosenberg 2003, 12–18.
14  Conant 1901.
15  Ibid., 34–35.
16  Ibid., 35–36.
17  Ibid., 56–57.
18  Ibid., 57–58.
19  Ibid., 58.
20  United States, War Department 1903, pt. 1, 109–10.
21  Ibid., 110.
22  Aguinaldo to the Philippine Commission (23 Nov. 1902); Root to the President of the Senate and the Speaker of the House (20 Jan. 1903); United States, House of Representatives 1903.
23  Ibid., 1–4.
24  For the agricultural condition at the early stage of the American occupation, see Willis 1970, 338–65; Escalante 2007, 235–38. Aguinaldo himself was interested in acquiring friar lands from the Philippine government. The official record of 1910 showed that he was granted a special lease of 1,056 hectares of the Imus estate in the province of Cavite. This was one of six special lease contracts involving larger lands. United States, House of Representatives 1911, vol. 1, 195–204.
25  Poblete to Taft and Roosevelt (27 Oct. 1904), BIA 6769-4.
26  *El Mercantil* (27 Oct. 1904), BIA 6769-4. The newspaper clipping contained an excerpt from an editorial that appeared in *El Grito del Pueblo* (26 Oct. 1904).
27  See for example, *Manila Times* (1 July 1905), BIA 6769-4.
28  For the role of W. Morgan Shuster in the collaboration with local elites, see Paredes 1989b, 41–69.
29  *Manila Times* (1 July 1905), BIA 6769-4.
30  "Appendix: Public Hearing in the Philippine Islands," in United States, House of Representatives 1906, 24–26.

31 United States, War Department 1903, pt. 2, 107; United States, War Department 1904, pt. 3, 290–91; United States, War Department 1905, pt. 3, 369–78.
32 Kemmerer 1916, 328; "Currency Division Ends" (the title of newspaper unknown) (31 Jan. 1906), Princeton University, Seeley G. Mudd Manuscript Library, Edwin W. Kemmerer Papers (hereafter cited as KP), Box 254. Kemmerer was a student of Jeremiah Jenks at Cornell University and directed Conant's currency system in the Philippines during 1903–1906. He jointed Jenks at Cornell and moved to Princeton in 1912. During the 1920s, Kemmerer was widely known as a "money doctor" and directed financial advising missions to many countries. Rosenberg 1985, 182, 195–96; Rosenberg 2003, 17–18; *Manila Times* (3 Sept. 1903), KP, Box 254.
33 "Currency Division Ends" (the title of newspaper unknown) (31 Jan. 1906); *New York American* (4 Jan. 1903); *Manila Times* (3 Sept. 1903), KP, Box 254.
34 This report was included in United States, War Department 1907, pt. 1, 487–641. See also United States, War Department 1906b.
35 United States, War Department 1907, pt. 1, 487. In Kemmerer's report, a detailed study on the opinions of provincial treasurers on the establishment of an agricultural bank (May 1903) was attached. Ibid., 510–25.
36 Ibid., 490.
37 Ibid., 491–94.
38 Ibid., 494–95.
39 Ibid., 501–9.
40 United States, War Department 1906c.
41 "Currency Division Ends" (the title of newspaper unknown) (31 Jan. 1906), KP, Box 254.
42 Ibid., 20–23.
43 Ibid., 25–26.
44 United States, War Department 1906a, pt. 4, 21–22.
45 *Manila Cablenews* (24 Oct. 1905); *Manila Times* (24 Oct. 1905); *Manila Cablenews* (25 Oct. 1905); *Manila American* (25 Oct. 1905); *Manila Cablenews* (26 Oct. 1905); *Manila Times* (26 Oct. 1905); *Manila Times* (27 Oct. 1905); *Manila Times* (8 Nov. 1905); all KP, Box 254.
46 Those involved in the process included Colonel Clarence R. Edwards (Chief of the Bureau of Insular Affairs), J. W. Jenks (Professor at Cornell University and U.S. Commissioner at the Commission on International Exchange), Senator J. C. Spooner, Senator F. G. Newlands, Senator W. B. Allison, Senator Henry Cabot Lodge, John Hubbard (Treasurer of the International Banking Corporation), and J. S. Tait (Manager of the International Banking Corporation). Jenks to Edwards (20 Dec. 1905); Edwards to Spooner (20 Dec. 1905); Edwards to Jenks (20 Dec. 1905); Edwards to Newlands (20 Dec. 1905), BIA 6769-18; Jenks to Edwards (3 Jan. 1906), BIA 6769-19; Newlands to Edwards (30 Dec. 1905); Edwards to Newlands (3 Jan. 1906), BIA 6769-20; Hubbard to Edwards (8 Jan. 1906) and his friend's comments

on a draft of the bill to establish an agricultural bank, BIA 6769-21, 22; Newlands to Edwards (9 Jan. 1906); Edwards to Allison (12 Jan. 1906), BIA 6769-23; Allison to Edwards (15 Jan. 1906); Edwards to Allison (18 Jan. 1906), BIA 6769-26; Jenks to Edwards (18 Jan. 1906), BIA 6769-27; Tait to Edwards (18 Jan. 1906) and a criticism against a bill to establish an agricultural bank by an unknown writer, BIA 6769-28; Jenks to Edwards (5 Mar. 1906), BIA 6769-30; Taft to Lodge (22 Mar. 1906), BIA 6769-31.

47 United States, House of Representatives, 59th Congress, 2d Session, "S. 6249. A Bill to provide for the establishment of an agricultural bank in the Philippine Islands, by Mr. Lodge, 22 May 1906, 2 Feb. 1907," BIA 6769-31.

48 Governor of Ilocos Sur to the Governor-General (18 June 1906); Governor of Ilocos Norte to the Governor-General (24 Jan. 1906); Diego Liñan of Ambos Camarines to the Governor-General (25 June 1906); 18 landowners of Negros Occidental to the Governor-General (26 June 1906); Acting Secretary to the Governor-General (28 July 1906), BIA 6769-47.

49 Lodge to Taft (19 June 1906), BIA 6769-35; "The Proposed Philippine Bank" (the title of newspaper unknown) (12 Feb. 1907), KP, Box 254.

50 United States, House of Representatives, 59th Congress, 2d Session "H.R. 23567. A Bill to encourage agriculture in the Philippine Islands, by Mr. Cooper, Jan. 10, 1907"; "H.R. 23937. A Bill to provide for the establishment of an agricultural bank in the Philippine Islands, by Mr. Cooper, Jan. 10, 1907"; "H.R. 25049. A Bill to encourage agriculture in the Philippine Islands . . . , by Mr. Garret, Jan. 28, 1908"; "H.R. 25053. A Bill to provide for the establishment of an agricultural bank in the Philippine Islands, by Mr. Cooper, Jan. 28, 1907," BIA 6769-31.

51 Cable from the Governor of Negros Occidental to Taft (11 Feb. 1907), BIA 6769-65.

52 Taft to Hale (4 Feb. 1907), BIA 6769-61; Lodge to Taft (5 Feb. 1907), BIA 6769-63; Cooper to Taft (19 Feb. 1907), BIA 6769-66.

53 "Public Law No. 24, An Act to provide for the establishment of an agricultural bank in the Philippine Islands," in United States, War Department (1907), pt. 1, 500a–500b.

54 Smith to Taft (14 Mar. 1907), BIA 6769-59.

55 Edward to Speyer (14 Mar. 1907), BIA-69; Speyer to Edwards (15 Mar. 1907), BIA 6769-70; Hubbard to Edwards (22 Mar. 1907), BIA 6769-71; Hubbard to Edwards (4 Apr. 1907); Edwards to Hubbard (11 Apr. 1907), BIA 6769-72; Jobes to Edwards (13 Apr. 1907), BIA 6769-73; Hubbard to Edwards (16 Apr. 1907), BIA 6769-75; Edwards to Jobes (24 Apr. 1907), BIA 6769-76; Jobes to Edwards (29 Apr. 1907), BIA 6769-77; Jobes to Edwards (7 May 1907), BIA 6769-79; Stanley (1974), 234; May (1984), 165–66.

56 This style of banking business was also followed by the International Banking Corporation. See Willis 1917a, 410–11.

57 Insular Treasurer to Secretary of War (25 Oct. 1907), BIA 6769-82; United States War Department 1908, pt. 3, 60–61.

58 Act No. 1730 ("An Act to authorize continuing annual appropriation to meet any obligation of the Philippine government . . . "), BIA 6769-80.
59 First Philippine Legislature, First Session, "Joint Resolution No. 9, Providing for the appointment of a committee for studying a plan to carry into effect the establishment of an agricultural bank in the Philippine Islands," BIA 6769-86.
60 Smith to Taft (19 Mar. 1908), BIA 6769-83.
61 Edwards to Smith (23 Mar. 1908); Taft to Attorney General (21 Mar. 1908), BIA 6769-83.
62 Act No. 1865 (1908), 1122–23.
63 *Agricultural Bank of the Philippine Government* 1908, 5–10, BIA 6769-90, 91.
64 Philippine Islands, Bureau of the Treasury 1910, 13.
65 United States, War Department 1910, 166.
66 Philippine Islands, Bureau of the Treasury 1910, 16; United States, War Department 1911, 153–54.
67 Fiscal years for 1909–1913 started from July of one year previous to the fiscal year and ended at June of the named fiscal year. In 1914–1915, the fiscal year started from January and ended at December of each year.
68 Philippine Islands, Bureau of the Treasury 1910, 16.
69 This took effect in October 1911. United States, War Department 1912a, 145; Philippine Islands, Bureau of the Treasury 1912, 23.
70 Philippine Islands, Bureau of the Treasury 1910, 16; Philippine Islands, Bureau of the Treasury 1912, 23; United States, War Department 1912b, 206. At first these agencies accepted only current accounts, and mainly served local merchants. In FY1913, 24 agencies of the bank were operating throughout the country, 13 having being newly established in various provinces (in this year, the Zamboanga agency was closed with the opening of an agency of the Bank of the Philippine Islands, following the bank's policy of not competing with commercial banks). In FY1913, all agencies accepted both current accounts and time deposits. As of June 1913, current accounts amounted to 191,010 pesos, and time deposits to 33,888 pesos. Philippine Islands, Bureau of the Treasury 1913, 42–43; United States, War Department 1914, 223.
71 Philippine Islands, Bureau of the Treasury 1913, 46; United States, War Department 1914, 223.
72 As will be later discussed, by Act No. 2214 (Feb. 1913) the maximum amount of each loan was increased to 35,000 pesos. Of the total 390 loans provided during FY1909–FY1913, the collateral for 259 loans consisted of land under Torrens titles, while the remaining 131 loans were provided under the Spanish title. See Philippine Islands, Bureau of the Treasury 1913, 46–47.
73 Archibald Harrison, "Report by the Chairman of the Investigating Committee on Conditions Affecting Agricultural Property in the Island of Negros which is Mortgaged to the Bank" (10 Aug. 1918), BIA 6769-634.

74 Cullinane 1971, 13; Salamanca 1984, 46–49. Cullinane points out that "in 1906, when Filipinos were given the majority control of the provincial Boards, the commissioners continued to emphasize the important role of the American provincial treasurer and the overall restraining power of the American-dominated Executive Bureau." Cullinane 1971, 21.
75 Salamanca 1984, 43, 47.
76 Act No. 1906 (1909), 986.
77 Act No. 2016, BIA 6769-110.
78 Philippine Islands 1913, 43–45. Before this decision was give, there was controversy over whether or not it was proper for provincial governments to earn interest by depositing their funds in the government agricultural bank, since they could not get interest by depositing funds with the Insular Treasury. Carpenter to McIntyre (16 Jan. 1913); McIntyre (21 Feb. 1913), BIA 6769-103.
79 Act No. 2214 ("An Act providing for certain changes in the general powers of the Agricultural Bank of the Philippine Government and for other purposes"), BIA 6769-106. See also Executive Bureau, the Government of the Philippine Islands, "Provincial Circular No. 60," BIA 6769-115.
80 In early 1913, the Insular Treasury had about 3 million pesos of provincial treasurers' current accounts while the Manila branch of the International Banking Corporation held more than 4 million pesos of those deposits, at an annual interest rate of three and one-half percent. Carpenter to McIntyre (16 Jan. 1913), BIA 6769-103.
81 Manning to McIntyre (10 June 1913), BIA 6769-110. It is not known how the International Banking Corporation agreed to give up a favorable position as depository of provincial government funds. However we may assume that the pressure from the local elite to increase the capacity of the Agricultural Bank was so intense that the U.S. government officials in the insular government ventured to persuade the International Banking Corporation to surrender its position as depository of provincial government funds in exchange for larger benefits in the future.
82 The prevailing annual interest at the Agricultural Bank during FY1913 was three percent of time deposits for six-month periods and 3.5 percent for yearly deposit periods. *Daily Consular and Trade Reports, Oct. 21, 1913*, BIA 6769-112.
83 "Provincial Circular No. 60," BIA 6769-115.
84 Philippine Islands, Bureau of the Treasury 1916a, 52–53; United States, War Department 1915, 243.
85 Philippine Islands, Bureau of the Treasury 1916b, 55; United States, War Department 1916, 187.
86 "Consolidacíon Nacional, Manila, Feb. 5, 1914, Timely Resolution," BIA 6769-116; "Consolidacíon Nacional, Manila, Feb. 24, 1914, Recommendations of the Agricultural Committee: The Resolution increasing capital of the Agricultural Bank before the Legislature," BIA 6769-118; *Philippines Free Press* (7 Mar. 1914), BIA 6769-118.

## CHAPTER 4: THE PHILIPPINE NATIONAL BANK AND LENDING IN AGRICULTURE

1. Forbes to McIntyre (16 Oct. 1911), BIA 6769-95; Forbes to Edwards (23 Oct. 1911), BIA 6769-96; Legarda to Edwards (7 Nov. 1911), BIA 6769-99; Assembly Bill No. 176, Third Philippine Legislature, First Session, BIA 6769-105.
2. McIntyre to Forbes (19 May 1913), BIA 6769-107.
3. Stanley (1974), 235; "A Draft of the Commission Bill Introduced by Commissioner Martin," BIA 6769-123B; "Insular Bank Proposed in Philippines," *U.S. Commerce Reports* (20 Oct. 1915), BIA 6769-A-3; *Consolidación Nacional* (translation) (14 Sept. 1915), BIA 6769-A-4.
4. Stanley (1974), 235–36; McIntyre, "Memoranda," BIA 6769-with 123; *La Democracia* (translation) (14 Sept. 1915), BIA 6769-A-2.
5. Stanley (1974), 236–37; McIntyre to Quezon (12 Nov. 1915), BIA 6769-126; McIntyre to Harrison (14 Dec. 1915); A bill creating an insular bank of the Philippine Islands drafted by Willis, BIA 6769-128; Willis to McIntyre (23 Apr. 1916), BIA 6769-143; McIntyre to Willis (20 June 1916), BIA 6769-153.
6. Act No. 2612 (1916), 1097–1102. See also *By-Laws of the Philippine National Bank* (Manila, 1917), Henry Parker Willis Papers, Rare Book and Manuscript Library, Columbia University (hereafter cited as WP), Box 17.
7. For U.S. Reserve Board, see Chapter 1.
8. Act No. 2747 (1918), 453–58. As will be discussed in Chapter 7, even by the mid-1920s almost all the stocks of the National Bank were owned by the Philippine government and private ownership of the stocks remained minimal.
9. Act No. 2938 (1921), 573–79. See also *By-Laws of the Philippine National Bank* (Manila, 1921), BIA 6769-667A.
10. Act No. 2612 (1916), 1097–1102.
11. Act No. 2938 (1921), 573–79.
12. Act No. 2747 (1918), 453.
13. Act No. 2938 (1921), 574.
14. Ibid., 573–79.
15. Initially the Bank was controlled by a board of seven directors, with H. Parker Willis as chairman and president, Samuel Ferguson as vice president, Charles C. Robinson as secretary and vice president, and Vicente Singson Encarnacion, W.H. Anderson, Leon Rosenthal, and Venancio Concepcion as directors. See Willis 1917a, 418.
16. *New York Times* (19 July 1937); *New York Herald Tribune* (21 July 1937), "H. Parker Willis," BIA Personnel File, Box 701; Stanley 1974, 240; Meltzer 2003, 70–71.
17. Willis 1917a. See also Willis 1917b and Willis 1917c.
18. Willis 1917a, 418–19.
19. Ibid., 415, 419.
20. Ibid., 419–22.
21. Ibid., 422.

22  Nagano 1986, 179–83. For the registration policy of land titles and its problems, see Umehara 1992, 96–112.
23  Willis 1917a, 430–31.
24  Ibid., 431.
25  Ibid., 432.
26  Ibid.
27  Ibid., 430–31.
28  Ibid., 412–13, 432–33; Willis to Harrison, 9 Aug. 1916, BIA 6769-153; WP, Box 17. In the discussion by Willis, it is unclear whether local private banks directly offered crop loans to the planters, or the foreign trading firms or larger domestic merchants got involved in crop loan business by lending funds from private banks. The Bank of the Philippine Islands provided loans directly to the planters, while the Hongkong Shanghai Banking Corporation conducted crop loan business through foreign trading firms or larger merchants. On the other hand, the Agricultural Bank of the Philippine Government could have provided crop loans within the limit of 40 percent of the market value of crops harvested. The deposits of the Philippine government in the private banks as of 31 May 1916 were as enumerated below.

| Bank | Fixed Deposits (in pesos) | Current Deposits (in pesos) |
| --- | --- | --- |
| Hongkong Shanghai Banking Corp. | 1,243,849 | 1,191,409 |
| Chartered Bank of India, Australia and China | 800,000 | 1,185,332 |
| International Banking Corporation | 1,100,000 | 1,490,896 |
| Bank of the Philippine Islands | 1,100,000 | 122,030 |
| Total | 4,243,849 | 3,989,667[a] |

[a]3,989,666 pesos in the original document.
*Source:* Willis to Harrison (15 June 1916), BIA 6769-152.

29  Willis 1917a, 433; Willis to Harrison (9 Aug. 1916), BIA 6769-153; WP, Box 17.
30  Willis 1917a, 433–34.
31  Ibid., 434–36. For the changes in Philippine sugar processing from *muscovado* sugar production to the centrifugal sugar production, see Nagano 1986, 16–19, 97–98, 210–12.
32  Stanley 1974, 240–41. Samuel Ferguson went to the Philippines in 1902 as court

stenographer. He later became secretary to the governor-general when Francis Burton Harrison took office in September 1913. See "Samuel Ferguson," BIA Personnel File, Box 194.

33 "Archibald Harrison," BIA Personnel File, Box 267.
34 Memorandum about the motion of Archibald Harrison before the Executive Committee of the Philippine National Bank, May 1918, Philippine National Library, Manuel L. Quezon Papers, Series IV, Subject File (hereafter cited as QP), Box 439.
35 "Confidencial: Documentos y correspondencias relacionados con el 'Comite de Revisión de Préstamos Agricolas,' presidido por el Sr. Archibald Harrison, Ex-Secretario y Director del B.N.F.," BIA 6769-634; Francis Burton Harrison Papers, Manuscript Division, Library of Congress, Box 42.
36 Report by the Chairman of the Investigating Committee on Conditions Affecting Agricultural Property in the Island of Negros which is Mortgaged to the Bank, 10 Aug 1918, In "Confidencial: Documentos y . . . ," 107–65. The investigating committee headed by Harrison was later called in Spanish the Comite Investigador de Prestamos Agricolas or Comite Revisor de Prestamos Agricolas.
37 Ibid., 108–11.
38 Ibid., 124–25, 128.
39 Ibid., 125–26.
40 Ibid., 131–35.
41 Ibid., 135–38.
42 Ibid., 138–40.
43 The Guanco mill was established in 1920 with a capital of 1 million pesos. See Nagano 1986, 113.
44 Report by the Chairman of the Investigating Committee . . . , 141–45.
45 Ibid., 145–50.
46 Ibid., 150–52.
47 Ibid., 152–58.
48 Ibid., 158–60.
49 Ibid., 160–61.
50 Seaver to Harrison (9 Aug. 1918), In "Confidencial: Documentos y . . . ," 46–54; QP, Box 439. For a full transcription of this letter, see Larkin (1993), Appendix D.
51 Seaver to Harrison (12 Aug. 1918), In "Confidencial: Documentos y . . . ," 176–85; QP, Box 439.
52 Ibid., 176.
53 Ibid., 180.
54 Memorandum by Harrison (17 Aug. 1918), In "Confidencial: Documentos y . . . ," 199.
55 Memorandum Confidencial por V. Concepcion (18 Aug. 1918), In "Confidencial: Documentos y . . . ," 202–17.
56 Harrison to Concepcion (27 Aug. 1918), In "Confidencial: Documentos y . . . ," 298–99.
57 Memorandum Order (31 Aug. 1918), In "Confidencial: Documentos y . . . ," 309.

58 Copias de las contestaciónes de los Sres. Singson, Madrigal y Fernandez, miembros del Comite Agricola presidida por el Director Mr. Archibald Harrison, In "Confidencial: Documentos y . . . ," 313–14.
59 Harrison to Concepcion (13 Sept. 1918), In "Confidencial: Documentos y . . . ," 321.
60 Act No. 2938 (1921), 573–79.
61 Branches and agencies of the National Bank were opened in Iloilo in 1916; Cebu and Corregidor Island in 1917; Aparri (Cagayan Province), Bacolod (Negros Occidental), Davao (Mindanao), and Cabanatuan (Nueva Ecija) in 1918; Legaspi (Albay), Lucena (Tayabas), Vigan (Ilocos Sur) in 1919; and Dagupan (Pangasinan) and Naga (Camarines Sur) in 1920. The annual report of the National Bank as of September 1929 includes the balance sheets of eight domestic branches and thirteen agencies of the Bank. Report and Balance Sheet of the Philippine National Bank for the Year 1920, Manila, 1921, BIA 6769-with 150; Report on Philippine National Bank, Manila, as of 30 Sept. 1929, BIA 6769-with 187.
62 By the early 1930s, approximately a half million Torrens titles were issued. Umehara 1992, 107.
63 "Philippine National Bank, Bacolod, Examiner's Report of Condition at Close of Business, Sept. 5, 1927"; "Philippine National Bank, Bacolod, Examiner's Report of Condition at Close of Business, Oct. 16, 1929"; "Philippine National Bank, Bacolod, Examiner's Report of Condition at Close of Business, Sept. 5, 1930"; "Philippine National Bank, Bacolod, Examiner's Report of Condition at Close of Business, Apr. 20, 1931"; "Philippine National Bank, Iloilo, Examiner's Report of Condition at Close of Business, Oct. 10, 1929"; "Philippine National Bank, Iloilo, Examiner's Report of Condition at Close of Business, Apr. 25, 1932"; "Philippine National Bank, Iloilo, Examiner's Report of Condition at Close of Business, Oct. 16, 1933," BIA 6769-with 187.
64 Legarda 1999, part 3; Owen 1984a, 56–71; Owen 1984b, 201–30.
65 Wickberg 1965b.

**PART III. DEBACLE**
**CHAPTER 5: THE WOOD-FORBES MISSION AND THE FINANCIAL CRISIS**
1 Said 1993.
2 Ileto 1999.
3 Rafael 2000.
4 Quibuyen 1999.
5 Salman 2001.
6 After his resignation, Harrison led a secluded life in Scotland. For his view on the Philippine government's involvement in its economy and financial crisis, see Harrison 1922, chap. 17. See also "Francis Burton Harrison," *National Cyclopedia of American Biography*, vol. 46 (1963), 24; "Francis Burton Harrison," *Dictionary*

*of American Biography, Supplement 6, 1956–1960* (1980), 279–281; Golay 1997, 173–77, 181–82, 222–23.

7   Forbes 1928, vol. 2: 284–87; Agoncillo and Guerrero 1973, 362–65; Onorato 1988, 27–31; Ybiernas 2007, 345–48. Generally, it is thought that American policy toward the Philippines swung between Republican and Democratic presidents. However, Frank H. Golay suggests that Democratic President Wilson's policy toward the Philippines did not totally override the previous policy under Republicans. See Golay 1997, chap. 6.

8   For a detailed study of the Wood-Forbes Mission, see Onorato 1988, chap. 3.

9   This refers to President McKinley's instructions in April 1900 to the Philippine Commission. He ordered first Civil Governor Taft to construct civil governments at municipalities or provinces in various regions. At that time the Philippines was in a state of insurgency. See "Appendix C: Instructions of the President to the Taft Commission," In Elliott 1968, 485–90.

10  United States 1921, 6. See also United States Library of Congress, Manuscript Division, Journal of W. Cameron Forbes, Second Series II, 1921–1929, Appendix 6: 330–33.

11  Besides the report published in Manila, the Wood-Forbes Mission Report was published with a slight revision of its title by the Government Printing Office, Washington, DC in 1921 and 1922. It was also included in Philippine Islands, Governor General 1922, 13–43.

12  United States 1921, 12.

13  Ibid., 25.

14  Ibid., 21.

15  Due to a serious illness, Samuel Ferguson resigned from the presidency of the National Bank on 15 March 1918 and died a few days later at the age of 35. He was in the United States on business when he was stricken at his hotel in New York. "Samuel Ferguson," BIA Personnel File, Box 194.

16  His full name was Venancio Concepcion (following the common spelling in disregard of the accent mark). He became the third president of the Philippine National Bank in March 1918 and resigned in November 1920. At the time of the Philippine revolution he had been a prominent Visayan general and had served as a member of the Malolos Congress in 1899. For a brief biography, see Kalaw 1965, 109.

17  Before the term of Venancio Concepcion, Samuel Ferguson, who served as the second president of the National Bank (1916–1918), had preemptively committed the erroneous transfer of currency reserves. The Chief of the U.S. Bureau of Insular Affairs (BIA), Frank McIntyre, opposed the plan to allow the National Bank to take over the currency reserve fund, but in vain. He rather proposed an arrangement between the Philippine government and the National City Bank of New York whereby the fund would be placed in charge of the latter. See Mass 1971, 204.

18  United States 1921, 21–22.

[19] In fact, the financial condition of the Philippine government had begun to deteriorate during the administration of Governor-General Forbes in 1909–1913. See Casambre 1968, chap. V; Golay 1984, 231–60; Golay 1997, 155–65.
[20] Luthringer 1934, 96–113.
[21] Ibid., 121.
[22] Ibid., 123–24.
[23] It was arranged that Francis Coates, Jr. and his investigating party would leave for Manila on 30 October 1919. Coates to Baker (11 Oct. 1919), BIA 6769-347.
[24] Coates 1921, 101.
[25] The Philippine insular treasurer at this time was Albert P. Fitzsimmons. He had been an acting assistant surgeon in the U.S. Army, and was in the Army Medical Department in the Philippine Islands before 1914. He served on the Municipal Board of Manila from 1914 to 1916. In June 1916 he was appointed insular treasurer, a position he held until the end of 1919. From June 1919 to May 1921, he was the director of the mint in the Philippine Islands. "Albert P. Fitzsimmons," BIA Personnel File, Box 204; Philippine Islands, Bureau of the Treasury (1923), 2. For published articles by Fitzsimmons on Philippine currency and economy, see Fitzsimmons 1917a, 1917b, 1918.
[26] Wright 1921, 22A. It is interesting to note here that Fitzsimmons himself wrote about the confusion of the transfer of Liberty Loan and Alien Property funds in his memorandum as follows: "At the time the armistice was signed they [Philippine National Bank] had large loans on hemp and oil, which they were unable to realize upon.... It is true they conducted some very creditable activities, such as transmitting about ₱15,000,000.00 for the Alien Property Custodian and nearly ₱30,000,000.00 for the various Liberty Loan funds, which amounted to a total of about ₱45,000,000.00 transferred to the United States free of charge and reduced our trade balance to a like amount. It was perfectly well and proper to make large subscriptions for Liberty Loans and to close out the German properties, but when it comes to transmitting the funds to the United States, this should not have been done. The United States should have been required to accept delivery here and arrange for the transfer of the funds thru their own Treasury Department, and in this manner it would not have disorganized the financial activities of the Philippine Islands, by exhausting our gold reserve." A. P. Fitzsimmons, "Memorandum of the Relations of the Bureau of the Treasury with the Philippine National Bank" (undated), 6–7, BIA 6769-444.
[27] Walcutt to Yeater, cable (24 May 1919), BIA 6769-after 261; 6769-309.
[28] Yeater to Walcutt, cable (26 May 1919), BIA 6769-after 313.
[29] BIA Chief Frank McIntyre visited Manila in early 1920 and was very much concerned about Philippine financial conditions. Walcutt to McIntyre (6 Feb. 1920); "Frank McIntyre," BIA Personnel File, Box 408; Baker to Coates, cable (19 Mar. 1920), U.S. Library of Congress, Manuscript Division, Francis Burton Harrison Papers, Box 36.

30 Cruz 1974, 54.
31 Ibid., 55.
32 Ibid., 188–89; Stanley 1974, 251–52; "Maj.-Gen. Frank McIntyre: The Record-Breaking Colonial Manager Retires," *Our Army* (Feb. 1929); Frank B. McIntyre, "The Bureau of Insular Affairs of the War Department," *The Philippines* (15 Mar. 1929); "Frank McIntyre," BIA Personnel File, Box 408; "Frank McIntyre," *The National Cyclopedia of American Biography*, vol. 32 (1945), 333–34. For McIntyre's career, see also Biedzynski 1990.
33 Clarence R. Edwards, "Memorandum of Proposed Amendment Effecting Certificate Reserve in the Philippine Islands" (25 Jan. 1912), BIA 808-368.
34 Ibid.
35 Conant to McIntyre (26 Oct. 1914), BIA 808-392; "An Act to Establish a Currency Reserve Fund for the Maintenance of the Parity of the Philippine Currency," BIA 808-392A; Philippine National Library, Manuel L. Quezon Papers, Series IV, Subject File (hereafter cited as QP), Box 50.
36 Charles A. Conant, "Proposed Changes in the Monetary Law of the Philippine Islands" (27 Oct. 1914), 1, BIA 808-393A; QP Box 50.
37 Ibid., 1–2.
38 Ibid., 3.
39 Ibid., 4–5.
40 Ibid., 6.
41 McIntyre to Conant (16 Apr. 1914), BIA 808-374.
42 McIntyre to Harrison (21 May 1914), BIA 808-375.
43 Conant to Harrison (14 July 1914), BIA 808-378A.
44 Garrison to Harrison (28 July 1914), BIA 808-379.
45 Ibid.
46 The Jones Law was indeed passed in the U.S. Congress in February 1916 and approved by the president in August 1916. Elliot 1968, 427–28.
47 McIntyre to Harrison (31 Oct. 1914), U.S. Library of Congress, Manuscript Division, Francis Burton Harrison Papers, Box 33.
48 "Memorandum for the Secretary of War: Subject: Deposits in the United States of part of certificate reserve fund, Philippine Islands, by Judge Advocate General" (15 Aug. 1914), BIA 808-382; McIntyre to Harrison (17 Aug. 1914), BIA 808-after 381.
49 Act No. 2603 (4 Feb. 1916), BIA 808-421.
50 Luthringer (1934), 47.
51 Bernard Herstein served as insular collector of customs in the Philippines from November 1913 to July 1916. He then served as a member of the Board of Public Utility Commissioners in the Philippines until December 1916, when he resigned from the Philippine service. However, until September 1917 he was detailed to duty in the United States to draft a new tariff act and to make a study of a currency reserve system. He was a chemist with a doctor's degree. "Bernard Herstein," BIA Personnel File, Box 281.

52 Hershey to McIntyre (16 Dec. 1916), BIA 808-440; McIntyre to Harrison (25 Jan. 1917), BIA 808-440; draft of the bill for an Act to create the redemption fund and to amend the currency laws of the Philippines respecting the issue and redemption of treasury certificates, BIA 808-440A; Herstein to Hershey (14 Dec. 1916), BIA 808-440B; McIntyre to Harrison (12 Apr. 1917), BIA 808-443; draft of an Act to regulate the currency, to establish a gold parity fund in the treasury of the Philippine Islands and for other purpose, BIA 808-443; Herstein to Harrison, n.d., BIA 808-443A; McIntyre's Memorandum on Mr. Herstein's draft (12 Apr. 1917), BIA 808-443B; Fitzsimmons to McIntyre (9 Oct. 1917), BIA 808-448.

53 Osmeña to de Veyra (8 Nov. 1917), BIA 808-447; de Veyra to Kemmerer (8 Nov. 1917), BIA 808-447.

54 de Veyra to Osmeña (14 Nov. 1917), BIA 808-after 447.

55 Kemmerer to Osmeña (11 Jan. 1918), BIA 808-452; E. W. Kemmerer, "Memorandum Concerning Certain Proposals for Currency Legislation in the Philippine Islands Submitted to the Speaker of the Philippine Assembly" (12 Jan. 1918), BIA 808-452A.

56 Ibid., 2–10.

57 Ibid., 41–44.

58 Ibid., 50–63.

59 BIA to Harrison (14 Nov. 1917), BIA 808-after 447.

60 McIntyre to Kemmerer (8 Dec. 1917), BIA 808-449; Frank McIntyre, "Notes on Memorandum of Dr. Kemmerer Concerning Proposed Currency Legislation in the Philippine Islands Submitted to the Speaker of the Philippine Assembly January 11, 1918" (19 Jan. 1918), BIA 808-452.

61 "Memorandum re H. No. 834, May 1, 1918," BIA 808-with 457; Frank McIntyre, "Memorandum" (4 May 1918), BIA 808-457.

62 Hoyt 1963.

63 Wood and Forbes to SECWAR, cable (10 June 1921), BIA 22639-A-57; Hoyt (1963), 300–302.

64 Hoyt 1963, 302–4.

65 United States House of Representatives 1922b, 1.

66 Hoyt 1963, 304–5; *La Vanguardia*, Manila (24 June 1921), BIA 6769-A-39.

67 For the Board of Control, see Chapters 4 and 7.

68 Leonard Wood Papers, Diaries (4 June 1921); Hoyt 1963, 311.

69 "Record of Conversation with Mr. Manuel Quezon, President of the Senate, about July 5th," United States Library of Congress, Manuscript Division, Frank R. McCoy Papers, Box 19; Hoyt 1963, 311.

70 Kalaw 1965, 126–27.

71 For the Filipinos' rebuttal to the Wood-Forbes Mission Report, see de Veyra 1922. However, this article does not discuss the issues of the mismanagement of the Philippine National Bank and the currency crisis.

72 Kalaw 1965, chap. XVI; Agoncillo and Guerrero 1973, 354–57.

73   Kalaw 1965, chap. XVI; Agoncillo and Guerrero 1973, 357–59; McCoy 2009, 284–86.
74   For a similar argument that World War I created a watershed in American colonial rule of the Philippines, see McCoy 2009, 262–63. McCoy also suggests that World War I transformed the U.S. state itself by establishing an interlocking counterintelligence system. Ibid., 296–300.

## CHAPTER 6: THE PHILIPPINE NATIONAL BANK AND CREDIT INFLATION

1   Stanley 1974, 237–38.
2   Ibid., 240–41.
3   Coates 1920, 1–4.
4   Haskins & Sells 1922. This is the commissioned investigation report on the accounts of the Philippine National Bank assigned to the firm of Haskins & Sells by the Wood-Forbes Mission. See Luthringer 1934, 154.
5   Coates 1920, 19.
6   Ibid., 19–21.
7   Ibid., 21–22.
8   Ibid., 22–35.
9   Ibid., 35–38.
10  Ibid., 59–62.
11  Ibid., 61.
12  Hawes 1987, 59–60; Sullivan 1992, chap. 8.
13  This company was founded by Germans in 1910. In 1914 Philip C. Whitaker, an American financial adviser for the Archdiocese of Manila, persuaded the Archbishop to acquire the company. As a result, the stocks of the company were distributed to bishops and priests throughout the Philippines. The company expanded its production, establishing a new mill by importing equipment from the United States, yet its capacity could not meet the larger export demand of coconut oil. It was not until the war was over and prices of coconut oil crashed that the extravagant management of the company was revealed. Gleeck 1975, 74–75.
14  Coates 1920, 114–16.
15  Ibid., 52–57.
16  Following the Philippine Vegetable Oil Co., this company was established in 1914 as the second coconut mill in the Philippines. It was ultimately bought out by the American firm Procter & Gamble in 1935. Tiglao 1981, 2–3; Yoshihara 1985, 61.
17  Haskins & Sells 1922, 7.
18  A. R. Franklin, "Memo Re Philippine National Bank Loans to Oil Companies," 2, BIA 6769-708B.
19  Philippine National Bank 1923, 8, BIA 6769-711G.
20  Corpus to Quezon (3 Mar. 1925), 3, Philippine National Library, Manuel L. Quezon Papers, Series VII, Subject File (hereafter cited as "QP"), Box 447.

21 "Report on Philippine National Bank, Manila, Philippine Islands as of December 31, 1925," 14, BIA 6769-750.
22 The Philippine Vegetable Oil Co. was later absorbed by a British-German firm, the Philippine Refining Co. Since then, the Philippine Refining Co. and the Philippine Manufacturing Co. have remained the two major enterprises of the Philippine coconut processing industry. Gleeck 1975, 75; Yoshihara 1985, 78–79.
23 For the establishment and management of the Mindoro Development Co., see Nagano 1986, 60–80; Schult 1991, 458–74; Sullivan 1992, 128–36.
24 Nagano 1986, 97–101.
25 Willis to McIntyre (23 Apr. 1916), BIA 6769-143.
26 Coates 1920, 145–46.
27 Ibid., 126.
28 Ibid., 86.
29 Ibid., 89–90.
30 Ibid., 90.
31 Ibid., 90–92.
32 Ibid., 92.
33 Ibid., 92–93.
34 Ibid., 93–94.
35 Ibid., 94.
36 Ibid.
37 Ibid.
38 Nagano 1993, 225–26.
39 Haskins & Sells 1922, 7. See also "Memo Re Sugar Centrals Controlled by P.N.B.," BIA 6769-708B.
40 Nagano 1993, 226–27.
41 Coates 1920, 44.
42 Ibid., 3.
43 F. C. Fisher and Michael Camus, "Report Concerning Liability, Civil or Criminal of Former Directors of the Philippine National Bank Arising from Commissions Connected with the Management of Its Affairs" (28 Nov. 1923), QP, Box 445. For a study that discusses the problems of the National Bank's loans based on this report, see McCoy and Roces 1985, 320–25. See also McCoy 2009, 272.
44 Fisher and Camus, "Report Concerning Liability, Civil or Criminal," 152–55.
45 Ibid., 156–59.
46 Ibid., 168–70. Vicente Singson Encarnacion was president of Compañía Mercantil de Filipinas and Vicente Madrigal was its director. Coates 1920, 48, 50.
47 Fisher and Camus, "Report Concerning the Liability, Civil or Criminal," 160–61.
48 Ibid., 161–62.
49 Ibid., 162–63.
50 Ibid., 163–64.
51 Ibid., 165.

52 Ibid., 170–72. From the time of its establishment, the highest executive position of the National Bank had been president; however, during 1921 the title was changed to "general manager." "Philippine National Bank, Manila, P. I., July 1, 1936," 11, Harry S. Truman Library, J. Weldon Jones Papers, Box 41.
53 Fisher and Camus, "Report Concerning the Liability, Civil or Criminal," 172–73.
54 Ibid., 173.
55 Ibid., 174.
56 Ibid., 180–84.
57 Ibid., 185.
58 Ibid.
59 Wong 1999, 121–32.
60 Ibid., 132–42.
61 Ibid., 139.
62 Ibid., 142–46.
63 Ibid., 147.
64 The massive loan practice to the director-related corporations became an issue once more in the Philippines after World War II, when loans to directors, officers, stockholders, and related interests (called "DOSRI loans") were brought to light. DOSRI loans were regulated by the General Banking Act of 1948. In 1964 the Central Bank issued a circular to specify the requirement. In 1965, anti-DOSRI provisions were applied to the loans that were provided to corporations in which bank directors, officers, and stockholders held equity. Yet, DOSRI loans never disappeared. Hutchcroft 1998, 106–7.

## CHAPTER 7: RECONSTRUCTING THE PHILIPPINE NATIONAL BANK AND THE CURRENCY SYSTEM

1 Coates 1920a, 1920b, 1921.
2 Haskins & Sells 1922.
3 Wright 1921.
4 Wright 1922.
5 For the official view by Governor-General Wood in February 1923 and the general outline of the Wright report of 1922, see: "Bank's Millions Dissipated," *Manila Daily Bulletin* (17 Aug. 1923); "Philippine National Bank Conditions Bared by Wood Message," *Manila Times* (19 Aug. 1923); "The Governor's Message on the Philippine National Bank," *Philippine Herald* (19 Aug. 1923); "An Orgy of Mismanagement: The Story of the Philippine National Bank," *Far Eastern Review* (Sept. 1923), 584–85, 615–20, BIA 6769-A-80.
6 Concepcion 1927. Concepcion's Spanish memoir is available in English translation as "'The Tragedy' of the Philippine National Bank by Venancio Concepcion, Former President and General Manager thereof. Manila 1927," BIA 6769-804A.
7 [Translation] *El Ideal*, Manila, 20 June 1921, BIA 6769-A-41.

8   [Translation] *La Vanguardia*, Manila, 24 June 1921, BIA 6769-A-39. Note that BIA's translator retains the accent in Concepción, although postcolonial Philippine Spanish generally dispenses with it. "City fiscal" refers to the Manila city prosecutor.
9   [Translation] *El Comercio*, Manila, 25 June 1921, BIA 6769-A-42.
10  For Concepcion's remarks immediately after his arrest, see "General Venancio Concepcion Files Demurrer to First Complaint Against Him and Pleads Not Guilty to Second," *Manila Times* (10 July 1921); "Fiscal Torres Replies to Demurrer Saying Facts in Case Constitute a Cause for Action Against Concepcion," *Manila Times* (11 July 1921).
11  For the loan to this corporation provided by the National Bank, see Chapter 6.
12  Section 35 of Act No. 2747 prohibited the National Bank from granting loans directly or indirectly to members of the Bank's board of directors or agents of its branches. Act No. 2747 (1918), 457.
13  Decision of the Supreme Court [No. 18535, August 15, 1922], *Official Gazette*, vol. XXI, no. 86 (19 July 1923), 1543–49; "Venancio Concepcion," BIA Personnel File, Box 124.
14  For the National Bank's loan to this corporation, see Chapter 6.
15  Section 17 of Act No. 2747 provided that the board of directors should shoulder responsibility for the management of the National Bank. Act No. 2747 (1918), 455.
16  Decision of the Supreme Court [No. 18536, September 11, 1922], *Official Gazette* (Manila), vol. XXI, no.140 (22 Nov. 1923), 2938–45; "Venancio Concepcion," BIA Personnel File, Box 124.
17  Decision of the Supreme Court [No. 19190, November 29, 1922], *Official Gazette* (Manila), vol. XXI, no. 50 (26 Apr. 1923), 914–16; "Venancio Concepcion," BIA Personnel File, Box 124.
18  "Deposed Bank President, Leaving Prison, Plans Business Career," *Manila Daily Bulletin* (10 June 1925); "Venancio Concepcion," BIA Personnel File, Box 124.
19  Concepcion (1927); "'The Tragedy' of the Philippine National Bank," BIA 6769-804A.
20  For the loan business of the National bank to the exporters of Manila hemp including these three firms, see Chapter 6.
21  Concepcion (1927), 23–27; "'The Tragedy' of the Philippine National Bank," 11–12, BIA 6769-804A.
22  Concepcion (1927), 39–53; "'The Tragedy' of the Philippine National Bank," 16–23, BIA 6769-804A.
23  Concepcion (1927), 51–52; "'The Tragedy' of the Philippine National Bank," 22, BIA 6769-804A.
24  Williams (1925), 168.
25  George F. Luthringer's book 1934, still the best source on the financial crisis, uses two reports by Coates 1920a and 1921 and one report by Wright 1922 in chapters VII & VIII. Peter Stanley 1974 discusses the mismanagement of the National Bank

based on one report by Coates 1920a in chapter 9. Michael P. Onorato's work 1968, 1988 on the Wood-Forbes mission refers to one report by Coates 1920b and one report by Wright 1921.

[26] Coates 1921, 2.
[27] As has been discussed in Chapter 1, the revision of the Philippine currency law of 1918 (Act No. 2776) was the alignment of the revision of the regulation of the currency system (Secs. 2–6 of Chapter 41) in the Administration Code of 1917 (Act No. 2711).
[28] *Laws of the Fourth Philippine Legislature ... Including the Administrative Code together with Certain Resolutions of the Philippine Commission.* Washington, DC: Government Printing Office 1918, 178, BIA Library, Entry 95, vol. 365.
[29] Luthringer (1934), 97; Act No. 2603 (1916), 440.
[30] Coates 1921, 27.
[31] *The Federal Reserve Act (Approved December 23, 1913), as Amended August 4, 1914, August 15, 1914, March 3, 1915, September 7, 1916, June 21, 1917.* Washington, DC: Government Printing Office 1917, 30, BIA 17128-57.
[32] Coates 1921, 7.
[33] Act No. 2612 (1916), 1100. The phrase "That whenever in the judgment of the Governor-General it is in the public interest" in Act No. 2612 was changed into "That whenever in the judgment of the Secretary of Finance it is in the public interest" in Act No. 2747 (1918), 455.
[34] Coates 1921, 4.
[35] Act No. 2776 (1918), 880.
[36] Coates 1921, 25. See also Luthringer 1934, 100.
[37] Coates 1921, 47–55.
[38] Ibid., 60–62.
[39] Ibid., 101–7.
[40] Wright 1921.
[41] Ibid., 3.
[42] Ibid., 2–4.
[43] Ibid., 5–12.
[44] Ibid., 13.
[45] Ibid., 26.
[46] Ibid.
[47] Ibid., 13–15.
[48] Ibid., 15–16.
[49] Ibid., 25.
[50] Ibid., 25; Act No. 2939 (1921), 602.
[51] Wright 1921, 25, 27.
[52] Ibid., 27. See also Edwin W. Kemmerer, "Memorandum Concerning Certain Proposals for Currency Legislation in the Philippine Islands Submitted to the Speaker of the Philippine Assembly (12 Jan. 1918)," BIA 808-452A.

53  Wright 1921, 43–44.
54  United States Library of Congress, Manuscript Division, Francis Burton Harrison Papers, Boxes 33–36.
55  McIntyre to Baker (10 May 1919), BIA 6769-252; McIntyre to Harrison (1 August 1919), BIA 6769-after 306; McIntyre to Harrison (12 Aug. 1920), BIA 6769-after 494; McIntyre to Harrison (18 Sept. 1920), BIA 808-470; McIntyre to Harrison (30 Sept. 1920), BIA 6769-525; Frank McIntyre, "Memorandum: On Mr. Francis Coates, Jr. Report on Gold Standard Fund and the Certificate Reserve Fund of the Treasurer of the Philippine Islands Submitted to the Secretary of War on March 3, 1921" (28 Mar. 1921), BIA 6769-with 585A; McIntyre to Coates (5 Apr. 1921), BIA 6769-with 585A; McIntyre to Wood (28 Dec. 1922), BIA 808-after 579; Frank McIntyre, "Currency System in the Philippine Islands" (27 Apr. 1923), BIA with 808-585; Frank McIntyre's memo (26 May 1925), BIA 808-595.
56  For Conant's proposal, see Charles A. Conant, "Proposed Changes in the Monetary Law of the Philippines Islands" (27 Oct. 1914), BIA 808-393A; Philippine National Library, Manuel L. Quezon Papers, Series IV, Subject File, Box 50.
57  McIntyre to Baker (10 May 1919), BIA 6769-252.
58  Wood to Weeks (29 Nov. 1921), BIA 808-545; Wood to Weeks (18 Dec. 1922), BIA 808-557; Weeks to Wood (30 Jan. 1922), BIA 808-557; Wood to Weeks (24 Feb. 1923), BIA 808-582.
59  Act No. 3058 (1922), 1543–48.
60  Forbes 1928, II, 265–66; Agoncillo and Guerrero 1973, 352. For details of the management of the government corporations, see Apostol 1927, chaps. VIIII & IX.
61  See also Forbes 1928, II, 266.
62  Ibid.
63  United States 1921, 23.
64  Philippine Islands, Governor General 1922, 1.
65  Wood to Weeks (31 Aug. 1922), BIA 6769-710.
66  Weeks to Wood (18 Oct. 1922), BIA 6769-710.
67  Quoted in Apostol 1927, chap. X.
68  Philippine Islands, Governor General 1928, 36.
69  "Wood's Order to Abolish Board of Control Upheld by Philippines Tribunal," *Manila Daily Bulletin* (2 Apr. 1927); "Text of Supreme Court Decision in Bank and Coal Company Cases," *Manila Daily Bulletin* (2 Apr. 1927), BIA 6769-787; "Law Creating Control Board a Blunder, Says Sumulong; 'I Am Not at All Surprised by Court's Decision'–President Quezon," *Tribune* (2 Apr. 1927); "Full Text of Supreme Court's Decision on Board of Control," *Tribune* (2 Apr. 1927), BIA 6769-790B.
70  "Text of Supreme Court Decision," *Manila Daily Bulletin* (2 Apr. 1927), BIA 6769-787; "Full Text of Supreme Court's Decision," *Tribune* (2 Apr. 1927), BIA 6769-790B; Decision of Supreme Court [No. 27225, April 1, 1927], *Official Gazette*, vol. XXV, no. 67 (4 June 1927), 1489, BIA 6769-791A.

71 "Text of Supreme Court Decision," *Manila Daily Bulletin* (2 Apr. 1927), BIA 6769-787; "Full Text of Supreme Court's Decision," *Tribune* (2 Apr. 1927), BIA 6769-790B; Forbes (1928), II, 267.

72 "Text of Supreme Court Decision," *Manila Daily Bulletin* (2 Apr. 1927), BIA 6769-787; "Full Text of Supreme Court's Decision," *Tribune* (2 Apr. 1927), BIA 6769-790B; Forbes 1928, II, p. 266.

73 "U.S. Tribunal Will Review Court Ruling," *Manila Daily Bulletin* (5 Apr. 1927), BIA 6769-790C; Supreme Court of the United States, Nos. 564 and 573 – October Term 1927 [May 14, 1928], BIA 6769-801; Grunder and Livezey 1951, 167–68; Liang 1971, 148–50; Agoncillo and Guerrero 1973, 368; Golay 1997, 245–47, 275; McCoy 2009, 287–91.

# BIBLIOGRAPHY

## I. ARCHIVE COLLECTIONS
Francis Burton Harrison Papers, Manuscript Division, U.S. Library of Congress.
Edwin W. Kemmerer Papers, Seeley G. Mudd Manuscript Library, Princeton University.
Frank R. McCoy Papers, Manuscript Division, U.S. Library of Congress.
Manuel L. Quezon Papers, Philippine National Library.
Henry Parker Willis Papers, Rare Book and Manuscript Library, Columbia University.
Leonard Wood Papers, Manuscript Division, U.S. Library of Congress.
Record Group 350: Records of the Bureau of Insular Affairs, U.S. National Archives.

## II. LAWS AND STATUTES
Act No. 938. 1903. *Official Gazette* (Manila), vol. I, no. 62 (Nov. 11): 797–99.
Act No. 1865. 1908. *Official Gazette* (Manila), vol. VI, no. 32 (Aug. 5): 1122–23.
Act No. 1906. 1909. *Official Gazette* (Manila), vol. VII, no. 28 (July 14): 986.
Act No. 2067. 1911. *Official Gazette* (Manila), vol. IX, no. 32 (Aug. 9): 1316.
Act No. 2083. 1911. *Official Gazette* (Manila), vol. IX, no. 52 (Dec. 27): 2177–79.
Act No. 2603. 1916. *Official Gazette* (Manila), vol. XIV, no. 8 (Feb. 23): 440.
Act No. 2612. 1916. *Official Gazette* (Manila), vol. XIV, no. 24 (June 14): 1097–1102.
Act No. 2747. 1918. *Official Gazette* (Manila), vol. XVI, no. 12 (Mar. 20): 453–58.
Act No. 2776. 1918. *Official Gazette* (Manila), vol. XVI, no. 22 (May 29): 877–81.
Act No. 2938. 1921. *Official Gazette* (Manila), vol. XIX, no. 27 (Mar. 3): 573–79.
Act No. 2939. 1921. *Official Gazette* (Manila), vol. XIX, no. 28 (Mar. 5): 601–2.
Act No. 3058. 1922. *Official Gazette* (Manila), vol. XX, no. 87 (July 22): 1543–48.
Act No. 4199. 1935. *Official Gazette* (Manila), vol. XXX, no. 42 (Apr. 6): 737–38.
Public Law No. 137. 1903. *U.S. Statutes at Large*, vol. 32: 952–53.
Public Law No. 274. 1906. *U.S. Statutes at Large*, vol. 34: 453–54.

## III. GOVERNMENT PUBLICATIONS
*Agricultural bank of the Philippine government: Act of the Philippine legislature creating and establishing the bank and by-laws adopted by the board of directors.* 1908. Manila: Bureau of Printing (BIA 6769-90, 91).

Philippine Islands, Bureau of Banking. 1930. *Annual report of the bank commissioner of the Philippine Islands, 1929*. Manila: Bureau of Printing.

―――. 1931. *Annual report of the bank commissioner of the Philippine Islands, 1930*. Manila: Bureau of Banking.

―――. 1932. *Annual report of the bank commissioner of the Philippine Islands, 1931*. Manila: Bureau of Banking.

―――. 1933. *Annual report of the bank commissioner of the Philippine Islands, 1932*. Manila: Bureau of Banking.

―――. 1935. *Annual report of the bank commissioner of the Philippine Islands, 1934*. Manila: Bureau of Banking.

Philippine Islands, Bureau of Commerce and Industry. 1918. *Statistical bulletin*, no. 1. Manila: Bureau of Printing.

Philippine Islands, Bureau of the Treasury. 1904. *First annual report of the chief of the division of the currency*. Manila: Bureau of Printing.

―――. 1901. *Annual report of the treasurer of the Philippine Islands, FY1910*. Manila: Bureau of Printing.

―――. 1910. *Annual report of the treasurer of the Philippine Islands, FY1910*. Manila: Bureau of Printing.

―――. 1912. *Annual report of the treasurer of the Philippine Islands, FY1912*. Manila: Bureau of Printing.

―――. 1913. *Annual report of the treasurer of the Philippine Islands, FY1913*. Manila: Bureau of Printing.

―――. 1916a. *Annual report of the treasurer of the Philippine Islands, FY1914*. Manila: Bureau of Printing.

―――. 1916b. *Annual report of the treasurer of the Philippine Islands, FY1915*. Manila: Bureau of Printing.

―――. 1920. *Annual report of the treasurer of the Philippine Islands, 1919*. Manila: Bureau of Printing.

―――. 1923. *Annual report of the treasurer of the Philippine Islands, 1922*. Manila: Bureau of Printing.

―――. 1924. *Annual report of the treasurer of the Philippine Islands, 1923*. Manila: Bureau of Printing.

―――. 1925. *Annual report of the treasurer of the Philippine Islands, 1924*. Manila: Bureau of Printing.

Philippine Islands, Governor General. 1919. *Report of the governor general of the Philippine Islands, 1918*. Washington, DC: Government Printing Office.

―――. 1922. *Report of the governor general of the Philippine Islands, 1921*. Manila: Government Printing Office.

―――. 1923. *Report of the governor general of the Philippine Islands, 1920*. Washington, DC: Government Printing Office.

―――. 1927. *Annual report of the governor general of the Philippine Islands, 1925*. Washington, DC: Government Printing Office.

———. 1928. *Annual report of the governor general of the Philippine Islands, 1926.* Washington, DC: Government Printing Office.
Philippines (Commonwealth), Bureau of Banking. 1938. *Annual report of the bank commissioner of the Philippines, 1937.* Manila: Bureau of Printing.
———. 1939. *Annual report of the bank commissioner of the Philippines, 1938.* Manila: Bureau of Banking.
———. 1940. *Annual report of the bank commissioner of the Philippines, 1939.* Manila: Bureau of Banking.
Philippines (Commonwealth), Bureau of the Treasury. 1936–1941. *Annual report of the treasurer of the Philippines, 1935; 1936; 1937; 1938; 1939; 1940.* Manila: Bureau of Printing.
United States. 1921. *Report of the special mission on investigation to the Philippine Islands.* Manila: Bureau of Printing.
United States, House of Representatives. 57th Congress, 2d Session. 1903. *Establishing of an agricultural bank in the Philippine Islands. Letter from the secretary of war, transmitting petition of Emilio Aguinaldo y Famy asking legislation for the establishment of an agricultural bank in the Philippine Islands (Document No. 303).* (BIA 6769-1).
United States, House of Representatives. 59th Congress, 1st Session. 1906. *Philippine tariff: Hearings before the committee on ways and means.* Washington, DC: Government Printing Office.
United States, House of Representatives. 61st Congress, 3d Session. 1911. *Administration of Philippine Lands: Report by the committee on insular affairs of the house of representatives of interior department of the Philippine government touching the administration of Philippine lands and all matters of fact and law pertaining thereto pursuance of house resolution no. 795 (Report No. 2289).* Washington, DC: Government Printing Office.
United States, House of Representatives. 67th Congress, 2d Session, Committee on Insular Affairs. 1922a. *Hearings on H.R. 10442, February 21, 1922, and Part 2, March 7 and 22, 1922. Extending limit of indebtedness of the Philippine government.* Washington, DC: Government Printing Office.
United States, House of Representatives. 67th Congress, 2d Session. 1922b. *Extending limit of indebtedness of the Philippine government (Report No. 874).* Washington, DC: Government Printing Office.
United States, Senate, Committee on the Philippines. 1902a. *Hearings before a subcommittee of the committee on the Philippines . . . . A system of currency for the Philippine Islands, Feb. 13 & March 3, 1902.* Washington, DC: Government Printing Office.
———. 1902b. *Currency in the Philippines: Hearing before the subcommittee on the Philippines . . . March 24, 1902. Statement of Charles A. Conant.* Washington, DC: Government Printing Office.
United States, War Department, Bureau of Insular Affairs. 1900. *Report of the*

*Philippine commission to the president, January 31, 1900.* Washington, DC: Government Printing Office.

———. 1901. *Report of the United States Philippine commission to the secretary of war for the period from December 1, 1900 to October 15, 1901.* Washington, DC: Government Printing Office.

———. 1903. *Third annual report of the Philippine commission, 1902.* Washington, DC: Government Printing Office.

———. 1904. *Reports of the Philippine commission, the civil governor, and the heads of the executive departments of the civil government of the Philippine Islands (1900–1903).* Washington, DC: Government Printing Office.

———. 1905. *Fifth annual report of the Philippine commission, 1904.* Washington, DC: Government Printing Office.

———. 1906a. *Sixth annual report of the Philippine commission, 1905.* Washington, DC: Government Printing Office.

———. 1906b. *Report of the chief of the division of the currency to the treasurer of the Philippine Islands concerning the availability of establishing a government agricultural bank in the Philippines.* Washington, DC: Government Printing Office (BIA 6769-24, 25).

———. 1906c. *Report on the agricultural bank of Egypt to the secretary of war and to the Philippine commission.* Washington, DC: Government Printing Office (BIA 6769-48, 49).

———. 1907. *Seventh annual report of the Philippine commission, 1906.* Washington, DC: Government Printing Office.

———. 1908. *Eighth annual report of the Philippine commission, 1907.* Washington, DC: Government Printing Office.

———. 1910. *Report of the Philippine commission, 1909.* Washington, DC: Government Printing Office.

———. 1911. *Report of the Philippine commission, 1910.* Washington, DC: Government Printing Office.

———. 1912a. *Report of the Philippine commission, 1911.* Washington, DC: Government Printing Office.

———. 1912b. *Report of the Philippine commission, 1912.* Washington, DC: Government Printing Office.

———. 1914. *Report of the Philippine commission, 1913.* Washington, DC: Government Printing Office.

———. 1916. *Report of the Philippine commission, 1915.* Washington, DC: Government Printing Office.

## IV. BOOKS, ARTICLES, AND UNPUBLISHED MATERIALS

Abelarde, Pedro E. 1947. *American tariff policy toward the Philippines, 1898–1946.* New York: King's Crown Press.

Adas, Michael. 1974. *The Burma Delta: Economic development and social change on an Asian rice frontier, 1852–1941.* Madison: University of Wisconsin Press.
Agoncillo, Teodoro A., and Milagros C. Guerrero. 1973. *History of the Filipino people.* Quezon City: R. P. Garcia Publishing Co.
Allen, G. C., and Audrey G. Donnithorne. 1968a. *Western enterprise in far eastern economic development.* New York: Augustus M. Kelly (reprint, 1st ed. 1954).
———. 1968b. *Western enterprise in Indonesia and Malaysia: A study in economic development.* New York: Augustus M. Kelly (reprint, 1st ed. 1954).
Apostol, Jose P. 1927. *The economic policy of the Philippine government: ownership and operation of business.* Manila: University of the Philippines.
Baba, Keinosuke, ed. 1961. *Firipin no kinyu to shihon keisei* [Finance and capital formation in the Philippines]. Tokyo: Institute of Developing Economies.
Balanon, Angelita B. (n.d.). "The role of banking in the Philippine colonial economy, 1851–1896." Unpublished manuscript.
Balmaceda, Julian C. 1924. *Agricultural credit coöperative associations in the Philippines.* Manila: Bureau of Printing.
*Banco de las Islas Filipinas, LXXV aniversario: Remembratorio del primer banco establecido en el extremo oriente.* 1928. Manila: [Banco de Las Islas Filipinas].
Bankers Association of the Philippines. 1957. *Banking in the Philippines.* Manila.
"The Bank of the Philippine Islands." 1918. *The Bankers Magazine* 96, no. 3: 371–376.
Banyai, Richard A. 1974. *Money and banking in China and Southeast Asia during the Japanese military occupation, 1937–1945.* Taipei: Tai Wan Enterprises Co.
Barrows, David P. 1914. *A decade of American government in the Philippines, 1903–1913.* Yonkers-on-Hudson, NY: World Book Co.
Beckhart, Benjamin Haggott. 1972. *Federal reserve system.* New York: Columbia University Press.
Biedzynski, James Christopher. 1990. "Frank McIntyre and the Philippines." Ph.D. dissertation, Ohio University.
Blanco, John D. 2009. *Frontier constitutions: Christianity and colonial empire in the nineteenth-century Philippines.* Berkeley: University of California Press.
Brown, Ian. 1979. "Siam and the Gold Standard, 1902–1908." *Journal of Southeast Asian Studies* 10, no. 2: 381–399.
———. 1988. *The Élite and the economy in Siam c. 1890–1920.* Singapore: Oxford University Press.
———. 1997. *Economic Change in South-East Asia, c.1830–1980.* Kuala Lumpur: Oxford University Press.
Brown, Rajeswary Ampalavanar. 1993. "Chettiar capital and Southeast Asia credit networks in the inter-war period." In *Local suppliers of credit in the third world, 1750–1960*, ed. Gareth Austin and Kaoru Sugihara, pp. 254–287. New York: St. Martin's Press.
———. 1994. *Capital and entrepreneurship in South-East Asia.* New York: St. Martin's Press.

Buencamino, Victor. 1977. *Memoirs of Victor Buencamino*. Mandaluyong, The Philippines: Jorge B. Vargas Filipiniana Foundation.

Butcher, John, and Howard Dick, eds. 1993. *The rise and fall of revenue farming: Business elites and the emergence of the modern state in Southeast Asia*. New York: St. Martin's Press.

Casambre, Napoleon Jimenez. 1968. "Francis Burton Harrison: His administration in the Philippines, 1913–1921." Ph.D. dissertation, Stanford University.

Central Bank of the Philippines. [1974]. *Central bank of the Philippines: January 3, 1949–January 3, 1974*. [Manila: Central Bank of the Philippines].

"Charles Arthur Conant (July 2, 1861–July 5, 1915)." 1930. *Dictionary of American biography*, vol. IV: 334–335. New York: Charles Scribner's Sons.

"Charter of the Bank of the Philippine Islands, Act No. 1790." (n.d.). In *Manual of the bank of the Philippine Islands, 1851–1918*, vol.1, pp. 13–45. Manila: n. p.

"China banking corporation: Golden anniversary." 1970. *Chronicle Business Report*, Aug. 16.

China Banking Corporation, Manila, P. I. (n.d.). *Articles of incorporation and by-laws, incorporated July 20, 1920*. Manila: [s.n.].

Churchill, Bernadita Reyes. 1983. *The Philippine independence missions to the United States, 1919–1934*. Manila: National Historical Institute.

Coates, Francis, Jr., 1920a. "Report of an examination of the Philippine national bank Manila, P. I. as of at close of business Nov. 30, 1919" [BIA 6769-565A].

_____. 1920b. "Report to the secretary of war containing twenty-nine consecutive folios & signed sheets" (Aug. 30) [BIA 22639-57, Confidential "B" File].

_____. 1921. "Report to the honorable, the secretary of war–United States of America, Washington, D.C., covering an investigation of the operation in the gold standard fund and the certificate reserve fund of the treasurer of the Philippine Islands in connection with the operations of the Philippine national bank of the Philippine Islands" (Mar. 3) [BIA 6769-585A].

Cohen, Paul A. 1984. *Discovering history in China: American historical writing on the recent Chinese past*. New York: Columbia University Press.

Colayco, Maria Teresa. 1984. *A Tradition of leadership: Bank of the Philippine Islands*. Manila: Bank of the Philippine Islands.

Conant, Charles A. 1901. *A special report on coinage and banking in the Philippine Islands made to the secretary of war*. Washington, DC: Government Printing Office.

_____. 1902. "The Currency of the Philippine Islands." *Annals of the American Academy of Political and Social Science* 20, no. 3: 44–59.

Concepcion, Venancio. 1927. *"La tragedia" del banco nacional Filipino*. Manila: n.p.

Corpuz, Arturo G. 1999. *The Colonial iron horse: Railroads and regional development in the Philippines, 1875–1935*. Quezon City: University of the Philippines Press.

Cruz, Romeo V. 1974. *America's colonial desk and the Philippines, 1898–1934*. Quezon City: University of the Philippines Press.

Cullather, Nick. 1992. "The United States, American business, and the origins of the Philippine central bank." *Bulletin of the American Historical Collection* 20, no. 4: 80–99.

Cullinane, Michael. 1971. "Implementing the 'new order': The structure and supervision of local government during the Taft era." In *Compadre colonialism: studies on the Philippines under American rule*, ed. Norman G. Owen. Michigan Papers on South and Southeast Asia no. 3, pp. 9–34. Ann Arbor: Center for South and Southeast Asian Studies, University of Michigan.

———. 2003. *Illustrado politics: Filipino elite responses to American rule, 1898–1908*. Quezon City: Ateneo de Manila University Press.

Cushman, Jennifer W. 1991. *Family and state: The formation of a Sino-Thai tin-mining dynasty, 1797–1932*, ed. Craig J. Reynolds. Singapore: Oxford University Press.

de Veyra, Jaime C. 1922. "The Filipinos' answer to the Wood-Forbes report. Extension of remarks, Hon. Jaime C. de Veyra." *Congressional Record* 62, pt. 13: 13263–13268.

Diokno, Maria Serena. 2000. "The Maldito Mexican peso and the currency crisis a century ago." Paper presented at the 6th International Philippine Studies Conference. July 10–14. Quezon City: Philippine Social Science Center.

Dixon, Chris. 1991. *South East Asia in the world-economy: A regional geography*. Cambridge: Cambridge University Press.

Doeppers, Daniel F. 1983. "Mortgage loans and lending institutions in pre-war Manila." *Philippine Studies* 31, no. 2: 189–215.

———. 1984. *Manila 1900–1941: Social change in a late colonial metropolis*. Quezon City: Ateneo de Manila University Press.

Edwards, Clarence R. 1900. *Memorandum on currency and exchange in the Philippine Islands*. Washington. DC: Government Printing Office.

"Eighty Years of Public Service": A Brief history of the Monte de Piedad savings bank. 1962. Manila: Monte de Piedad Savings Bank.

Elliot, Charles Burke. 1968. *The Philippines: To the end of the commission government: A study in tropical democracy.* New York: Greenwood Press (reprint, 1st ed. 1917).

Elson, Robert. 1992. "International commerce, the state and society: Economic and social change." In *The Cambridge history of Southeast Asia, Vol. 2: The nineteenth and twentieth centuries*, ed. Nicolas Tarling, pp. 131–195. Cambridge: Cambridge University Press.

Eng, Pierre van der. 1993. *The silver standard and Asia's integration into the world economy, 1850–1914*. Canberra: Australian National University. Working Papers in Economic History no. 175.

———. 1996. "Introduction." In *Currency and the economy of Netherlands India, 1870–95*, by N. P. van den Berg, pp. vii–xxvi. Singapore: Institute of Southeast Asian Studies.

Escalante, Rene R. 2007. *The bearer of pax Americana: The Philippine career of William H. Taft, 1900–1913*. Quezon City: New Day Publishers.
Espiritu, Augusto P., and Mila Magno-Mijares. 1957. *Rural banking*. Manila: [s.n.].
Fitzsimmons, A. P. 1917a. "The monetary system of the Philippine Islands." *The Philippine Review* 2, no. 8: 22.
_____. 1917b. "Our silver situation." *The Philippine Review* 2, no. 9: 17–20.
_____. 1918. "The phenomenal growth of the banking business in the Philippine Islands during the past two years." *The Philippine Review* 3, no. 5: 320–326.
*Firipin ni okeru ginko-hattatsushi* [A history of the development of banking in the Philippines]. 1942. Yokohama: Yokohama Specie Bank, Research Department.
Forbes, W. Cameron. 1928. *The Philippine Islands*. Boston: Houghton Mifflin.
Foster, Ann L. 2010. *The Projections of power: The United States and Europe in colonial Southeast Asia, 1919–1941*. Durham, NC: Duke University Press.
Foucault, Michel. 1990. *The history of sexuality: An introduction*. New York: Vintage Books.
Fukuda, Shozo, 1995. *With seat & abacus: Economic roles of Southeast Asian Chinese on the eve of world war II*, ed. George Hicks. Singapore: Select Books.
Galang, Zoilo M., ed. 1938. *Philippine business library, vol. V: Business leaders miscellanea*. Manila: Imprenta Los Filipinos.
Giesecke, Leonard F. 1987. *History of American economic policy in the Philippines during the American colonial period, 1900–1935*. New York: Garland Publishing Co.
Gleeck, Lewis E., Jr. 1975. *American business and Philippine economic development*. Manila: Carmelo & Buermann.
Go, Julian. 2008. *American empire and the politics of meaning*. Durham, NC: Duke University Press.
Go, Julian, and Anne L. Foster, eds. 2003. *The American colonial state in the Philippines: Global perspectives*. Durham, NC: Duke University Press.
Golay, Frank H. 1984. "The search for revenues." In *Reappraising an empire: New perspectives on Philippine-American history*, ed. Peter W. Stanley, pp. 231–260. Cambridge, MA: Harvard University Press.
_____. 1997. *Face of empire: United States-Philippines relations, 1898–1946*. Quezon City: Ateneo de Manila University Press.
Gonjo, Yasuo. 1985. *Fransu teikokushugi to Ajia: Indoshina ginkoshi kenkyu* [French imperialism and Asia: A study of the banque de l'Indochine]. Tokyo: University of Tokyo Press. (The French version is published as *Banque coloniale ou banque d'affaires: La Banque de d'Indochine sous la III République*. Paris: Comité pour l'histoire économique et financière de la France, 1993).
Greenberg, Michael. 1951. *British trade and the opening of China*. Cambridge: Cambridge University Press.
Grunder, Garel A., and William E. Livezey. 1951. *The Philippines and the United States*. Westport, CT: Greenwood Press.

Hamashita, Takeshi. 1990. *Kindai Chugoku no kokusaiteki keki: Choko shisutemu to kindai Ajia* [International impetus of modern China: Tribute trade system and modern Asia]. Tokyo: University of Tokyo Press.

Hanna, Hugh H., Charles A. Conant, and Jeremiah W. Jenks. 1903. *Stability of international exchange: Report on the introduction of the gold-exchange standard into China and other silver-using countries.* Washington, DC: Government Printing Office.

———. 1904. *Gold standard in international trade: Report on the introduction of the gold-exchange standard into China, the Philippine Islands, Panama, and other silver-using countries and on the stability of exchange.* Washington, DC: Government Printing Office.

Harden, Edward M. 1898. *Report on financial and industrial conditions in the Philippine Islands.* Washington, DC: Government Printing Office.

Harrison, Francis Burton. 1922. *The corner-stone of Philippine independence: A narrative of seven years.* New York: Century.

"Harrison, Francis Burton." 1963. *National cyclopedia of American biography*, vol. 46, p. 24. New York: James T. White & Co.

"Harrison, Francis Burton." 1980. *Dictionary of American biography, supplement 6, 1956–1960*, pp. 279–281. New York: Charles Scribner's Sons,

"Haskins & Sells report of examination of P.N.B. as of May 19, 1921, with 16 Exhibits." 1922 [BIA 6769-708A].

Hawes, Gary. 1987. *The Philippine state and the Marcos regime: The politics of export.* Ithaca, NY: Cornell University Press.

Hayden, Joseph Ralson. 1945. *The Philippines: A study in national development.* New York: Macmillan.

Hernandez, Jaime. 1937. *Philippine currency legislation reform.* San Juan, Rizal, The Philippines: Oriental Commercial Co.

Herrera, José Cabezas de. 1883. *El marqués de campo y la sucursal del banco peninsular ultramarino establecida en Manila.* Madrid: Velero.

Hicks, George L., ed. 1993. *Overseas Chinese remittances from Southeast Asia: 1910–1940.* Singapore: Select Books.

Hoyt, Frederick Gilman. 1963. "The Wood-Forbes mission to the Philippines, 1921." Ph.D. dissertation. Claremont Graduate School and University Center.

Huff, W. G. 1989. "Bookkeeping barter, money, credit, and Singapore's international rice trade, 1870–1939." *Explorations in Economic History* 26, no. 2: 161–189.

Hutchcroft, Paul D. 1998. *Booty capitalism: The politics of banking in the Philippines.* Ithaca, NY: Cornell University Press.

Ide, Henry C. 1907. "Banking, currency and finance in the Philippine Islands." *The Annals of the American Academy of Political and Social Science* 30: 27–37.

Ileto, Reynaldo C. 1999. *Knowing America's colony: A hundred years from the Philippine war.* Philippine Studies Occasional Paper Series no. 13. Honolulu: Center for Philippine Studies, University of Hawai'i at Manoa.

Ingram, James C. 1971. *Economic change in Thailand, 1850–1970.* Stanford, CA: Stanford University Press.

Inoue, Tatsumi. 1995. *Kinyu to teikoku: Igirisu teikoku keizaishi* [Finance and imperialism: A study of the economic history of the British empire]. Nagoya: Nagoya University Press.

"In the lives of these people, there is a bank. . . . " 1971. *Citibank: A Manila chronicle special report* (July) [Newspaper clipping file, Lopez Museum, Manila].

Ishii, Kanji. 1979. "Igirisu shokuminchi ginkogun no saihen: 1870–80 nendai no Nihon, Chugoku o chushin ni [Reorganization of British colonial banks: With special references to Japan and China in the 1870s and 1880s (I) and (II)]." *Keizaigaku Ronshu* [Journal of Economics] (University of Tokyo: Faculty of Economics) 45, no. 1: 20–60 and 45, no. 3: 18–46.

Jenks, Jeremiah W. 1907. "Agricultural bank for the Philippine Islands." *Annals of the Academy of Political and Social Sciences* 30: 38–44.

Ji, Zhaojin. 2003. *A history of modern Shanghai banking: The rise and decline of China's finance capitalism.* Armonk, NY: M. E. Sharpe.

Kalaw, Maximo M. 1916. *The case for the Filipinos.* New York: The Century Co.

———. [1921]. *The present government of the Philippines.* Manila: [McCullough Print. Co.].

———. 1926. *The development of Philippine politics (1872–1920).* Manila: Oriental Commercial Co.

Kalaw, Teodoro M. 1965. *Aide-de-camp to freedom.* Trans. Maria Kalaw Katigbak. Manila: Teodoro M. Kalaw Society.

Kemmerer, Edwin W. 1905a. "The Establishment of the gold exchange standard in the Philippines." *Quarterly Journal of Economics* 19: 585–609.

———. 1905b. "Two years of gold exchange standard in the Philippines." *Journal of the American Asiatic Association* 5, no. 10: 302–304.

———. 1907. "The Philippine postal savings bank." *The Annals of the Academy of Political and Social Science* V, no. 30: 45–51.

———. 1908. "Agricultural bank for the Philippines." *The Yale Review* 16: 262–279.

———. 1916. *Modern currency reform: A history and discussion of recent currency reforms in India, Port Rico, Philippine Islands, Straits Settlements and Mexico.* New York: Macmillan.

Keynes, John Maynard. 1924. *Indian currency and finance.* London: Macmillan (reprint, 1st ed. 1913).

King, Frank H. H. 1988a. *The Hongkong bank in the period of imperialism and war, 1895–1918: Wayfoong, the focus of wealth (The history of the Hongkong and Shanghai banking corporation, Vol. II).* Cambridge: Cambridge University Press.

———. 1988b. *The Hongkong bank between the wars and the bank interned, 1919–1945: Return from grandeur (The history of the Hongkong and Shanghai banking corporation, Vol. III).* Cambridge: Cambridge University Press.

Klein, P. W. 1990. "Dutch monetary policy in the East Indies, 1602–1942: A case of changing continuity." In *Money, coins and commerce: Essays in the monetary history of Asia and Europe (From antiquity to modern times)*, ed. E. H. G van Cauwenberghe, pp. 419–453. Leuven: Leuven University Press.

Kramer, Paul A. 2006. *The blood of government: Race, empire, the United States and the Philippines.* Chapel Hill: University of North Carolina Press.

Laanen, Jan T. M. van, ed. 1980. *Changing economy in Indonesia: Volume 6: Money and banking, 1816–1940.* The Hague: Martinus Nijhoff Publishers BV.

———. 1990. "Between the Java bank and the Chinese moneylender: Banking and credit in colonial Indonesia." In *Indonesian economic history in the Dutch colonial era*, ed. Ann Booth, W. J. O'Malley, and Anna Widemann, pp. 244–266. New Haven: Yale University Southeast Asia Studies.

Larkin, John A. 1993. *Sugar and the origin of modern Philippine society.* Berkeley: University of California Press.

Legarda, Angelita Ganzon de. 1976. *Piloncitos to pesos: A brief history of coinage in the Philippines.* Manila: Bancom Development Corporation.

Legarda, Benito J., Jr., 1999. *After the galleons: Foreign trade, economic change and entrepreneurship in the nineteenth-century Philippines.* Quezon City: Ateneo de Manila University Press.

Liang, Dapen. 1971. *Philippine parties and politics: A historical study of national experience in democracy.* San Francisco: Gladstone Company.

Licuanan, Virginia Benitez. 1985. *Money in the bank: The story of money and banking in the Philippines and the PCIBank story.* Manila: PCIBank Human Resources Development Foundation.

Lindblad, Thomas. 1998. *Foreign investment in Southeast Asia in the twentieth century.* New York: St. Martin's Press.

Luthringer, George F. 1934. *The gold-exchange standard in the Philippines.* Princeton, NJ: Princeton University Press.

Mackenzie, Compton. 1954. *Realms of silver: One hundred years of banking in the East.* London: Routledge & Kegan Paul.

Malcolm, George A., and Maximo M. Kalaw. 1923. *Philippine government: Development, organization and functions.* Manila: The Associated Publishers.

Mass, Eugene H. 1971. "Francis Burton Harrison, governor general of the Philippine Islands, 1913–1921." Ph.D. dissertation, Catholic University of America.

Matsuoka, Koji. 1936. *Kinkawase honisei no kenkyu* [A study of the gold exchange standard]. Tokyo: Nihon Hyoronsha.

May, Glenn Anthony. 1984. *Social engineering in the Philippines: The aims, execution, and impact of American colonial policy, 1900–1913.* Quezon City: New Day Publishers (reprint, 1st ed. 1980).

McCoy, Alfred W. 1982. "A queen dies slowly: The rise and decline of Iloilo City." In *Philippine social history: Global trade and local transformations*, ed. Alfred W. McCoy and Ed. C. de Jesus, pp. 297–358. Quezon City: Ateneo de Manila University Press.

_____. 2009. *Policing America's empire: The United States, the Philippines, and the rise of the surveillance state*. Madison: University of Wisconsin Press.

McCoy, Alfred W., and Alfredo R. Roces. 1985. *Philippine cartoons: Political caricature of the American era, 1900–1941*. Quezon City: Vera-Reyes.

McCoy, Alfred W., and Francisco A. Scarano, eds. 2009. *Colonial crucible: Empire in the making of the modern American state*. Madison: University of Wisconsin Press.

"McIntyre, Frank." 1945. *The National cyclopedia of American biography*, vol. 32, pp. 333–334. New York: James T. White & Co.

Meltzer, Allan H. 2003. *A history of the federal reserve, volume 1, 1913–1951*. Chicago: University of Chicago Press.

"Monte de Piedad's 106th year." 1988. *Manila Chronicle*, Supplement (Aug. 2).

Nagano, Yoshiko. 1986. *Firipin keizaishi kenkyu: Togyo shihon to jinushi-sei* [A study of Philippine economic history: Capitalism and hacienda in the sugar industry]. Tokyo: Keiso Shobo.

_____. 1988. "Oligopolistic structure of the Philippine sugar industry during the great depression." In *The international sugar economy in war and depression, 1914–40*, ed. Bill Albert and Adrian Graves, pp. 170–181. London: Routledge.

_____. 1993. "The Philippine national bank and sugar centrals during the American colonial period." *Philippine Studies* 41, no. 2: 217–231.

_____. 1997. "The agricultural bank of the Philippine government, 1908–1916." *Journal of Southeast Asian Studies* 28, no. 2: 301–323.

_____. 1999. "Politics and Philippine banking during the American period." *Philippine Political Science Journal* 20, no. 43: 61–82.

_____. 2010. "Philippine currency system during the American colonial period: Transformation from the gold exchange standard to the dollar exchange standard." *International Journal of Asian Studies* 7, no. 1: 29–50.

Nawata, Seiichi. 1943. *Firipin no tsuka oyobi kinyu* [Currency and finance in the Philippines]. Tokyo: Toa Kenkyujo.

Nihon Ginko Chosa-kyoku (Bank of Japan, Research Section), ed. 1948. *Firipin chuoginko ho, beihi godo kinkyu iinkai houkoku oyobi kankoku* [Act of the central bank of the Philippines, report and recommendations of the joint Philippine-American finance commission]. Tokyo: Bank of Japan.

Onorato, Michael P. 1968. *A brief review of American interest in Philippine development and other essays*. Berkeley, CA: McCutchan Publishing Co.

_____. 1988. *Leonard Wood and the Philippine cabinet crisis of 1923*. Marikina, Metro Manila: J. C. Palabay Enterprises (revised ed.).

Orosa, Sixto L., Jr. 1988. *Banking, anyone? (A retired banker reminisces)*. Manila: J. V. Development Corp.

Owen, Norman G. ed. 1971. *Compadre colonialism: Studies on the Philippines under American rule*. Michigan Papers on South and Southeast Asia no. 3. Ann Arbor: Center for South and Southeast Asian Studies, University of Michigan.

_____. 1984a. "Americans in the abaca trade: Peele, Hubbell & Co., 1856–1875." In *Reappraising an empire: New perspectives on Philippine-American history*, ed. Peter W. Stanley, pp. 201–230. Cambridge, MA: Harvard University Press.

_____. 1984b. *Prosperity without progress: Manila hemp and material life in the colonial Philippines*. Berkeley: University of California Press.

Paredes, Ruby R., ed. 1989a. *Philippine colonial democracy*. Quezon City: Ateneo de Manila University Press.

_____. 1989b. "The Origin of national politics: Taft and partido federal." In *Philippine colonial democracy*, ed. Ruby R. Paredes, pp. 41–69. Quezon City: Ateneo de Manila University Press.

Parrini, Carl L. 1993. "Charles A. Conant, economic crises and foreign policy, 1896–1903." *Behind the throne: Servants of power to imperial presidents, 1898–1968*, ed. Thomas J. McCormick and Walter LaFeber, pp. 35–66. Madison: University of Wisconsin Press.

Pérez, Miguel, et al. [1887]. "Cronica semi-historia de Filipinas y en especial de las Yslas Bisayas desde 1877 a 1887." [Manila]: Unpublished manuscript.

Perkins, E. A. 1947. *History of the Philippine currency system*. Manila (typescript) [Rizal Library, Ateneo de Manila University].

Philippine National Bank. 1923. *Annual report to stockholders by the board of directors of Philippine national bank for the year 1922*. Manila [BIA 6769-711G].

Quibuyen, Floro C. 1999. *A nation aborted: Rizal, American hegemony, and Philippine nationalism*. Quezon City: Ateneo de Manila University Press.

Rafael, Vicente L. 2000. *White love and other events in Filipino history*. Durham, NC: Duke University Press.

_____. 2008. "Reorientation: Notes on the study of the Philippines in the United States." *Philippine Studies* 56, no. 4: 475–492.

Raventos, Emili Girat. 1981. *La compañía general de tabacos de Filipinas, 1881–1981*. Barcelona: [La Campañía General de Tabacos de Filipinas].

Regidor, Antonio M., and J. Warren Mason. 1950. "Commercial progress in the Philippines." In *Encyclopedia of the Philippines*, ed. Galang M. Zailo, 3rd ed., vol. V, pp. 72–123. Manila: Exquiel Floro.

Reyes, Jose S. 1967. *Legislative history of America's economic policy towards the Philippines*. New York: AMS Press (reprint, 1st ed. 1923).

Reyes-McMurray, Marisse. 1998. "The first Filipino private bank." In *Kasaysayan: The story of the Filipino people, vol. 6: Under stars and stripes*, ed. Milagros C. Guerrero. [Hong Kong]: Asian Publishing Co.

Romero, Ma. Fe Hernaez. 1974. *Negros Occidental between two foreign powers (1888–1909)*. Bacolod City: Negros Historical Commission.

Romualdez, Eduardo Z. 1962. "Financial problems created by the war." *Journal of History* 10, no. 4: 448–518.

Rosenberg, Emily S. 1985. "Foundations of United States international financial power: Gold standard diplomacy, 1900–1905." *Business History Review* 59, no. 2: 169–202.

_____. 2003. *Financial missionaries to the world: The politics and culture of dollar diplomacy: 1900–1930*. Durham, NC: Duke University Press.
Rothbard, Murray N. 2002. *A history of money and banking in the United States: The colonial era to world war II*. Auburn, AL.: Ludwig von Mises Institute.
Said, Edward W. 1979. *Orientalism*. New York: Vintage Books.
_____. 1993. *Culture and imperialism*. New York: Alfred A. Knopf.
Salamanca, Bonifacio S. 1984. *The Filipino reaction to American rule, 1901–1913*, Quezon City: New Day Publishers (reprint, 1st ed. 1968).
Salman, Michael. 2001. *The embarrassment of slavery: Controversies over bondage and nationalism in the American colonial Philippines*. Berkeley: University of California Press.
Schult, Volker. 1991. "The San Jose sugar hacienda." *Philippine Studies* 39, no. 4: 458–474.
*Senzen ni okeru hito no zaisei, kinyu, tsuka, boeki-ippan* [Overview of finance, banking, currency and trade]. 1942. Yokohama: Yokohama Specie Bank, Presidential Research Section.
Shafer, Neil. 1964. *A guide book of Philippine paper money*. Racine, WI: Whitman Publishing Co.
Shaw, Angel Velasco, and Luis H. Francia, eds. 2002. *Vestiges of war: The Philippine-American war and the aftermath of an imperial dream, 1899–1999*. New York: New York University Press.
Spalding, William F. 1918. *Eastern exchange currency and finance*, 2nd ed. London: Sir Isaac Pitman & Sons.
Stanley, Peter W. 1974. *A nation in the making: The Philippines and the United States, 1899–1921*. Cambridge, MA: Harvard University Press.
_____, ed. 1984. *Reappraising an empire: New perspectives on Philippine-American history*. Cambridge, MA: Harvard University Press.
Stine, Leo C. 1966. "The economic policies of the commonwealth government of the Philippine Islands." *Journal of East Asiatic Studies* 10: 5–136.
Suehiro, Akira. 1989. *Capital accumulation in Thailand, 1855–1985*. Tokyo: The Centre for East Asian Cultural Studies.
Sugihara, Kaoru. 1996. *Ajia-kan boeki no keisei to kozo* [Formation and structure of intra-Asian trade]. Kyoto: Minerva Publishing Co.
Sullivan, Rodney J. 1992. *Exemplar of Americanism: The Philippine career of Dean C. Worcester*. Quezon City: New Day Publishers.
Takanashi, Hiroaki, ed. 1971. *Firipin no kinyu jijo* [Financial conditions in the Philippines]. Tokyo: Institute of Developing Economies.
Tate, D. J. M. 1979. *The making of modern South East Asia, vol. 2: The western impact: Economic and social change*. Kuala Lumpur: Oxford University Press.
Tiglao, Rigoberto. 1981. *The Philippine coconut industry: Looking into coconut export-oriented agricultural growth*. Davao City: ARC Publications.

Tirona, Mary Grace A. 1987–1988. "Financial entrepreneurship and monopoly capitalism." *Journal of History* V, no. 32–33: 34–64.
Treadgold, Malcolm L. 2003. "The Philippine currency board arrangement, 1945–48: A case of deflationary bias?" *Financial History Review* 10, no. 1: 57–74.
Tyrrell, Ian. 2009. "Empire in American history." In *Colonial crucible: Empire in the making of the modern American state*, ed. Alfred W. McCoy and Francisco A. Scarano, pp. 541–556. Madison: University of Wisconsin Press.
Umehara, Hiromitsu. 1992. *Firipin no noson: Sono kozo to hendo* [Philippine villages: Structure and transformations]. Tokyo: Kokon Shoin.
Valdepeñas, Vicente B., Jr. 2003. "Central banking in historical perspective." In *Money and banking in the Philippines*. Manila: Bangko Sentral ng Pilipinas.
Vergara, Araceli P. 1954. "The bank of the Philippine Islands." Unpublished manuscript, College of Business Administration, University of the Philippines, Diliman.
Vibal, H. P. 1960. "Philippine banking history." *Banking, finance and investments annual & directory for 1959.* Manila: [Insurance & Finance Pub.].
Villalon, Brigido G. 1926. "The banking system of the Philippines and the Philippine national bank." Masters thesis, George Washington University.
Wickberg, Edgar. 1965a. "The Chinese mestizo in Philippine history." *Journal of Southeast Asian History* 5: 62–100.
_____. 1965b. *The Chinese in Philippine life, 1850–1898.* New Haven, CT: Yale University Press.
Willis, H. Parker. 1917a. "The Philippine national bank." *The Journal of Political economy* 25, no. 5: 409–441.
_____. 1917b. "The Philippine national bank." *Bankers Magazine* 95, no.2: 251–252.
_____. 1917c. "The Philippine national bank." *The Philippine Review* 2, no. 3: 45–63.
_____. 1970. *Our Philippine problem: A study of American colonial policy.* New York: Arno Press (reprint, 1st ed. 1905).
Williams, D. R. 1925. *The United States and the Philippines.* Garden City, NY: Doubleday, Page & Co.
Wolters, Willem G. 2001. "Flooded with foreign coins: Spanish and American administrators dealing with currency problems in the Philippines, 1890–1905." *Bijdragen tot de Taal-, Land- en Volkenkunde* [Journal of the Humanities and Social Sciences of Southeast Asia and Oceania] 157, no. 3: 511–538.
_____. 2007. "How were labourers paid in the Philippine Islands during the nineteenth century?" In *Wages and currency: Global comparisons from antiquity to the twentieth century*, ed. Jan Lucassen, pp. 139–167. Bern: Peter Lang.
Wong, Kwok-Chu. 1999. *The Chinese in the Philippine economy: 1898–1941.* Manila: Ateneo de Manila University Press.
Wright, Ben F. 1921. "Memorandum concerning the development of the currency system of the Philippine Islands with special reference to existing conditions

and to the Philippine national bank" (Aug. 1). United States Library of Congress, Manuscript Division, Leonard Wood Papers, Box 219; and also Princeton University, Seeley G. Mudd Manuscript Library, Edwin W. Kemmerer Papers, Box 250.

_____. 1922. "Report on the Philippine national bank being a summary of the report of Francis Coates, Jr. as of November 30, 1919, the report of Haskins and Sells as of May 19, 1921 and a revaluation of the bank's assets as of June 30, 1922 by special bank examiner Ben F. Wright and national bank examiner Leo H. Martin" (Nov. 20) [BIA 6769-720; and also Princeton University, Seeley G. Mudd Manuscript Library, Edwin W. Kemmerer Papers, Box 247].

Yanaihara, Tadao. 1963. "Teikokushugi ka no Indo [India under colonial rule]." In *Yanaihara Tadao zenshu* [Collected works of Tadao Yanaihara], vol. III, pp. 459–706. Tokyo: Iwanami Shoten,

Ybañez, Roy C. 1983. "The Hongkong bank in the Philippines, 1899–1941." In *Eastern Banking: Essays in the History of the Hongkong and Shanghai banking corporation*, ed. Frank H. H. King, pp. 435–466. London: Athlone Press.

Ybiernas, Vicente Angel S. 2007. "Philippine Financial Standing 1921: The First World War Boom and Bust." *Philippine Studies*, 55, no. 3: 345–372.

Yoshihara, Kunio. 1984. "A note on information sources on Philippine business history." *Tonan Ajia Kenkyu* [Southeast Asian Studies] 22, no. 3: 307–315.

_____. 1985. *Philippine industrialization: Foreign and domestic capital.* Quezon City: Ateneo de Manila University Press.

# INDEX

## A

Abreu, Newberry and Reyes Bank, 55table7, 201n22
Adas, Michael, 14
Administration Code (1917), 31, 48, 172–73
Agency house, 9, 15, 61, 64, 82, 114, 163, 193: cash advances to growers, 144; Hubbell & Co., 9, 64; loans to, 82; Peele, 9, 64 Russell & Sturgis, 9, 64; Spanish tobacco firm Tabacalera, 64; Compañía de los Tranvias de Filipinas, 64
Agricultural and Industrial Bank, 54, 202n25
Agricultural Bank of the Philippine Government, 55table7, 69–90, 91, 208n81–82: Act No. (1865), 10, 16, 72, 83, 87; Act No. (2612) or transfer to Philippine National Bank, 93–96, 102, 172–74, 221n33; By-Law of the Agricultural Bank of the Philippine Government, 83–84; depository of provincial governments, as, 89; establishment, 9, 16: (Public Act No. 243), 72, 80; revised act (Act No. 1906), 88; revised act (Act No. 2016), 88; revised act (Act No. 2214) , 88, 89, 207n72, 208n79; revised law (Act No. 3610), 49–51
Agricultural financial institutions, 203n51
Aguinaldo, Emilio, 74: on friar lands, 204n24

Aldecoa & Co., 61
Allison, W. B., 205n46
American colonial period: debacle in the Philippines, 186, 189
American provincial treasurer, 78, 84–85, 87–88, 89, 103, 208n74
Anderson, W. H., 209n15
Asturias Sugar Central, Inc., 64
Atlantic Gulf & Pacific Co., 61

## B

Babcock & Templeton, 145
Bacolod-Murcia Milling Co., 155: loan, 152, 153table22, 154, 156table23
Banco Español Filipino, 9, 23, 62, 64, 72, 81
Banco Peninsular Ultramarino de Madrid, 55table7
Bank of the Philippine Islands, 60: branches, 58 table8; commercial bank, as, 57, 65; establishment, 9, 23, 55table7, 62–64; export business, supporting, 66; Gold Standard Fund, 28; issuance of bank notes, 203n46; loans to planters, 210n28; major stockholder, 202n26
Banking Law (Act No. 3154), 49, 50–51, 203n51. *See also* Guanco Act
Berry, Fred N., 105, 158
Binalbagan Estate, Inc.: loans, 152, 155, 169
Board of Control, 91, 97–98, 138, 140: abolition of, 180–85

240

Bowring Treaty (1855), 8
British banks, 163
British Malaya, 8, 10, 13, 14: Chinese in capital formation, 200–201n8; Chinese merchants credits, 162; tin/rubber import to United States, 194
Brown, Ian, 8
Building and loan association, 50–52, 201n19
Bulacan province, 52, 80, 105
Bureau of Banking, 49, 52, 55table7
Bureau of Insular Treasury, 26, 35, 98

C

Cadastral Act (1913), 85, 102, 110
Calamba Sugar Estate: credit from National Bank, 152
Camus, Michael, 157, 158
Capiz province, 105
Cebu province (and city), 57, 59, 64, 113table113, 160, 212n61
Central Azucarera de Bais: loans, 152, 154
Central Luzon Agricultural Students' Bank, 201n21
Chartered Bank of India, Australia and China, 8, 9, 28, 55table7, 57, 58table8, 72, 81, 210n28
Chettiar, 14
China Banking Corporation (CBC), 56table7, 57, 58table8, 65, 162
Chinese banks, 163: money lending practices, 161
Coates, Francis, Jr., 125, 126–27, 144, 145–46, 166: Report of 1920, 146, 151–52, 156; Report of 1921, 172, 175, 180
Coconut products (copra and coconut oil), 42, 43, 51, 65, 142: companies, loans from Philippine National Bank, 148–49 table20; export, 147; processing, 147–51
Colonial bank, 6, 9, 196n17
Colonial democracy, 18, 69, 71, 140, 191
Colonial nationalism, 5, 191

Commercial banking corporation, 50–51
Compañía de los Tranvias de Filipinas, 64
Compañía General de Tabacos de Filipinas, Tabacalera, 46, 61–62, 64, 111, 200n7
Compañía Maritima, 61
Compañía Mercantil de Filipinas, 145, 148, 158–61, 218n46
Compañía Naviera de Filipinas, 148, 157, 160
Colonial discourse, 5, 6, 17–18, 119, 140, 187–89, 197n43
Conant, Charles A.: amending Philippine currency law, 130–32, 136; financial and banking expert, 25; on gold exchange standard, 198n3; Philippine currency reform, 25–26, 72–74, 206n32; on single currency fund, 179
Concepcion, Venancio, 209n15, 213n16–17: arrest, 138–39, 166–71; on Compañía Mercantil de Filipinas, 159; on crop loan, 108–9, 112, 144, 152; on G. Martini Ltd., 146; gold reserve, 168; management style, 105, 111; resignation, 5, 167; "*La Tragedia del Banco Nacional Filipino*," 169–71
Cooper, Henry A., 80
Copra, 43, 45, 46table5, 61, 62, 64, 142, 148
Corporation Law (Act No. 1459), 49, 96: revised law (Act No. 3610), 49, 50–51
Corpus, Rafael, 150
Cristobal Oil Co., 148, 149table 20–21, 150
Cronyism, 193
Crop loan, 15, 64, 103–4, 105–11, 112, 113table 15, 113–15, 153, 193, 210n28
Cruz, Romero V., 128
Currency law (1918): revision of, 165, 171–80
Currency policy: failure, 187
Currency Reserve Fund, 7, 52, 120, 126–37, 213n 17, 215n35: abolition, 180; combination of two currency reserves, 136–37, 165–66, 186; deposit in New York agency of Philippine National Bank, 2–3, 32, 35, 127, 178, 185; mismanagement, 35; minimum

level of, 36, 177, 178; transfer from New York to Manila, 35, 174
Cuyugan, Carlos, 157

## D

De la Rama, Esteban, 106–7
De Veyra, Jaime C., 134, 136
Delaney, J. Elmer, 1, 145–46, 152, 158, 171: in Concepcion's memoir, 170
Division of Insular Affairs. *See* U.S. War Department. Bureau of Insular Affairs
Dollar exchange standard, 16, 22, 32, 38–40
Domingo, Jose E., 111
DOSRI loan, 219n64
Dutch East Indies, 7–8, 10, 13, 14, 45 table 4, 194: Gold exchange standard, 131

## E

Edwards, Clarence R., 129–30, 205n46
*El Comercio*. "The First Arrest in the Bank Case," 168–69
*El Ideal*. "The Conduct of General Concepcion as President of the National Bank," 168
Elites, Filipino, 189: on abolition of Board of Control, 184; corruption, 186
Exchange Standard Fund, 39

## F

Federal Reserve Act (U.S.), 34, 173, 174–75, 186
Federal Reserve Bank (U.S.), 36, 39, 94, 174–77
Federal Reserve Board (U.S.), 34, 92, 99
Federal Reserve System (U.S.), 32, 34, 173, 174, 180
Ferguson, Samuel, 105, 146, 151, 211–12n32, 213n15, n17
Fernandez Hermanos, 146, 147table19, 148
Fernandez, R. J., 111, 158
Ferrer, Francisco, 111
Filipinization policy, 181, 185
Filipino landowners/entrepreneurs, 124, 186
Fisher and Camus Report, 158, 160, 161

Fisher, F.C., 157, 158
Fitzsimmons, Albert P., 126–27, 134, 214n25–26
Forbes, W. Cameron, 4, 91–92, 121, 137, 214n19
Francis Burton Harrison Papers, 179
French Indochina, 10, 11–13, 43, 192
Froehlich Kuttner, 159

## G

G. Martini Ltd., 145–46, 147table19, 170
Garrison, Lindley M., 132–33
Germann & Co., 107
Gold exchange standard: currency system, 6, 10–11, 131; French Indochina, 13; fundamental principles, 176, 186; Gold Standard Fund and the Silver Certificate Reserve, 172, 175–78, 186; Philippine currency system, 16, 21–27, 37–39, 52, 134–37, 165, 177–80, 187; Thailand financial crisis, 192
Gold standard, 10, 13, 21–22, 24, 27, 72, 131, 132, 176
Gold Standard Fund, 34, 165, 177, 178, 179: abolition of, 131; deposit in private banks in Manila, 177; establishment of, 129, 180; on gold parity of the silver peso, 176; lending investment, 129; merger, 172, 175, 186; Philippine peso parity / conversion, 26–29, 28 table 1, 37–38, 134; Philippine currency reserve fund, 34–37, 121, 137, 165, 172, 176, 178–80, 186; Silver Certificate Reserve, 31, 32, 134–36
Gonjo, Yasuo, 12, 15: on Banque de l'Indochine, 192–93
Government corporations: reform and reconstruction, 182, 183
Governor General Office of the Philippines, 29, 32, 36, 88–89, 173, 174, 179
Guanco Act, 203n51
Guanco, E. 107–8, 153
Guaranty Trust Co., 55table7, 61

## H

*Haciendas*, 47, 104, 114, 200n5: family owned sugar central and mills, 106–12, 154
Hale, Eugene, 80
Hamashita, Takeshi, 15
Harding, Warren G., 120, 121
Harrison, Archibald, 105–6, 108–9, 111–12, 158, 210n28
Harrison, Francis Burton, 1–2, 5, 71, 90, 92, 120–21, 132–34, 169: economic policy, 123–24, 179; Filipinization policy, 181–88; on government-owned corporations, 181; Illegal bank management, 138–40, 169 recommendation of loans, 151; resignation, 167, 188, 212n6
Haskins & Sells Report (1922), 148, 217n4: on loan business of National Bank, 166
Hermanos, Levy, 62
Hermanos, Lizarraga, 62
Herstein, Bernard, 134, 215n51: Conant-Herstein bill, 136
Hijos de L. de la Rama, 106–7
Hinigaran Sugar Plantation, 153
Hongkong and Shanghai Banking Corporation, 8, 9, 15, 55table7, 58table8, 60–65, 81: branches in the Philippines, 59; crop loan business, 210n28
Hoyt, Frederick G., 137
Hubbard, John, 205n46

## I

Iloilo province (and city), 106, 160: Agricultural Banks' loans in, 86, 87 table 11, 106; crop loans, 103, 109, 113table16, 114; established banks in, 59, 61, 64; Bank of the Philippine Islands branch in, 57, 62, 171; National Bank branch in, 112, 171, 212n61; sugar plantations, 105
Ilustrado, 70

Ingram, James C., 11: on Thai economic history, 192
Insular Treasurer, 25, 26, 32, 36, 48, 52, 199n40, 214n25: agricultural bank, 77, 82–84, 89; currency and exchange crisis, 125–27; National Bank, 95
Insular Treasury (Manila), 180, 208n80
Insurance companies, 201n19
International Banking Corporation, 55table7, 59, 61, 81, 89, 208n80–81, 210n28: National City Bank of New York, merged with, 92, 202n33; sugar industry loans, 151
Intra-Asian trade, 13
Irving National Bank (New York City), 35
Isabela Sugar Co., 152, 153table22, 154, 155, 156table23
Isabela Sugar Factory, 108

## J

Jenks, Jeremiah W., 21, 198n3, 205n46
Jones Law (1916), 31, 215n46

## K

Kabankalan Sugar Co., 153table22
Kemmerer, Edwin W., 11, 21, 23, 178, 198n3, 199n27, 205n32: establishment of agricultural bank, 71–72, 77–79, 81, 84; Gold exchange standard, 134, 178–80; Gold Standard Fund, 135–36; Philippine currency, 134, 178–80, 198n3
Kopp, Adolph, 171

## L

La Banque de l'indonchine, 8, 12–13, 15, 192–93
*La Vanguardia*: on Venancio Concepcion, 168, 169
Land Registration Act (1902), 79, 102
Legarda, Benito, 9–10, 91
Liberty Loan bond, 2–3, 35, 214n26
Liongson, Francisco, 76–77

## 244  Index

Lodge, Henry Cabot, 80, 205n46
Luthringer, George F., 27, 31, 35, 126: currency crisis in the Philippines, 126; on Currency Reserve Fund, 35, 125; *The Gold-Exchange Standard in the Philippines*, 3–4, 6, 11, 125; Gold Standard Fund, 27, 31, 125
Luzon Rice Mills, 62
Luzuriaga, Jose Ruis, 73

## M

Ma-ao Sugar Central Co., 152, 153table22, 154, 155, 156table23
Macleod & Co., 61
Madrigal, Vicente, 105, 111, 146, 158, 218n46
Manila: banks, 23, 28, 54, 55–56table 7, 59
*Manila Bulletin*: on the release of Concepcion, 169
Manila hemp, 13, 16, 42, 43, 46table5, 47table 6, 51, 61, 64, 65, 70: agricultural loans, 113table 16; exports, 141–43, 143table 17, 170; prices, 146; trading, 144–47, 158
Manila Railroad Company, 29, 132, 181
Martin, Henderson, 92–93
McIntyre, Frank., 92, 129, 132–36, 139, 179–80, 191–92, 196n15, 213n17, 214n29
McKinley, William, 22, 121, 213n9
Member bank, of the Federal Reserve System, U.S., 32, 34, 39, 173, 180
Mercantile Bank of China (MBC), 56table7: lending policy, 162
*Mestizo*, 47–78, 200n8
Mindoro Development Co., 151–52
Monte de Piedad and Savings Bank, 55 table 7, 57, 58 table 8, 202n26
Montilla, Emilio, 108
Montilla, Gil, 108
Montilla, Remigio, 108

## N

National Bank: annual report of 1925, 150; Board of Control, 181; branches and agencies, 212n61; depletion of currency reserve, 171; as depository of the Philippine Government, 172, 174, 175; Filipinization, 169; lawsuit, 185; loans, 148, 151; mismanagement, 176, 188; on Manila hemp transactions, 146; stocks, 209n8; violation of regulations, 161
National Bank of Egypt, 78
National Cement Company, 181
National City Bank of New York, 58table8, 59, 65, 213n17: International Banking Corporation, merged with, 92, 202n33
National Coal Company, 181, 184–85
National Development Company, 181
Nederlandsch Indische Handelsbank, N.V., 56table7, 58table8, 59
Nederlandse Handel Mij. (NHM), 8
Negros Occidental province: agricultural loans in, 86, 106, 153; *haciendas*, 106–11; landowners in, 80; sugar industry, 105
Nepotism, 193
New York, 195n4: banks, 120; currency reserve, 2, 166; National Bank, 174–75, 180; Philippine National Bank, 2, 7, 125, 141, 180, 186, 192, 195n4
New York banking law, 175
Newlands, F. G., 205n46
Nolan, Ricardo, 111
North Negros Sugar Co., 64

## O

*Obras pías*, 9, 62
Oriental Bank Corporation, 196n17, 201n22
Osmeña, Sergio, 2, 5, 18, 134, 136–40, 181, 183, 191
Overseas Chinese, 13–15, 24, 41, 114, 200n8

## P

Palma Central, 152, 153table22, 155, 156table23
Pampanga province: agricultural banks loans, 86, 87table11; banks branches, 57; sugar industry, 76, 105, 152–53, 156

Index 245

Pampanga Sugar Development Co., 152–53, 155table 22, 156table23
Partido Democrata, 124, 138, 140
Partido Nacionalista, 5, 18, 92, 138, 139, 140, 191
Partido Nacionalista Colectivista, 5, 139, 140, 152
Partido Nacionalista Consolidado, 5, 140
Payne-Aldrich Tariff Act, 42, 70, 142
Peele, Hubbell Co., 9, 64
Peoples Bank and Trust Company, 57, 58table8
Philippine Assembly, 18, 22, 70, 82, 92
Philippine Bank of Commerce, 56table7, 58table8
Philippine coconut industry, 150–51
Philippine Coinage Act of 1903 (Public No. 137), 22, 23, 26, 30, 129–30, 132: revised act (Act No. 2776), 31, 36, 136, 172, 174, 177–78, 221n27; revised act (Act No. 2938), 93, 95, 96, 181; revised act (Act No. 3058), 36, 38, 180; revised act (Act No. 4199), 22, 38
Philippine Commission, 22, 23–26, 76, 129, 136, 191: agricultural Bank, 72, 77–80, 82, 84; agricultural loans, 73, 88; banking system, 74–75; establishment of Bureau of Treasury, 48; Gold Standard Fund, 129, 136
Philippine Commonwealth, 22, 38, 49
Philippine Currency Law (1918): revision, 128–37, 172, 174–78, 221n27
Philippine currency policy, 52, 188
Philippine currency system, 5, 16, 22, 31, 32, 37, 39, 129, 165, 176–80, 196–97n29
Philippine economy, 42, 163, 193–94: collapse, 35; development, 92, 194; export sector, 64, 125, 142; inflation, 4, 11, 120;
Philippine Fiber and Produce Co., 145, 147table19, 170
Philippine financial crisis (1919–1922), 5–6, 128, 166, 167, 172, 193: and corruption of the Philippine National Bank, 16, 18, 128, 187; causes, 177, 186, 192; on Filipinization, 185; and Philippine politics, 187, 188; role of gold exchange standard system, 179
Philippine financial policy, 179
Philippine Gold Standard Act of 1903 (Act No. 938), 26, 77, 129, 132, 177–78
Philippine government, 24: bond sale, 2; deposits in private bank, 210n28; fiscal revenues and expenditures, 190; response to financial crisis, 16, 20; on silver standard, 24, 25, 26. *See also* Philippine legislature
Philippine Guarantee Co., 148
Philippine Islands: American influences, 189; expenses of civil administration, 123–24; legal currency, 25, 31, 130; military pacification, 190; sovereignty of, 21–22. *See also* Philippines
Philippine legislature, 2, 186: 1919–1922 Financial Crisis, 186; Agriculture Bank Act, 72, 81–83, 88, 90; coins, 32; crisis in, 17; crop loans, 103; currency law, 179–80; establishment, 22, 191; Filipinization, 182; on Kemmerer's recommendation, 178; National Bank Act, 91; Philippine National Bank, 93. *See also* Philippine government
Philippine Manufacturing Co., 149–50, 149table 21
Philippine National Bank: agricultural loan, 15, 46, 103–4, 106–12, 113table15–16; Bacolod branch (agency), 105–6, 112, 113table 16, 212n61; board of directors, 96–98, 106, 152, 155–57, 182, 184, 220n15; branch, 57, 58table8; corruption, 5–6, 17–18, 119, 124–25, 137, 140, 167, 180–81, 185, 187–88; Currency Reserve Fund, 32; currency reserves, 2–4, 7, 17, 34–35, 120, 124, 125, 127–28, 141, 166–67, 171–72, 178–79; dual lending,112–15;

establishment, 2–3, 9, 16, 34, 53table7, 91–99, 120, 123; Iloilo branch, 61, 103, 105–6, 112, 113–14, 113table6, 159–60, 171, 212n61; losses of loans, 110, 146, 147table19, 149table21, 154, 157, 163, 167; Manila office, 3, 120, 125, 166, 175; mismanagement, 2, , 4, 124, 128, 141, 166–67, 179, 187–88; nepotism in business practice, 193; New York agency, 2, 7, 34–35, 125, 137, 141, 166–67, 174–75, 179–80, 185–86, 192, 195n4; revised act (Act No. 2747), 93–94, 96, 156, 169, 172, 209n8, 220n12, 221n33; revised act (Act No. 2939), 36, 178
Philippine National Bank Act (Act No. 2612), 93, 94–96, 102, 172–74, 221n33
Philippine National Bank Act (1916), 172, 173–74
Philippine National Bank Act (1918), 156–57
Philippine National Bank Act (1921): revised charter, 181
Philippine National Bank Law, 175
Philippine Organic Act (1902), 25, 48 183, 199n21
Philippine Refining Co., 218n22
Philippine Revolution, 9, 70, 74, 191
Philippine Sugar Centrals Agency, 155: liabilities, 156 table23
Philippine Treasurer: annual report, 199n27
Philippine Treasury, 180: on currency reserves, 166, 192
Philippine Trust Company, 57, 58table8, 202n26
Philippine Vegetable Oil Co., 62, 147, 148, 149table21, 217n16, 218n22: loans, 147, 149table20, 150, 169
Philippine-American War (1899–1902), 9
Philippines: American colonial state debacle, 180, 186; American colonial system, 192; coconut mills, 147, 150; colonialism, 69, 71, 119, 196n15; commercial banks, 41, 51, 52, 54, 57, 58table8, 82, 142, 162; DOSRI loans, 219n64; free trade partnership with the United States, 189–90; money lending practices, 161, 163, 193; political system, 166. *See also* Philippine Islands
Poblete, Pascual H., 75
Postal Savings Bank, 54, 55table7, 83, 94, 202n25
Prieto, Mauro, 201n21
Procter & Gamble, 217n16
Public Land Act (1903), 102
Public Law No. 24, 206n53
Puno y Concepcion, S. en C.: extension credit, 169

Q

*Quedans*, 145, 148, 152
Quezon, Manuel L., 1–2, 5, 18, 92, 111, 138–40, 150, 181, 183, 185, 191

R

Recto, Claro M., 140
Reyes, Fidel A., 90
Rice, 8, 11–12, 13, 49, 62, 64, 94, 108, 111, 113table6
Robinson, Charles C., 171, 209n15
Rodriguez Bank, 201n22
Roosevelt, Theodore, 75
Root, Elihu, 25, 72, 75
Rural credit institutions, 203n51
Rural Credit Law (Act No. 2508), 203n51
Russell & Sturgis, 9, 64

S

Salamanca, Bonifacio S., 70
San Jose Estate (Mindoro), 151
Savings and mortgage bank, 50–51, 52, 54, 57, 201n19
Seaver, George, 109–11
Serra, Salvador, 109
Shuster, W. Morgan, 76
Siam Commercial Bank, 8
Siguenza, Victoriano, 107, 153
Silver certificate, 20, 26–27, 30–32, 34–35,

129, 132, 135–37, 165, 176–78. *See also* Treasury certificates
Silver Certificate Reserve, 30–32, 34–35, 120, 129–37, 165, 172: appropriation, 179; convertibility into silver domestically, 176; deposit in Federal Reserve Bank, 177; merger, 172, 175, 186
Silver standard, 26: currency law in 1918, 166; currency system, as, 10–13, 22–24, 25, 192; foreign exchange, 176; fundamental principles, 176
Singson Encarnacion, Vicente, 105, 111, 157–59, 209n15, 218n46
Small-scale financial institutions, 203n51
Smith, Bell & Co., 61, 62
Smith, James F., 82
Southeast Asia: banking system, 6–10; colonial economies, 17, 41, 60; currency system, 192; financial crisis, 192; financial history, 13–15, 66, 114, 193; silver to gold exchange standard, 10–13; under British economic sphere of Asia, 194
Spalding, William F. *Eastern Exchange Currency and Finance*, 11
Spanish banks, 163
Spanish capital, 200n7
Speyer and Co., 81
Spooner, J. C., 205n46
Stanley, Peter W., 105: *A Nation in the Making: The Philippines and the United States (1899–1921)*, 5, 71; *Reappraising American Empire: New Perspectives on Philippine-American History* (1984), 69
Sugar: central, 151–56; exports, 13, 16, 42–47, 51, 61, 70, 142–43, 175; industry, 46, 62, 104; loans, 49, 86, 94, 105–13, 155, 170; mills, 29–30, 46, 104, 200n7; Negros Occidental, 73, 86; non-liquid assets, 4; plantations, 64, 105–13; processing, 151–56; tariffs, 77

T

Tabacalera. *See* Compañía General de Tabacos de Filipinas
Taft, William H., 62, 73–75, 80, 82, 204n9
Tait, J. S., 205n46
Talisay-Silay Milling Co., 152, 153table22, 155, 156table23
Tayabas province: agricultural Bank loans, 86–87
Thailand, 6, 8–9, 45 table 4: Chinese merchants credits, 162; currency for trade, 196n16; exports, 13, 15, 17; financial crisis, 12; gold exchange standard, 10–11, 192
Tobacco, 13, 42, 46–47, 49, 196n16: export, 46 table 46, 61, 70, 76–77; industry, 46; loans, 64, 94, 111, 145
Torrens title, 85, 102, 207n72, 212n62
Treasury certificate, 31–32, 34–37, 38–39, 136, 165, 177–78, 180, 216n52
Treasury Certificate Fund, 36–37, 37 table 37, 38–39, 180
Trust corporation, 50
Tydings-McDuffie Act, 42

U

U. de Poli, 145, 147table19, 170
Underwood-Simmons Act, 42, 142
Unipersonalistas, 5, 139
United States: army and navy expenditures in the Philippines, 27, 31, 190; on autonomy of Philippine government, 190; free trade partnership with the Philippines, 189–90; trade domination in Asia-Pacific area, 194
U.S. Congress: on official aid to the Philippines, 198n8
U.S. Federal Reserve Act (1913), 173, 174, 175
U.S. Philippine Commission, 191
U.S. War Department. Bureau of Insular Affairs (BIA), 1–7, 81, 91, 92, 124, 132, 144 186: 1919 Currency crisis, 17, 126–28; on currency system, 125,

188; on depletion of currency reserve, 166, 167; establishment, 21–22; policy toward Philippine currency system, 128–37, 179–80; role of, 191

U.S. War Department. Bureau of Insular Treasury, 207n70

## V
V. Madrigal & Co., 146
Victorias Milling Co., Inc., 64

## W
Walcutt, Charles C., Jr., 127, 129
Warner, Barnes & Co., 61–62
Weeks, John W., 120–22, 137–38, 180, 182–83
Whitaker, Philip C., 217n13
Willis, H. Parker, 92, 99, 102–5, 151, 171
Wilson, E. W., 160–61, 170
Wilson, Woodrow, 121, 213n7
Wong, Kwok-chu. *The Chinese in the Philippine Economy: 1898–1941*, 161
Wood regime: on Board of Control, 181–83; on Filipinization, 182
Wood, Leonard, 4–5, 121, 139, 183: on financial crisis, 166; on Philippine currency system, 180; reconstruction of the National Bank, 180–81
Wood-Forbes Mission, 4, 5, 17, 120–40, 167, 181
Wright, Ben F., 126–27, 166, 176–80: "Memorandum Concerning the Development of the Currency System of the Philippine Islands with Special Reference to Existing Conditions and to the Philippine National Bank," 175–76; on Philippine currency system, Wright Report, 166, 172, 175

## X
*Xinyong* (trustworthiness), 161–62, 163

## Y
Yeater, Charles E., 1–2, 120, 127
Ynchausti & Co., 62, 109

## Z
Zamboanga province: banks, 57, 59, 85, 207n70; copra, 64